WINGING IT

INTERNATIONAL MARINE / McGRAW-HILL EDUCATION

Camden, Maine | New York | Chicago | San Francisco | Lisbon | London | Madrid | Mexico City |
Milan | New Delhi | San Juan | Seoul | Singapore | Sydney | Toronto

WINGING IT

ORACLE TEAM USA'S INCREDIBLE COMEBACK TO DEFEND THE AMERICA'S CUP

DIANE SWINTAL, R. STEVEN TSUCHIYA, AND ROBERT KAMINS

1 2 3 4 QFR/QFR 1 9 8 7 6 5 4 3
ISBN   978-0-07-183412-4
MHID   0-07-183412-5
E ISBN 0-07-183446-X (four-color ebook)

Library of Congress Cataloging-in-Publication Data is available from the Library of Congress.

McGraw-Hill Education books are available at special quantity discounts to use as premiums and sales promotions or for use in corporate training programs. To contact a representative, please e-mail us at bulksales@mcgraw-hill.com. This book is printed on acid-free paper.

Questions regarding the content of this book should be addressed to
www.internationalmarine.com

Questions regarding the ordering of this book should be addressed to
McGraw-Hill Education
Customer Service Department
P.O. Box 547
Blacklick, OH 43004
Retail customers: 1-800-262-4729
Bookstores: 1-800-722-4726

Page ii: ORACLE TEAM USA's two AC72 catamarans training in August, 2013.
(© 2013 ACEA/Photo: Abner Kingman)

CONTENTS

ACKNOWLEDGMENTS

The authors would like to thank the sailors and designers mentioned in this book for taking time to share their perspectives. Additionally, we express our appreciation to Isabel Genis, Daniel Ferrando, Jane Eagleson, Alex Murray and all of the media center staff for their tireless help onsite; and to the team and event media officers for their cooperation. Many thanks for the incredible work by the talented photographers covering the America's Cup; a particular appreciation to Gilles Martin-Raget for his help.

Among those people we wish to thank for assistance, guidance, and support that directly or indirectly made this book possible are Stuart Alexander, Brad Butterworth, Mike Drummond, Laurent du Roure at OTUSA, Bob Fisher, Jack Griffin at *Cup Experience.com*, Ellen Hoke, Sam Hollis at ACEA, John Mangino, Dave Reed at *Sailing World*, JoAnn Roth, Lisa Ramsperger at OTUSA, Hamish Ross at ACRM, John Rousmaniere, Stuart Streuli at *Sailing World* and NYYC, and David Tillett.

Much credit is due Molly Mulhern for her editing, and her vision that made this book possible, and Shannon Swanson for her design skills.

Thanks also to Cheeko Matsusaka for setting a high standard; to Matt, Greg, and Bob at *CupInfo.com* for sharing the voyage (and much else); to Chuck Lantz for his service as tour guide to the Cup world in San Francisco and on the Internet; and to Jim Swintal.

And we ask forgiveness from our families for the time spent on yet another America's Cup project. Thank you.

**Please consider supporting the
Andrew Simpson Sailing Foundation, founded
in 2013 in Andrew's memory to introduce children
to sailing and encourage their enjoyment of the sport.
Learn more at *andrewsimpsonsailing.org***

INTRODUCTION
A Cup Like No Other

August 29 in New Zealand is the middle of winter. Six thousand, five hundred miles from San Francisco, one year and eight days before the 2013 America's Cup match, Emirates Team New Zealand skipper Dean Barker was learning how to sail, in his words, "a monster."

This was the fourth day of test sailing their first AC72 class yacht, the boat having been launched at the end of July. Just warming up, they had already topped an astounding 31 knots.

Meanwhile, ETNZ's competitors were spying on the Kiwi's new boat. In fact they had been spying on ETNZ for many months, monitoring the progress from small test-bed designs to the full-fledged AC72. All the teams kept an eye on their rivals—it was permitted as long as a minimum distance was maintained—but no one wanted to show their cards to their opponents too early. ETNZ sometimes took care of the problem by pretending to test conventional designs when they were being watched, playing coy until the spies gave up and went home for a while. Today ETNZ had more than the usual reasons to want some privacy.

Eleven sailors were onboard, plus technicians armed with computers to monitor structural loads in real time. Flanking the AC72 were their own chase boats, with dozens of design and technical staff keeping tabs.

It was time to fly.

The crew made adjustments to the daggerboards, Glenn Ashby trimmed the wing into position, Dean Barker at the helm turned the wheel down, and the big cat began to gather speed.

A catamaran normally sails fastest when heeling only slightly, leaning just enough to get the windward hull clear out of the water, cutting the underwater drag nearly in half. With the efficiency of the wing sail, the boat could fly the windward hull even in 6-8 knots of breeze. Today they had another trick in mind, too.

As the AC72 picked up speed, the apparent wind, the combination of the true, atmospheric wind and the motion of the boat itself through the air, angled forward and grew in speed.

Two 72-foot-long hulls, built of carbon-fiber and other composite materials, stretched away on both sides of the yacht, connected by two giant crossbeams, all kept stiff by a web of bracing structures. The "platform," as it was termed in Cup-speak, was wider than a tennis court and nearly as long, the spaces between crossbeams covered with a trampoline of open netting for the sailors to walk on.

The wing trimmer looked up at the wingsail, over 13 stories into the sky. The forward half of the wing was the spar, the structure that gave it the strength to stand upright, anchored by stays and shrouds. The second half of the wing, trailing just behind the spar, was comprised of flaps, which pivoted independently in several sections, adjusted in combination with the spar for efficient air flow over the two sections of the wing to suit conditions. Constructed of carbon fiber ribs covered with industrial heat-shrink film, the wing was more powerful than a soft sail of the same area, typically 50-85% more efficient depending on conditions.

It took two years to design and 20,000 man-hours to build just the wing itself. The rest of the boat, the first of two yachts ETNZ would build, took over twice that, not counting 140,000 man-hours of design.

The wing was the new toy on the AC72, the most visibly high-tech feature, expected to be the focus of sophisticated engineering development for all of the teams chasing the historic yachting trophy for 2013. Until today.

As the speed edged over 10-12 knots and kept climbing, the boat settled in at a comfortable angle of heel. And then something else happened. The leeward hull began to rise from the water, too. The entire tennis-court-sized platform and 131-foot wingsail, 15,000 pounds including the crew, were a meter or more in the air, being lifted by the daggerboard and rudder foils.

Nearly 21 feet tall, a pair of the oddly shaped daggerboards for the boat cost $400,000 just by themselves, and took three months to build.

The boat came out of the water, and now with no hulls in the water, just the lifting foil of the leeward daggerboard and a sliver of rudder foils in contact with the sea, an enormous amount of drag vanished. The boat leapt ahead, 10 knots faster, 15 knots faster. The faster she went, the more the apparent wind built. Boats of her kind had been planned to sail at 30-35 knots. With these lifting foils before long they would be flirting with 45 knots and more, over 50 miles per hour, the wind across the deck like putting a hand out the car window on the highway. When she was out of the water, the boat rode steadier on the foils than sailing on the hulls, and quieter, too.

Despite their success, the team kept quiet on August 29. No publicity photos or press releases. They had been spotted from shore, though, and predictably a photo was posted on the Internet. The image caught

ETNZ flying on her foils. That the Kiwi team had managed this feat was stunning. That they had managed it at all was a shock to some, including designers on other teams. A few people even wondered if the photo was a hoax. Less than a week later, ETNZ let a television crew film from the team's 1200-hp support boat, as the cat jumped out of the water and sped away, accelerating, leaving slack-jawed journalists speechless.

ETNZ was nearly two months behind schedule, but none of the other teams had launched their own cats yet. The New Zealand team had barely ten months until they had to be ready to race, and there was still a second new boat to come.

Back in San Francisco, the team that would defend the America's Cup, ORACLE TEAM USA, was in the process of stepping their new wingsail for the first time, and taking their first boat for its own early trials. They had some flying in mind, too.

The AC72s had become foiling catamarans. The teams needed faster chase boats, just to keep up. The crews needed helmets, body protection, and a long list of safety equipment that would continue to grow. Photographers had to acquire faster and longer lenses to deal with the subject's greater speeds and distances. A whole new technology would be used to apply the rules, and to make races on TV intelligible. Everything would happen quicker, and be more complicated, and expensive, in a tougher competition than anyone ever expected.

After her triumph in the waters around the Isle of Wight on another August day in 1851, when that silver prize was hauled aboard the schooner *America,* would anybody present then have thought that 162 years later there would be people still trying to win the Cup? Let alone hydrofoiling multihulls with wingsails? But an element of these AC72s racing each other at speeds often over 40 knots would have been familiar.

From the very beginning, at its core, the Cup is a history of innovation, of advanced technology in yachting. That's why the Cup was won in the first place, why it was defended, and why it still compels attention.

One person, after more than 25 years of involvement with the America's Cup, observed that winning the America's Cup is not about excellence. Excellence is the starting point. If you were to try to win the Cup and be merely excellent, you would lose. Winning the America's Cup has always been about going beyond.

ONE

Challengers and Defenders: A Brief History of the America's Cup

THE YACHT *AMERICA* AND THE DAWN OF THE AMERICA'S CUP

In the summer of 1851, Great Britain hosted "The Great Exhibition" to bring together art, culture, and technology from all corners of the globe. This international exposition was an early solution to bridge the gulf that separated nations before the advent of airplanes and advanced telecommunications.

One of the products of technology designed in conjunction for this exposition was the schooner yacht *America*, built by a group of New Yorkers led by industrialist John Cox Stevens. Upon arriving in England that summer, *America* captured the attention of British yachtsmen because of her distinct features that were markedly different from British yachts: *America* had a sharp bow, her widest point amidships, a full stern, low freeboard, and raked-backed masts. British boats, on the other hand, were characterized by fuller bows and narrower sterns. One yachtsman, the Marquis of Anglesey, noted, "If she is right, then all of us are wrong." The Marquis's observation was proven correct on August 22, 1851, when *America* outran her British counterparts in the most celebrated yacht race in history. Stevens and his fellow owners were awarded a silver cup. While Stevens was pleased with winning the cup, the gambler and competitor in him yearned for a match race for big cash stakes. Throughout that summer Stevens challenged the British to a match race but was met with silence. Eventually, a friend picked up the gauntlet—likely out of charity. *America* won that match race, and Stevens quickly sold high-flying *America* for a profit, but he kept the silver cup.

Upon returning to New York, Stevens and his associates were honored as heroes for defeating the superpower of the day. The celebrated U.S. statesman Daniel Webster crowed, "Like Jupiter among gods, America is first and there is no second!" Swayed by the nationalistic fervor and the adventure of winning an international race, Stevens donated the cup to the New York Yacht Club (NYYC) under the condition it serve as a perpetual challenge trophy for international competition between nations.

Defenders and Challengers

As a challenge trophy, the America's Cup is unlike the typical modern championships seen in other sports. Defending is a confrontation between the nation that holds the Cup and the rest of the world, one country holding it and all the others trying to take it away. It is the Defender's prize to lose against the best boat and sailors that the world can send against them. For 132 years since 1851, or, as some count, 113 years since the first defense in 1870, America never lost a match, a feat often regarded as the longest winning streak in sports.

For 100 years, foreign countries came one at a time, represented by their designers, builders, sailors, and yachtsmen. Since 1970, by agreement the Defender faces the best of a fleet of multiple challengers who first compete against each other for their shot at taking away the trophy, and indeed taking the entire event, too.

The Defender, also known as The Trustee, holding the Cup is required to face any foreign yacht club that files a legitimate Notice of Challenge. The Deed of Gift sets out a few conditions for the racing (see below), but almost all those restrictions can be modified if the Challenger and Defender mutually agree, as has nearly always been the case, in 33 of 35 defenses.

The first defense of the America's Cup was held in 1870, and the number of races, the length and configurations of the racecourses, the types of yachts, and even the locations of the races were established through back and forth negotiation, a bit of compromise, and eventually agreement between Challenger and Defender.

If the Defender and Challenger cannot negotiate and agree on the conditions of the Match, the Defender has 10 months to face the Challenger under the strict terms of the Deed or else forfeit the trophy.

Beginning in 1970, rather than accept a single Notice of Challenge, and racing one opponent, the defending NYYC and the Challenger community adopted a system of accepting multiple challenges and having all the prospective challengers compete against each other in a selection series for the right to face the Defender.

The first Challenger accepted by the Defender is termed the Challenger of Record (COR), and all sides agree that the Challenger of Record will cede their position to the ultimate winner of a challenger selection regatta.

Generally the initial Challenger of Record and the Defender establish the detailed rules for the new America's Cup cycle, with various degrees of input from additional groups who also have intentions of becoming Challenger or Defender candidates, and then once the general rules are laid out, the additional teams are formally accepted. Once the new entries gain official status, they also have a say in any further changes to the rules.

The Deed of Gift

The rules attached to the Cup are contained in the Deed of Gift, a legal document that governs the competition for the trophy (see page 209). There are two rules in particular that have made a lasting impact:

One, the Cup serves as a competition between yachts of foreign nations. In the spirit of the Great Exhibition and in the spirit of the race between *America* and the British boats, the Cup races were meant to be a contest of competing technologies. As the world became increasingly globalized, the nationalistic element became less relevant, but the Cup remains to this day the ultimate contest of yacht design technology. That is why the America's Cup is not a one-design sailboat race and why the 2013 America's Cup match featured the most advanced racing sailboats in the world.

Two, the Challenger always has the right to sail a match against the Defender; and if the two parties cannot agree to the terms of a match via mutual consent, then a match would be held following the default terms specified in the Deed of Gift. This condition, which was born out of the frustration that Stevens experienced in 1851 when British yachtsmen ignored his challenge to race *America*, proved to be critical for keeping the Cup alive. This rule was responsible, albeit indirectly, for the creation of the tradition-breaking AC72 catamaran class.

FIVE REASONS THE NEW YORK YACHT CLUB HELD THE CUP FROM 1851 TO 1980

An invitation to challenge the NYYC for the Cup was sent to leading yacht clubs of the world in 1857. But eleven years passed before they received a challenge: in October 1868, Sir James Ashbury, on behalf of the Royal Thames Yacht Club of Great Britain, challenged with the schooner yacht *Cambria*. The first defense of the Cup was held in 1870 and the America's Cup was on the road to becoming yachting's Holy Grail. The Cup rose to mythic status in part because challengers could not wrest the elusive Cup away from the New York Yacht Club. For 132 years, the NYYC's defenders won 24 straight matches between the first defense in 1870 and the last successful defense in 1980: a total of 81 races won and a mere 8 races lost. The club managed to hold the Cup due to the combination of the following five factors:

1. The Club Was Represented by a Cadre of Skilled and Experienced Sailors

In the vast majority of the matches, the Defender's sailors were superior to those of the Challenger. In the rare cases where they were not better, the Defender's were equal in skill to the Challenger's crew. Charlie Barr,

Nathanael Herreshoff, Hank Haff, Charles Francis Adams, Mike Vanderbilt, Rod Stephens, Sherman Hoyt, Bus Mosbacher, Briggs Cunningham, Dennis Conner, Ted Turner, and Gary Jobson are just a handful of names of talented and experienced sailors who skippered or crewed for the New York Yacht Club.

The Americans' excellent tactics and boat-handling skills were a key reason for the lopsided record of 81 races won and 8 races lost. Having the advantage of superior crew made the difference during the few matches when the NYYC boat was inferior to the Challenger's. One of the most notable demonstrations of these yacht racing talents was the third race of the 1934 match. The Challenger *Endeavour*, a faster boat, led the Defender *Rainbow* around the bottom mark by six minutes, 39 seconds; both boats were now sailing upwind in light wind to the finish line hidden by fog. Aboard *Rainbow*, skipper Mike Vanderbilt handed the helm to Sherman Hoyt, a light air specialist. Hoyt, assisted by navigator Zenas Bliss, saw that both boats were laying the finish line. However, Hoyt, suspecting that *Endeavour*'s inexperienced navigator was unable to determine the precise location of the finish, decided to play a trick: Hoyt steered high as if he had to change direction to hit the finish. Hoyt was right. The afterguard of *Endeavour* wasn't sure about the location of the finish line and took the bait: the Challenger, who was ahead and to leeward, tacked to cover and then, after she crossed *Rainbow*, tacked back. These costly tacks scrubbed *Endeavour*'s speed; *Rainbow* then promptly eased her sheets, sailed lower, slipped by the Challenger, and won the race.

By the 1970s, the sailors of the Challengers began to catch up to the standards of the NYYC's Defenders; by 1983, the sailors of Challenger and Defender were evenly matched in skill.

2. Defender Selection Trials

Beginning with the third defense of the Cup in 1881, the NYYC held intra-club selection trials to determine the best yacht and crew to defend the Cup. These trials, which pitted an average of three Defender candidates, honed the skills of the crew; sharpened the afterguard; served as a proving ground to test tactics, boat-handling techniques, and boat design; and helped maintain "institutional memory" from defense to defense.

Thus, these trials were largely responsible for why American sailors were often better than the Challengers. The 1958 trials, as an example, featured a series with four candidates that raced from June to August to determine the Defender. Not only did the series help the Club that year, it also served as a boot camp for future Cup sailors such as Bus Mosbacher, who returned in 1962 and 1967 to successfully defend the Cup.

By contrast, the Challenger often arrived at the Cup match un-tested until the 1960s, when they began running their own intra-club selection series and, more significantly, beginning in 1970, the Challengers would run their own international selection series.

3. Commitment to Advancing Yacht Design Technology Ensured That the NYYC Always Had a Boat Fast Enough to Win

Up until the mid-1970s, the designers and engineers of the NYYC Defenders placed a priority on technology—be it hull design, sail design, or gear design; this priority led to the development of boats that were often faster than the Challenger. The NYYC enjoyed having the clearly faster boat in 15 out of the 24 defenses.

But, crucially, in the six defenses where the NYYC was hobbled with a slower boat, they were not significantly slower than the Challenger; and, thus, superior tactics and boat handling were able to overcome the deficiency in boat speed.

Whenever the NYYC had a faster boat, it simply resulted in overkill. In the second race of the 1881 match, the defender *Madeleine* crushed the challenger *Countess of Dufferin* by over 27 minutes; in the 1964 match, *Constellation* humiliated the challenger *Sovereign* by a margin of over 20 minutes in the second race.

Technological advancements include Nathanael Herreshoff's yachts such as *Reliance,* the 1903 Defender, which featured, among other things, innovative winches and hull design. W. Starling Burgess's J-Class yacht *Enterprise* sported an advanced duralumin mast that was lighter than the Challenger's outdated wooden design.

These and other technological advancements ensured that the NYYC's Defenders never fell far behind . . . until 1983.

4. NYYC and Its Defenders Maintained a Business-like Attitude (While the Challengers Often Embraced a Sporting Attitude)

The America's Cup is a complex endeavor that requires managing people and resources in a limited amount of time. Running an effective Cup campaign is like running a mini-corporation. The NYYC and the defender campaigns helped keep the Cup in America due in large part to its business-like approach. It is not surprising that captains of industry were often involved in the NYYC's defense of the Cup: these business leaders included merchant banker J. Pierpont Morgan, railroad executive Charles J. Paine, oil magnate William Rockefeller, and chemicals industry executive Peter du Pont.

By contrast, most of the Challengers embraced a relaxed or sporting attitude, particularly the British Challengers, who made up the majority of Challengers. Winning wasn't everything to them. This attitude was a combination of cultural differences and—because the concept of challenging the Cup, which meant trading an active yachting season at home for a single match abroad—romantic appeal, which didn't always attract the most practical of people.

This contrast in approach to the Cup is illustrated by the 1885 match.

British yacht designer J. Beavor Webb challenged the NYYC on behalf of one of his clients, Sir Richard Sutton. Sutton, a member of England's landed gentry, approached the Cup adventure purely as a sporting diversion.

The NYYC, by contrast, prepared for the match in its typical serious manner, holding a defender selection trial with four candidates. The America's Cup committee selected the yacht *Puritan*, from Massachusetts's Eastern Yacht Club; the committee, acting in an impartial business-like manner, selected the boat from Massachusetts over the other three, which were NYYC boats.

The *Puritan* campaign itself demonstrated an organized, business-like approach. Unlike the Challenger, the American campaign was efficiently directed by a three-man committee instead of a single individual: shipping and railroad magnate J. Malcom Forbes, the vice commodore of the Eastern Yacht Club, was its chairman; railroad executive Charles J. Paine was the campaign manager; and William Gray, Jr. also joined. This organization resembled a business and operated like one: Paine told a reporter, "You know it is one thing to get a boat out to use for your ordinary pleasure sailing and quite another thing to get her down to the fine edge necessary for international competition. The first is fun; the second is work."

At one point in the campaign, Paine, concerned about the boat's weight, ordered his crew to plane exactly a quarter inch off the deck's surface. In the following year, the interior of Paine's defender, *Mayflower,* was not only spartan but there were gaps between the wooden planks of the floor below to save weight. By contrast, the interior of the British Challenger was lavishly appointed with many creature comforts and looked like a Victorian drawing room.

The races in the 1885 match itself provided another illustration of the differences in attitude. At the start of one of the races, *Genesta*, on starboard tack (and having the right-of-way), was accidently rammed by *Puritan*. The Cup race committee immediately disqualified *Puritan* and signaled *Genesta* to complete the race on her own to collect a win. But Richard Sutton, in an act of sportsmanship, refused to do so.

The Americans' cutthroat approach certainly helped them win time after time, but it sometimes bordered on the comical. Prior to the 1934 match, the defending skipper, Mike Vanderbilt, and his challenging counterpart, T.O.M. Sopwith, agreed to furnish their Cup yachts with toilets, bathtubs, and other amenities. However, when Sopwith inspected Vanderbilt's boat belowdeck, he could not find the required amenities and accused the Defender of ignoring the rules. Vanderbilt countered back by taking the Challenger further below, where he revealed the toilet and bathtub stuffed in the boat's bilge to keep the weight low; Vanderbilt defended his ploy by stating that there was nothing in the agreement about a *functional* bathroom.

After World War II, there was a new breed of Challengers, and many embraced an approach shared by the NYYC. Australian Alan Bond's campaigns of the 1970s and early 1980s matched the business-like attitude of the Defender; and it was no surprise that they eventually beat the NYYC at their own game.

5. NYYC's Control of the Rules: "Britannia Rules the Waves, America Waives the Rules"

The playing field of the America's Cup was not always level. At the dawn of the Cup's history, the field of play was vastly in favor of the NYYC, the Defender. The story of the Cup is in part about the playing field becoming more level over time.

The NYYC, as founder and Defender, exercised great power over the rules. For the first match in 1870, the Club gave itself an overwhelming advantage: the NYYC would defend the Cup with a fleet of 15 yachts against the lone challenger. It was meant to "re-create" the 1851 race, but the Challenger, Sir James Ashbury, didn't see it that way. Ashbury reluctantly agreed to the onerous terms because he didn't want to sail back home without having a race. His boat finished sixth. Ashbury returned the next year with a fresh challenge but demanded that his yacht race one-on-one and not against a fleet. NYYC member George Schuyler, the sole surviving donor of the Cup and principle author of the Deed of Gift, sided with Ashbury. So the 1871 race became a match-race—a duel between two yachts. But there was a twist: the NYYC insisted on having two boats as part of their stable of Defenders—one that performed better in strong wind and another that did better in light; and the Club reserved the right to select one or the other prior to the start of each race based on the day's forecast. Naturally Ashbury did not like these unfair terms, but he raced anyway. He lost and never returned.

Starting with the next match, in 1876, the NYYC came to its senses and selected only one yacht to defend the Cup for the duration of a match.

During the 12-meter era (1958 to 1987), the NYYC unilaterally imposed a series of rules (known as the "Interpretative Resolutions") that supplemented the Deed of Gift. The 1958 resolutions relaxed some of the rules to allow Challengers to use American sails and deck gear (which at the time were among the best in the world) in a gesture of generosity. For the 1962 match, the Australian Challenger used sails and certain deck components built in America; the yacht was also tested in American tank-testing facilities. The Australian boat proved to be fast. And despite being the first challenge in that country's history, they were able to beat the Americans in one of the races that year and kept the other races relatively close. The NYYC, shaken by the closeness of the match, rescinded the 1958 resolutions: Challengers had to source their components from their own country once again.

After the 1974 match, which was won by their 12-meter class yacht *Courageous*, it was discovered that the boat actually rated as a 12.25-meter (caused by an unintentional error by the designer or builder). The Challenger, Alan Bond of Australia, demanded a rematch, but the NYYC refused.

Bond relented to the NYYC's decision but returned with a vengeance.

And three Cup matches later, in 1983, Bond's *Australia II* achieved the unthinkable and became the first Challenger to win the America's Cup.

AUSTRALIA II WINS THE CUP (1983)

How did the Australian team led by Alan Bond, a scrappy entrepreneur from Western Australia, achieve what no Challenger had previously accomplished? The Australians won the Cup in a manner reminiscent of the best Defenders—the NYYC: they had an effective management team armed with a business-like attitude; an experienced and highly skilled sailing team; and a boat that was significantly faster (except on a reach) and more maneuverable than the NYYC's defender.

Alan Bond and his management team oversaw a methodical yacht-design program that produced an excellent boat; and, through the most demanding training program in challenger history, they built a crew to take advantage of their boat's awesome speed. They also took a serious approach to the campaign. Warren Jones, the team's manager, said, "We train like commandos. I first came here in 1974 and it was a lot of fun. Now that has gone. The whole thing has become deadly, deadly serious."

The Defender's skipper, Dennis Conner, had a great crew, but their boat, *Liberty*, was hopelessly outclassed by Australia's revolutionary boat.

If it wasn't for mechanical breakdowns suffered by *Australia II* in the first two races and a near-win that was called off when time expired, Australia could have won the Cup 4-1 in dominating fashion. Instead, the match went to a seventh and final race. In that historic race, Dennis Conner and his crew were able to superhumanly lead *Australia II* at the penultimate mark by 57 seconds, but knowing that it wasn't a big enough lead against the superboat, they were forced to take a chance and find a windshift. *Liberty* was unable to find one, and *Australia II* passed her on that downwind leg, sailing lower and faster; the final upwind leg to the finish saw a tacking duel, but the Australians prevailed, crossing the finish line 41 seconds ahead.

The Challenger Selection Series Helped the Australians Gain Experience

The highly skilled and experienced sailing team of *Australia II* that took the Cup in 1983 was a product of a campaign that competed in three consecutive Cup matches from 1974 to 1980 and had the benefit of racing in the challenger selection series.

NYYC's Challenger Selection Series —Post WWII Racing Goes International

Beginning in 1970 the NYYC instituted an international challenger selection series to handle the ever-increasing influx of challenger candidates

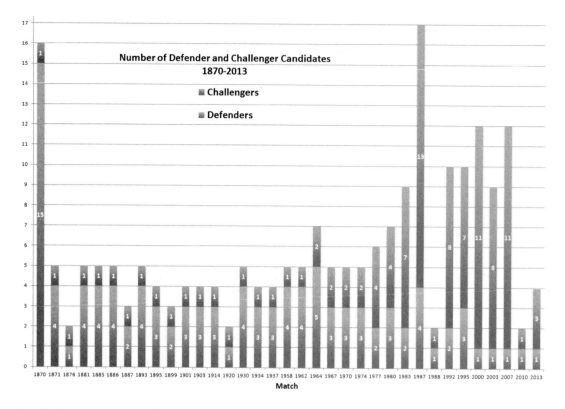

from around the world and with the hopes of improving the quality of Challengers (the 1964 and 1967 matches were embarrassing walk-overs by the NYYC against the Challengers).

The post-war years saw a rise in the number of potential challengers. After the war, the Cup was revived in 1956 with the modest-sized International 12-meter class, a more economic alternative to the J-Class, which was used before the war; by comparison, the median cost of a 12-meter campaign in the 1958 match was less than half the median cost of a J-Class campaign in the 1937 match, adjusted for inflation. The lower entry cost of competing for the Cup combined with increased globalization brought several Challengers to the doors of the NYYC to compete for the Cup. Beginning in the 1960s, it became common for the NYYC to postpone one challenge to accommodate another that challenged first: for the 1962 match, the NYYC had selected an Australian Challenger over a British Challenger, who had to wait until 1964. To prevent bickering among potential Challengers about who challenged first, the NYYC issued a memorandum in December 1962 that considered all challenges received within 30 days of the completion of the 1964 match to be considered simultaneous.

After the 1967 match, the NYYC received four challenges: the Royal Sydney Yacht Squadron, the Royal Dorset Yacht Club, the Yacht Club D'Hyères, and the Royal Yacht Club of Greece (although the challenges from the Royal Dorset and Greece soon dropped out). Initially, the club selected Australia's Royal Sydney Yacht Squadron to compete for the next match in 1970 but French ballpoint pen industrialist Baron Marcel Bich (on behalf of the Yacht Club D'Hyères) would not agree to a postponement of his campaign, so a series of negotiations between the challengers and the NYYC led to the establishment of a challenger selection series for the 1970 match.

This was the most important turning point in the history of the challengers' quest for the Cup, and it marked the beginning of the end of the NYYC's hold on the Cup. The challenger selection series (known as the Louis Vuitton Cup since 1983) helped level the playing field by improving the quality of the Challenger in the same manner the defender selection series had benefitted the NYYC.

As the chart on page 12 reveals, the ratio of challenger candidates to defender candidates has changed dramatically over time. After World War II, challenging the Cup was more accessible to more yacht clubs. And commencing with the 1970 challenger selection series, the number of Challengers rapidly began to outnumber the defender campaigns. (Note that for the 1964 and 1967 matches, there were two challenger candidates each; in those years, there was a single challenging yacht club, but it held an intra-yacht club selection series; these series were a forerunner to the international challenger series.)

It was the Australians led by Alan Bond who took most advantage of the challenger selection series. By the time Bond's *Australia II* team faced *Liberty*, they were the beneficiaries of a decade of experience, having sailed scores of races against sixteen different opponents. Of the fifteen members of Australia's sailing team, seven had experienced at least one America's Cup match; three of those had competed in three matches.

Having logged many hours racing in the elimination trials and Cup matches in Newport, Rhode Island, the crew of *Australia II* developed an understanding of the conditions of the America's Cup course, and this proved decisive. During the first windward leg of Race 6, with *Australia II* trailing *Liberty* on the same tack, Australian crew member Phil Smidmore predicted that the south-westerly thermal sea breeze would soon replace the gradient north-westerly breeze on the left side of the course; so *Australia II* changed course and headed left. By the time *Liberty* decided to cover, it was too late: Smidmore's call was correct. *Australia II* was lifted by the wind, grabbed the lead, and went on to win the race.

Seeking a Breakthrough in Yacht Design

After the 1980 match, Bond's team unanimously agreed that seeking a breakthrough in 12-meter yacht design should be a top priority. Australian Jones argued, "If we have only the same boat speed as them we will be incredibly lucky to beat them. To beat them we must be even faster." Therefore Bond's team implemented a deliberate program to design an experimental 12-meter and, as a hedge, a conventional twelve. In the spring of 1981, Lexcen began design work. But he did not do it alone. Instead, Ben Lexcen's creative brilliance was complemented with a design team that included hydrodynamicist Peter van Oossanen of the Netherlands

Ship Model Basin, aerodynamicist Joop Slooff, and sail designer Tom Schnackenberg. The team conducted extensive tank testing and computational fluid dynamics research on a scale not achieved before and yielded a boat design that was truly revolutionary.

Australia II's most salient features were her short length, low hull, large sail area, and "upside down" winged keel that endowed her with more stability than a conventional 12-meter. These features made her fast in light winds and in a breeze, and made her very maneuverable. She also benefited from having the best sails among the competitors. Schnackenberg invented vertical panel mains and tri-radial jibs—a design adopted by every Cup sail-maker after 1983.

Meanwhile, Dennis Conner and other leaders of American campaigns since the mid-1970s embraced the conventional wisdom that 12-meter yacht design had peaked and that a more conservative approach to yacht design paid better dividends. Conner said, "I've never been interested in being the first, the pioneer. Give me a competitive design, and I think I can do all right with it. My experience is that people on the leading edge pay the price more often than they reap the rewards." Conner's thinking was influenced in part by his experience sailing defender candidate *Mariner* in 1974, a 12-meter with an unusual hull design that was supposed to have been a breakthrough design but ended up being one of the slowest 12-meters ever designed. A misinterpretation of the tank-test results was the culprit according to *Mariner's* designer, Britton Chance. Legendary American yacht designer Olin Stephens, who designed several Cup winners, reflected,

> The bad tank test results and the coming of aluminum boats, which are easier to alter than wooden ones, led to the generally accepted feeling, which I think was pushed by the sailmakers and the sailors, that if you just get any good 12-meter, tune it up very well, get the sails right, get to know the boat and get a good crew, this was about the most you could do. Of course as a designer I couldn't be expected to subscribe to that point of view, and I always thought there was some possibility of some kind of breakthrough, maybe bigger, maybe smaller. There was less and less chance to demonstrate that possibility during the two or three matches of the 1970s, however.

Johan Valentijn designed *Liberty*—a conventional design that borrowed from previous 12-meters: she had a bow like *Freedom*, a keel like *Enterprise*, a deck plan like *Magic*, and a long counter like *Courageous*. In stark contrast to *Australia II*, *Liberty* was drawn in a mere ten days, and no tank testing was done.

Australia II's incredible maneuverability and speed forced Conner to take chances. Because *Liberty* couldn't engage *Australia II* in tacking duels without losing ground, the Americans had to play the windshifts to win. This risky strategy paid off in Race 1 and Race 4, but it cost them dearly in the last two races. It took seven races, but *Australia II* edged *Liberty* to win the America's Cup on September 26, 1983, breaking the longest sports streak in history.

A NEW WORLD: 1983 TO PRESENT

The Australian victory was the most important moment in the Cup's history after the original 1851 victory by the yacht *America*. It marked the end of the NYYC's long and relatively stable regime and the beginning of a more rough-and-tumble America's Cup punctuated with short regimes averaging only six years. In the thirty years since the NYYC lost the Cup, there have been five different owners of the Cup.

HOLDERS OF THE AMERICA'S CUP

Owner	Nation	Tenure	Record
New York Yacht Club	USA	1851-1983	24-1
Royal Perth Yacht Club	Australia	1983-1987	1-1
San Diego Yacht Club	USA	1987-1995	3-1
Royal New Zealand Yacht Squadron	New Zealand	1995-2003	2-1
Société Nautique de Genève	Switzerland	2003-2010	2-1
Golden Gate Yacht Club	USA	2010-present	2-0

The 1987 America's Cup match, the 26th Defense, was held in Fremantle, Western Australia, on the Indian Ocean. This edition of the Cup captured the interest of the public worldwide; there were an unprecedented thirteen Challengers from the United States, Canada, Great Britain, Italy, France, and a new contender, New Zealand.

Dennis Conner was on a mission to regain the Cup for America. Having been dropped by the NYYC, he sailed on behalf of his hometown yacht club, the San Diego Yacht Club.

New Zealand, an island nation of only 3.3 million people, made an impressive debut. Their Challenger, skippered by the young and brash Chris Dickson, managed to reach the Louis Vuitton finals, having achieved an astonishing 37-1 record. The Kiwis faced Conner's *Stars & Stripes* (31-7). The finals were raced in heavy wind and heavy seas, conditions that suited *Stars & Stripes*'s design, and the Americans went on to win 4-1. A lack of experience led New Zealand to unwisely shut down their design program after their boat was launched; meanwhile, Dennis Conner's experienced team continuously tinkered with the boat and sail design, even after sweeping their opponent in the semi-finals. Dickson lamented that, "Thirteen years' experience beat thirteen months' experience." Nevertheless, the Kiwis' amazing performance in 1987 laid the foundation for their eventual success in later years.

Conner's *Stars & Stripes* went on to beat the Australians 4-0, completing his comeback. The San Diego Yacht Club (SDYC) was thrilled to become the third trustee of the Cup, but their happiness would not last. Conner and his supporters became embroiled in a power struggle with the leadership of the SDYC over the details of the next match. In the meantime, surprisingly, no one had yet challenged the club. Many teams were expecting another 12-meter regatta in three or four years, but frustration mounted among would-be Challengers as months went by and they heard nothing but silence from the SDYC.

New Zealand merchant banker Michael Fay, one of the leaders behind the New Zealand team, decided to take action. His attorney, Andrew Johns, who studied the Deed of Gift, realized that the Cup is a challenge-driven sport and that their New Zealand–based yacht club, the Mercury Bay Boating Club (MBBC), had a right to a match. On July 17, 1987—five months after the SDYC won the Cup—Fay personally delivered a challenge to the SDYC commodore on behalf of the MBBC; Fay elaborated that he would meet the Defender with a sloop, 90 feet on the waterline, reminiscent of the magnificent J-Class. The SDYC was not amused and took Fay to court to challenge the legality of Fay's bid. The judge ruled in favor of New Zealand.

Absent a mutual agreement, SDYC and MBBC were forced to race under the terms of the Deed of Gift:

- The Defender is required to race the Challenger in a best-of-three match utilizing a 40-mile windward/leeward course for the first race, a 39-mile triangular course for the second race, and, if necessary, back to a windward-leeward course for the third race. The Defender has the right to select the location of the match.
- The Challenger selects the type of yacht: a single-masted vessel not to exceed 90 feet on the waterline or a multi-masted vessel not to exceed 120 feet on the waterline.

Time allowance is prohibited (in other words, a rating rule cannot be used to handicap one yacht over another).

The SDYC struck a defiant stance and decided to defend the Cup with a catamaran. No matter how fast MBBC's monohull was, it would not stand a chance against a multihull.

In September 1988, the MBBC's 120-foot (90-foot-waterline) sloop met SDYC's 60-foot catamaran. Needless to say, the American boat trounced the Kiwi boat in two races to successfully retain the Cup. The issue went back to court as Fay challenged the legality of a catamaran. Finally in April 1990, the sordid saga was put to rest as the court ruled in favor of SDYC. And the Cup remained in San Diego.

A positive result of the ordeal was the creation of a new class to replace the venerable but tired 12-meter class. Later that year a convention of yacht designers formulated the International America's Cup Class (IACC). Compared to the 12-meter, the new class of sloop carried two times the sail area, was 25 percent longer, and weighed slightly less.

(continued on page 22)

Significant Changes in the America's Cup Since 1983

There have been significant and lasting changes that occurred after Australia captured the Cup in 1983.

THE AMERICA'S CUP RACES HAVE BEEN MORE COMPETITIVE

With the exception of the Deed-of-Gift matches (1988 and 2010), the America's Cup has become more competitive. The average margin of victory in the 2013 match was 0.6 minute. (See chart on page 26.)

Research and Design Is Critical Because Boat Speed Is Now the Deciding Factor

The world was mesmerized by *Australia II*'s revolutionary design, and it caused future Cup campaigners to place a priority on research and design, using increasingly professional methods and expanding its scope.

Australia II was a product of a collaborative method where no one person was responsible for the whole design. The design was the product of a team of specialists: Joop Slooff, an aerodynamicist, who worked on NATO aircraft, used his high-end scientific knowledge about fluid dynamics to help Ben Lexcen execute the design of the winged keel; van Oossanen contributed the concept of a short, low-displacement boat.

Dennis Conner, learning from his 1983 mistake, built a team of yacht designers and specialists for his 1987 campaign and future campaigns. In 1992, Bill Koch and his *America*[3] team took the design approach even further by building a design and construction team of unprecedented size, around a hundred specialists. Koch's success attracted the attention of Russell Coutts, who interviewed members of *America*[3]'s design team. Coutts, trained as an engineer, was soaked in the methodologies used by the team, such as the application of a velocity prediction program (VPP), which is a software program that solves for the performance of a sailboat in various wind conditions by balancing the forces on the hull and the sails. The first VPP was developed at the Massachusetts Institute of Technology in the early 1970s; the research was funded by NYYC commodore Irving Pratt. But the use of VPPs was not widespread in the America's Cup until the past twenty years.

Research and design has become more critical than ever because boat speed has become perhaps the deciding factor. So far, since 1983, the faster boat has won every match because the sailors aboard the Defender and the Challenger have been evenly matched. (Before 1983 the NYYC Defenders were able to beat a challenger with a faster boat because they could out-wit or out-sail the Challenger.)

The Decline of Nationalism

Throughout most of the history of the Cup, the Challengers and Defenders were distinctly national.

For the vast majority of the Cup's history, the design and construction of the boats have long been the products of citizens of the country associated with the challenge or defense.

This nationalism extended to the sailors as well: the overwhelming majority of sailors who manned the yachts sailed for their country (there were exceptions before World War II, when the NYYC hired Scandinavian sailors on occasion to crew on their Defenders, but this did not raise any concern at the time because the Deed of Gift did not require crews to be sailing for their nation). But during the 12-meter era, it became customary for the crew to hold their club's nationality.

But as globalization took greater hold in the latter half of the twentieth century, this signature element of the America's Cup began to falter. For the 1977 match, American sailor Andy Rose was hired by Alan Bond to sail aboard *Australia*, which prompted the NYYC to issue a new rule requiring crew members to hold their club's nationality.

There were other signs of this when the Dutch collaborated with both the Australians and the Americans in 1983. But the 1980s remained overall true to the nationalistic spirit of the Cup, and the 1987 match in Fremantle, Australia, was in many ways the pinnacle of nationalism in the America's Cup.

While the 1992, 1995, and 2000 series were largely nationalistic, high-visibility exceptions became more common. In 1992, two out of the ten teams featured prominent hired guns from outside the country of the Challenger: *Il Moro di Venezia* of Italy and *Nippon* of Japan. The rule at that time stipulated that the designer and crew be "nationals" of the Challenger's country. To qualify as a national, though, the individual simply had to be domiciled in the country or have it be their principal residence for at least two years prior to the match.

But it was after New Zealand's successful defense in 2000 that the America's Cup witnessed a collapse of the spirit of nationalism. The spring of 2000 became a watershed moment. The ball got rolling when skipper Russell Coutts and tactician Brad Butterworth of Team New Zealand reluctantly resigned from Team New Zealand on May 19, 2000, due to a conflict with the team's

NATIONALITIES OF CREW ABOARD 1992 AC CHALLENGERS
IL MORO DI VENEZIA (CHALLENGER)

CEO and skipper	Paul Cayard	USA/France
Chief designer	German Frers	Argentina
Technical/research coordinator	Robert Hopkins	USA
Operations manager	Laurent Esquier	France
Coach	Steve Erickson	USA
Coach	John Kolius	USA

NIPPON (CHALLENGE CANDIDATE)

Skipper	Chris Dickson	New Zealand
Afterguard	John Cutler	New Zealand
Afterguard	Erle Williams	New Zealand

sponsors. Three days later, the Swiss Challenger, Alinghi, announced that they had hired the two Kiwi legends. Soon after, they were joined by four more members of New Zealand's core group of sailors; in addition, the Australian Grant Simmer and Dutch designer Rolf Vrolijk signed up for the Swiss team. Next, Laurie Davidson, the great New Zealand yacht designer, left Team New Zealand to lead the design team for the One World challenge of the United States; joining Davidson were about a dozen other Kiwi sailors.

Other teams also filled their rosters with international hired guns. The Italian Prada challenge sported Brazilian Torben Grael and Kiwi Rod Davis in the afterguard. American billionaire Larry Ellison's Oracle BMW Racing hired Peter Holmberg of the British Virgin Islands and John Cutler of Australia.

Russell Coutts, sailing for Alinghi, won the 2003 match, bringing the Cup to Europe for the first time. Coutts then abolished, with the blessing of Larry Ellison, as Challenger of Record, the nationality rules for the 2007 match. The rules were eliminated because Coutts and Ellison realized the farce and expense of having to maintain residences for their foreign members in the country of the challenge. And it has since remained this way.

The increased use of foreign talent by campaigns has changed the dynamic of the sport.

It had diminished the thrilling "nation versus nation" drama that imbues popular international events such as the Olympics and the World Cup. Consider that it was difficult for some American fans to feel proud of the 2013 ORACLE TEAM USA given that only one crew member (out of the eleven members) of the team was American.

It has also enabled campaigns to quickly become competitive. On a small scale, foreign advisors have helped teams new to the America's Cup learn the basics in a relatively short time; a notable example of this is New Zealand's first challenge in 1987, which benefited from the tutelage of experienced French 12-meter campaigner Laurent Esquier, who trained the Kiwis to sail a 12-meter. But on a large scale, it could launch a team straight to the Cup, as in the case of Team Alinghi.

A Sharp Increase in the Cost of Campaigns

Over four-hundred million dollars were spent by the four teams that competed in 2013 cycle; a staggering figure that approaches the total amount—adjusting for inflation—spent by the 123 teams that competed for the Cup from 1870 to 1980.

ESTIMATED CAMPAIGN COSTS FOR THE 34TH AMERICA'S CUP

Luna Rossa Challenge 2013	$65 million
Emirates Team New Zealand	$105 million
Artemis Racing	$115 million
ORACLE TEAM USA	$156 million

As majestic as the J-Class boats were, and are, the costs of a one-boat campaign in the 1930s were very modest by today's standards. For the 1934 America's Cup, the victorious *Rainbow* defense syndicate spent $500,000 ($8.7 million in 2013 dollars). The Challenger, T.O.M. Sopwith's *Endeavour*, spent $315,000 ($5.5 million). A single AC72, with two wings and three sets of appendages, runs around $13 million. By contrast, Dennis Conner's campaign for the 1983 defense spent around $12 million in 2013 U.S. dollars for a two-year campaign that included the building of three 12-meter yachts.

As the chart on page 20 illustrates, a sharp escalation in costs commenced after the 1983 America's Cup.

Four primary factors have contributed to the exponential rise in costs: payroll costs, longer campaigns, multiple boats, and increased R&D spending.

Payroll

Today's sailors are well paid. The rank-and-file crew earn anywhere from the upper five figures to the mid-six figures annually, with substantial bonuses for winning the Cup. Top afterguard talent can earn millions.

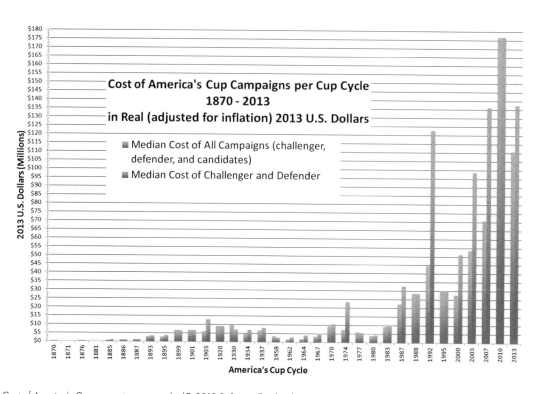

Cost of America's Cup campaigns per cycle. (© 2013 R. Steven Tsuchiya)

During the 12-meter era, which covered ten matches from 1958 to 1987, the vast majority of Cup sailors were amateurs, greatly reducing the payroll costs for the campaigns. But beginning with Dennis Conner's two-year campaign for the 1980 match, longer campaigns meant the need for professional crew over time. Other campaigns began following suit: at least half of the seventeen contenders for the 1987 America's Cup in Perth, Australia, employed professional crew. The Cup match pitted Dennis Conner's Sail America, the last largely amateur American team, against Taskforce America's Cup Defense, one of the first all-professional Australian teams. Conner's team won. However, the bridge had been crossed. After the 1987 Cup, every campaign—save Syd Fischer's *Young Australia* crew in 2000—has fielded a professional team.

Crew salaries rose gradually at first. The typical annual salary for an afterguard member for the New Zealand team, says Brad Butterworth, went from NZD$40,000 to $50,000 for the 1987 *Kiwi Magic* campaign to NZD$80,000 to $90,000 for the 2000 Team New Zealand defense.

Another watershed moment came on the heels of the 2000 regatta. American billionaire Craig McCaw decided to give the America's Cup a try. To jump-start his One World campaign, McCaw lured the most experienced sailors with extremely generous pay packages, easily five times more than the existing salaries. Ernesto Bertarelli, a rival billionaire from Switzerland, got into the game as well, prying many elite sailors away from Team New Zealand. Since then, a keen competition for top talent has driven salaries through the roof. The cost of personnel now accounts for 60 to 70 percent of the cost of a campaign, making it the most important factor in the escalating costs.

Conspiring with higher pay to increase budgets has been the lengthening of Cup campaigns. The longer a campaign, the more it costs. BMW Oracle Racing, which won the 33rd Cup in February 2010, had been at it continuously with no break since 2000. It hasn't always been this way.

Campaigns from the 1880s to the 1970s lasted anywhere from five months to a year and a half, with sailing teams being hired and terminated typically within a six-month period. Bob Bavier, the skipper of the *Constellation* in 1964, recalled that he "devoted six months to the . . . sailing effort—three months of weekends—three more months of sailing everyday, all day." Nowadays, that's not enough practice time for even the lowest-budget teams.

The current standard for the "endless campaigns" was invented by Dennis Conner's *Freedom* campaign, which stretched 1978 to 1980. Alinghi's America's Cup campaigns for 2003, 2007, and 2010 were essentially part of one continuous campaign that ran virtually non-stop from 2001 through the spring of 2010.

Multiple Boats

For the past 30 years, constructing multiple boats has been standard operating procedure for a serious campaign. For most of the history of the Cup, however, this was not the case. Of the 120 syndicates across 24 matches from 1870 to 1980, only one constructed more than one yacht for a Cup bid.

The 1983 Cup cycle broke that "one-boat-is-enough" methodology. For that Cup cycle, three of the nine contenders built at least two new boats for their effort to win the Cup. Dennis Conner's campaign built three. After nearly winning in 1980, Alan Bond commissioned a highly experimental design (*Australia II*) and a backup yacht of a more conventional design (*Challenge 12*).

As a result, the median cost of a campaign in 1983 was more than double that of the previous cycle.

For the 1987 Cup, nine of seventeen syndicates—thirteen Challengers and four Defense syndicates—built two or more boats. For the 1992 contest, ten teams constructed an astonishing twenty-five boats. The Defender, Bill Koch's *America*[3] syndicate, built four, while Challenger Raul Gardini's Il Moro di Venezia built five.

After the outrageous 1992 yacht-building contest, protocols between the Challenger and Defender have limited teams to two boats. However, that hasn't curtailed the escalating cost of a campaign. Rather than building new boats, the teams simply keep refining their existing ones.

Research and Development Costs

For most of the Cup's history before the 1987 campaign, America's Cup R&D meant a yacht designer with a small support staff, who on occasion would hire a tank-test specialist or another type of specialist, such as an aerospace engineer.

Nathanael Herreshoff designed six Cup winners between 1893 and 1920. The hull design for his yacht *Reliance* was formed in just one evening, when he carved a wooden half-hull to create the template for the final design. He personally designed most of the fittings for the boat and a suit of sails as well. Herreshoff's hull contract for *Defender*, in 1895, amounted to $75,000 ($2,040,000); his design fee was imbedded in the cost of the construction of the hull.

Olin Stephens, who designed six Cup winners from 1937 to 1980, employed a staff of several designers and draftsmen; he also used tank-testing services at the Stevens Institute of Technology. For the yacht *Courageous* in 1974, his firm's design fees amounted to $125,000 ($588,000) and the tank-testing cost was approximately the same, at $125,000 ($588,000). In today's dollars, the total cost of R&D and design fees for that campaign was $1.2 million. For the *Freedom* campaign in 1980, the total design cost was a mere $73,000 ($178,500).

As noted earlier, the *Australia II* campaign pioneered the strong marriage between yacht designers and scientists in the aerospace and hydrodynamics fields. Dennis Conner took things to yet another level in 1987, continually researching refinements well after the boat was launched.

"Dennis Conner also kept modifying boats during the [1987] campaign right up until racing," says veteran America's Cup designer Mike Drummond.

"So subsequent campaigns increased their building costs, and designs kept coming through the campaign, so more parts were built."

The BMW Oracle Racing campaign for the 33rd America's Cup in 2010 employed about 35 design staff plus a network of consultants that included multihull designers, aerospace engineers, and hydrodynamicists, that, including boat builders, involved over 120 people.

Multihulls Earn Respect and Find a Place in the America's Cup

Throughout the history of the Cup, monohulls were the standard, from the yacht *America* to the America's Cup Class sloops. Racing multihulls under mutual agreement was never taken seriously until after the 2010 match. And even after the spectacular racing in 2013, there are some sailors who would like to see a return to monohull racing.

Multihulls are not new to sailing, though. In fact, Cup founder John Cox Stevens owned one, *Double Trouble*, back in 1820. In 1876 the great yacht designer Nathanael Herreshoff, whose boats won six America's Cups, entered and raced a catamaran of his own design, *Amaryllis*, in the NYYC's Centennial Regatta. His revolutionary 24-foot cat handily beat her monohull opponents to take line honors. Unfortunately for Herreshoff and fans of multihulls, the NYYC derisively considered *Amaryllis* a freak and not a true yacht.

Fast-forward to the 2010 match: the sailors aboard BMW Oracle Racing's trimaran *USA* had a ride of their lives. Most of them had been monohull sailors until that point. After the match, Larry Ellison and Russell Coutts collaborated with yacht designers to develop a new class of boat for the 34th America's Cup, asking designer Bruce Nelson to develop a monohull and simultaneously asking multihull design firm Morrelli & Melvin to design a multihull class boat. The team's exhilarating experience in 2010 helped pave the way for selecting the multihull design, which would eventually become the AC72 catamaran class.

1992: 28th Defense of the America's Cup

The new International America's Cup Class energized the yachting world, and the 1992 match in San Diego attracted eight Challengers and two defense candidates. Michael Fay was back with a New Zealand syndicate. The other Challengers hailed from Italy, Australia, France, and Sweden, and there were two new players: Japan and Spain.

The brand-new class made an auspicious debut in May 1991 at the IACC World championship in San Diego. The winds, 15 to 20 knots, were strong for San Diego and meant a heavy sea-state. Carnage ensued: among other damages, the Japanese boat was dismasted and lost a man overboard; and the Spanish boat broke its steering system. The head of one of the American teams, Bill Koch, remarked that the IACC yachts were "incredibly dangerous." These difficulties, while not as severe, were echoed in the difficulties suffered by the AC72 class in its first year.

Team New Zealand initially dominated the 1992 challenger finals against Il Moro di Venezia, the Italian team. But Italians turned the tables by protesting the legality of Team New Zealand's bowsprit. The International Jury deemed the sprit illegal, and the New Zealanders were annulled one race. The ruling forced the team to re-learn how to sail without the bowsprit in the middle of the series. It raised the spirits of skipper Paul Cayard and his Italian team, which went on to roll over the Kiwis. But *Il Moro* was no match for the Defender, *America³*, losing 4-1. The Cup remained in SDYC's hands.

The *America³* campaign, led by industrialist Bill Koch, was a success because it was well managed and developed a sophisticated approach to designing the sailboats. Koch's campaign took what the *Australia II* design team did and multiplied it to an industrial scale. More than a hundred designers, engineers, and specialists made up the design and construction teams. Koch allowed for creativity but rigorously tested ideas using scientific methods. Eventually the ambitious team built four boats, in a no-stones-unturned program.

1995: 29th Defense of the America's Cup

Seven Challengers bid for the 1995 Cup. Team New Zealand was back again, managed by the noted ocean-racing yachtsman Sir Peter Blake and a rising star, Russell Coutts, who would become the greatest skipper and team manager in the history of the Cup.

Peter Blake won the 1989-90 Whitbread race as skipper of *Steinlager 2* in an unprecedented sweep of line, handicap, and overall honors on each of the race's six legs. For the 1992 America's Cup, he was brought in during the middle of the campaign to manage the team.

Russell Coutts, born in Wellington, New Zealand, in 1962, grew up sailing dinghies. At age seven, he sailed his first race with his older brother and never looked back. After having won a string of youth championships, Coutts won a gold medal in the Finn class in the 1984 Olympics at age 22. In 1986, Coutts made his foray into the America's Cup, serving briefly as a crew member for the original New Zealand challenge; but he departed the team before the racing started to earn his engineering degree. In 1992, he took part in various roles as a backup helmsman and tactician, and he even helmed the boat in a few races in the challenger finals.

For the 1995 Cup, Coutts leveraged the team's deep bench of experienced sailors and utilized the principles that made Bill Koch's design team successful. The design team was led by Tom Schnackenberg (who was part of the legendary *Australia II* team), Laurie Davidson, and Doug Peterson. They developed a very narrow boat, *Black Magic, NZL-32*. A Kiwi crew member, upon seeing the unusual boat for the first time, cried, "[The designers] either got it horribly wrong or it's terrifically right!" It echoed the words uttered by the Marquis of Anglesey when he first saw the yacht *America*: "If she is right, then all of us are wrong." *Black Magic* proved to be one of the best Cup yachts ever built. With Russell Coutts at the helm, *Black Magic* marched through the trials, achieving a record of 38-1 to win the Louis Vuitton Cup.

In the Cup match, New Zealand faced an old foe, Dennis Conner, who had ruined their party in 1987. This time, it was New Zealand who dominated. In the best of nine series, *Black Magic* swept the series 5-0, leading at all 30 marks. The New Zealand boat could sail higher *and* faster than the American boat. New Zealand, on their fourth attempt over the course of a decade, finally won the Holy Grail of yachting.

2000: 30th Defense of the America's Cup

For the 30th Defense of the America's Cup, eleven challengers from seven nations arrived in Auckland. And for the first time since 1876, there was only one defender campaign. Team New Zealand stood alone; and as it turned out, it was the start of a new trend. There has been only one Defender per Cup cycle since 2000.

Among the Challengers was a new face, Patrizio Bertelli, the CEO of the fashion house Prada. Bertelli's Italian challenge, the Luna Rossa Prada Challenge, made an impressive debut by winning the Louis Vuitton Cup, defeating Paul Cayard's *AmericaOne* team 5-4 in a closely fought series.

For the first time in the history of the America's Cup, there would be no American team battling in the match.

Team New Zealand was once again skippered by Russell Coutts. The new *Black Magic*, a product of Laurie Davidson's design team, featured an innovative "knuckle bow," which gained an additional eight inches of waterline length over a conventional design.

Black Magic went on to crush *Luna Rossa* 5-0 to keep the Cup in Auckland. In the last race, Russell Coutts handed the helm over to his protégé, 28-year-old Dean Barker.

2003: 31st Defense of the America's Cup

The 31st Defense was a watershed moment in the Cup's history. This was the series that saw nationalism go out the door. After their successful defense of the Cup in 2000, Russell Coutts and his core group of sailors departed Team New Zealand to join the Swiss Alinghi Challenge, led by billionaire Ernesto Bertarelli. According to Coutts, he was not able to achieve Team New Zealand's objectives given the budget constraints set by their sponsors, so he departed in frustration to a foreign Challenger.

There were nine Challengers for this series and, once again, Team New Zealand was the lone Defender.

This Cup cycle witnessed American billionaire Larry Ellison's first challenge. Ellison, a successful amateur skipper who had followed the Cup for decades, finally decided to throw his hat in the ring. He hired Bruce Farr and Associates to design his boats, and he built a sailing team led by Chris Dickson (Australia) and Peter Holmberg (British Virgin Islands). Ellison's first attempt was not a bad start—his team managed to race in the Louis Vuitton finals, but they lost 5-1 to Team Alinghi, helmed by the now legendary Russell Coutts.

At the Cup final, with many New Zealand fans angry about the departure of Coutts and company, the Kiwi-led *Alinghi* faced Team New

Zealand, skippered by Dean Barker. *Alinghi* swept the match 5-0. Russell Coutts had now won a record fourteen out of fourteen America's Cup races since 1995.

Ernesto Bertarelli's victory brought great attention to Switzerland, and he was hailed as a hero for bringing the Cup to Europe for the first time. However, his relationship with Coutts crumbled after the victory: Coutts wanted to take on more responsibilities and had a vision for the Cup that was not shared by his boss. In a startling turn of events, Coutts was eventually fired from the team and prevented from joining another team for the next Cup cycle due to a non-compete clause in his contract.

2007: 32nd Defense of the America's Cup

Given that landlocked Switzerland had no adequate venue to host an America's Cup match, it held an Olympic-style bidding contest to determine the next venue. Valencia, Spain, won the bid as host city. Although Russell Coutts departed, the other Kiwis remained with Team Alinghi. Brad Butterworth, longtime tactician, took over as skipper. *Alinghi* would be the sole Defender on behalf of the Swiss yacht club, Société Nautique de Genève.

Ernesto Bertarelli introduced a bold, new regime of running the America's Cup: AC Management, a division of Team Alinghi, would operate the *entire* event, including the challenger selection series. The Challenger of Record, Larry Ellison's Golden Gate Yacht Club (GGYC), agreed to this format given the fact that the umpires and jury members remained independent of Alinghi.

One of the changes brought by Alinghi and Ellison's team, BMW Oracle Racing, was the introduction of the Louis Vuitton Acts, regattas with fleet races and match races held in various ports (such as Marseille, France; Malmö, Sweden; Trapani, Italy; and Valencia, Spain) in the years leading up to the Match in 2007. The Acts served as a warm-up for Cup sailors and helped publicize the America's Cup.

In the Louis Vuitton Cup semi-finals, Luna Rossa defeated BMW Oracle, and Team New Zealand defeated the Spanish team Desafío Español. In the finals, Team New Zealand routed Luna Rossa 5-0.

The America's Cup match of 2007 was the most exciting since 1983. *Alinghi* won the series 5-2, but the races were incredibly close. In a freak finish in the last race, *Alinghi* won by a mere second.

And so the Cup remained with Société Nautique de Genève. With the 2007 match over, Russell Coutts was available for hire. Larry Ellison offered Coutts the role of CEO of BMW Oracle Racing, and the Kiwi sailing legend accepted.

2010: 33rd Defense of the America's Cup

Soon after his successful defense in the summer of 2007, Ernesto Bertarelli, emboldened by his experience in the previous cycle, attempted

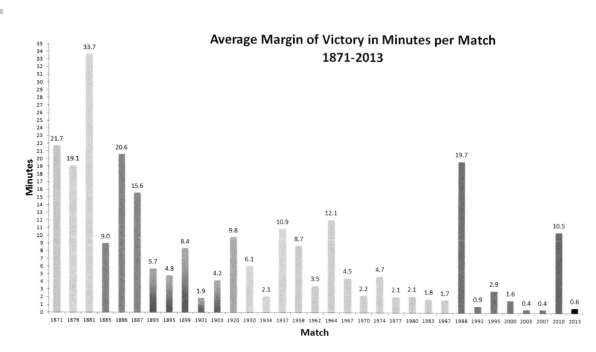

Average Margin of Victory in Minutes per Match
1871-2013

Average margin of victory in minutes, America's Cup matches, 1870-2013. The bars are shaded to reveal the different ratings of the yachts that competed. For example, the period from 1958 to 1987 represent the 12-metre class era. See page 211 for additional information about these ratings. (© 2013 R. Steven Tsuchiya)

to gain more control of the next edition. In a startling move, his team collaborated with individuals of the city of Valencia, Spain, establishing Club Náutico Español de Vela (CNEV), a paper yacht club to "challenge" Société Nautique de Genève (SNG), the Cup's holder. Because the Challenger and Defender negotiate the terms of a match, Bertarelli was able to craft terms that would essentially give the Defender nearly unchecked power. CNEV was more than happy to agree to SNG's terms for the prospect of keeping Valencia as the host city potentially for years to come.

The terms of the Match included the following:

Umpires and race officials would be employees of Alinghi's management company, and could reject or eject competitors at any time.

Alinghi would set the rules for racing and could restrict or sanction competitors as it saw fit.

Alinghi would select the umpires on the water and the jury who would judge the races.

Potential challenger candidates were appalled by these self-serving terms. The most vocal was Larry Ellison and his yacht club, the Golden Gate Yacht Club. Ellison tried to talk sense to Bertarelli, but after discussions failed, his team took SNG to court to challenge the validity of CNEV. Based on the Deed of Gift, the Challenger must be an "organized yacht club of a foreign country, incorporated, patented, or licensed by the legislature, admiralty or other executive department, having for its annual regatta an ocean water course on the sea, or on an arm of the sea, or one which combines both. . . ."

The court ruled in favor of the Golden Gate Yacht Club, and it replaced CNEV as the Challenger of Record.

As was the case in 1988, a Deed-of-Gift match was to be held, and a race date was eventually set for February 2010. As Challenger, BMW Oracle Racing had the prerogative to set the waterline length and type of yacht; Coutts and Ellison opted for a 90-foot-waterline sloop, with a maximum beam of 90 feet.

Meanwhile, though incensed by the decision, Team Alinghi refused to agree on a compromise that would revert to the balance of power of the previous match and prepared to defend against the Golden Gate Yacht Club and BMW Oracle Racing. With at least one lesson learned, unlike 1988, this Deed-of-Gift match would pit two multihulls against each other.

It was a design team's dream: they were free to spend millions to design the world's fastest around-the-buoy racing yacht. No class rules. No restrictions on materials. As long as it was a sloop with a 90-foot waterline, nearly anything was permissible.

At BMW Oracle Racing, Coutts marshaled design and construction efforts that involved over 120 people working to create the ultimate racing yacht. The design team, led by Mike Drummond, developed *USA-17*, a monster trimaran. Her center hull measured 90 feet on the waterline to comply with the Deed of Gift, but her outer hulls, which she sailed on, measured over 113 feet. Her signature feature was her 224-foot-tall carbon fiber wingsail. It remains the largest wing ever made, for a boat or an airplane, and the tallest mast ever built for a Cup yacht (three feet taller than the previous record-holder, the mast of the gigantic 1903 defender *Reliance*). The primary benefit of the wing was that it allowed *USA-17* to efficiently and effectively change gears in any condition.

Mike Drummond described the difference between *USA-17*'s wing and a traditional "soft" sail: "In general, both the soft sail and the wingsail provide a lifting surface that drives the boat forward. As the sail gets big-

Alinghi 5 versus BMW Oracle Racing's *17* in the first race of the 2010 America's Cup. (© 2010 Gilles Martin-Raget)

ger, it becomes more and more difficult to maintain an optimum shape. You can only tension a triangular [traditional soft] sail from three points, so as it gets bigger, it becomes harder to prevent the shape from distorting from the optimum. With a hard wing, you can control the shape to a very precise degree, which is a big advantage, and the shape doesn't distort. It is a much more efficient shape."

Alinghi launched a 110-foot catamaran, *Alinghi 5*, with a 203-foot-tall mast that carried 3DL sails built by North Sails. Her mainsail measured approximately 6,000 square feet, her headsail about 4,000 square feet, and the gennaker about 11,800 square feet. *Alinghi's* stiff network of struts, kingposts, and beams was a forerunner to the AC72 design.

As awesome as these boats were, the match was not interesting from a racing standpoint. *Alinghi* was hopelessly outclassed by *USA-17*, losing both races. At the helm of *USA-17* was skipper Jimmy Spithill, who earned his first Cup win.

With BMW Oracle Racing's victory, Russell Coutts had now achieved an incredible streak: winning and defending the Cup for New Zealand in 1995 and 2000, taking the Cup out of New Zealand's hands as skipper of *Alinghi* in 2003, and then beating *Alinghi* in 2010 as CEO of BMW Oracle Racing. Coutts was beginning to resemble a one-man version of the New York Yacht Club. And like the NYYC, Coutts was also shaping the rules of the game.

TWO Defending the 34th America's Cup

PICKING UP THE CUP

On February 14, 2010, BMW Oracle Racing, representing Golden Gate Yacht Club, won the America's Cup.

Still dripping in celebratory champagne, Larry Ellison, Russell Coutts, and other team members were pressed about their plans for defending the Cup, and the answer was that they had poured so much into preparing their challenge and winning the Cup that the next defense had not been the subject of serious discussion at all. A Challenger of Record (COR), Italy's Club Nautico di Roma, had been accepted, and Vincenzo Onorato, the main patron of the COR's Mascalzone Latino team, shared similar opinions with Larry Ellison on many aspects of the America's Cup.

The details of what to do next, however, were very much still to be determined.

Two questions loomed even as BMW Oracle's victory was still being celebrated. Where would the next America's Cup be held, and would it be in multihulls or would it go back to the traditional monohulls?

With San Francisco, California, being the home of the Golden Gate Yacht Club, and Larry Ellison living nearby, just south of the city, certainly San Francisco was the first city that came to mind. San Francisco Bay is not just a huge and beautiful setting for a regatta, but the Bay and the Golden Gate function as a wind machine, producing nearly daily breezes that build to 20 knots or more for much of the year.

Since becoming involved in the America's Cup in 2003, whenever asked, Ellison had always expressed enthusiasm about the idea of bringing the event to his adopted hometown. Now, along with GGYC and OTUSA, the opportunity was at hand.

Ellison was noncommittal about the multihull versus monohull options. Much was involved in such a decision, and there had been vigorous debate in the sailing community about the path to choose.

But on February 14, 2010, the team was exhausted. They had driven themselves single-mindedly toward building the 90-foot trimaran, with an unprecedented 224-foot-tall wingsail, testing in California, shipping to Europe, and keeping the boat intact long enough to win the two needed races against Société Nautique de Genève (SNG) and Alinghi.

And that was not even counting the legal and public relations side of the battle. What BMW Oracle Racing had once hoped would de-escalate into negotiations and a return to a conventional America's Cup in 2009 had instead erupted into a 33-month-long slog through three levels of the New York Supreme Court before the Golden Gate Yacht Club was finally confirmed as the official Challenger, and then they still had to litigate against their opponent just to establish the rules of the Match firmly enough to be able to comply with them. Not knowing where it would end, they had been chasing moving goalposts since 2007.

Asked at the post-AC33 press conference in Valencia what their plans were for AC34, Ellison and others replied that they hadn't even discussed their plans. BMW Oracle began their reign as Defender by bringing the America's Cup home, holding a few victory parties, and giving everyone a month off.

With Larry Ellison's decade of chasing the Cup, Russell Coutts' many years of involvement, and the experience of other senior leaders like Tom Ehman, whose involvement with the regatta went back into the mid 1980s, BMW Oracle Racing's leadership also knew something else. The America's Cup as an event was ailing.

The severity of that diagnosis depended somewhat on the physician delivering it, but if the model was to make it reasonably possible for a team to find commercial sponsorship and have a chance of winning the Cup, the event was broken. And even if commercial sponsors weren't a priority, even with private sponsorship from the richest men of the world, the event was struggling to maintain visibility in an increasingly competitive media landscape.

Louis Vuitton Cup races from New Zealand often aired taped delayed in the middle of the night in other parts of the world, including the United States, which should have been a prime market. The 2003 America's Cup match had begun with live coverage, the networks securing blocks of satellite time, only to show hours of wind delays for days in a row. The 2007 Louis Vuitton Cup opened up with nearly the entire opening round schedule scratched because there was either too little wind or too much.

And when the races did start, the current rules led the two boats to go into a "dial-up," both sitting directly into the wind at a dead stop for several minutes, or maybe, just maybe, sailing backward. Sailing a boat backward in slow motion was actually a difficult feat but was symptomatic of how not to entice potential viewers to get interested in the Cup.

A race took two hours, sometimes longer, and was held so far offshore that the only people who could see it were those on other boats, and even then they couldn't tell what was going on much of the time.

Making the Cup Better

There isn't one time in memory when a new club won the America's Cup and didn't announce their plans to make the historic event better. The beginning of the 34th Defense was no different. The Golden Gate Yacht Club and BMW Oracle Racing had a lot of problems to solve.

Several priorities evolved. From the sporting side, the long-term vision was for a healthy-sized group of competitive Challengers coming from a wide range of countries around the world. The racing should be compelling viewing, accessible enough for the uninitiated but fascinating enough to sailors or serious fans to keep them watching. In order to remain the pinnacle of the sport, the event had to remain at the forefront of technology, and on a higher level than competing events in terms of what it demanded from competitors and how it rewarded their accomplishments if they won. The history, the prestige, the fame were important, but they had to continually be tended, too.

From the commercial and financial side, teams require funding. Throughout the history of the Cup, whenever there has been a match, there have been some wealthy enthusiasts to help pay for it. In the NYYC's heyday, even the wealthiest of backers like J. P. Morgan often tended to group together with other members, forming syndicates with other rich men to support the campaigns. Sometimes it was sole patrons like Sir Thomas Lipton or, in the Great Depression, Harold Vanderbilt who stepped up, doing what they saw as their duty to hold up the side for their country. Fortunately, the "Cup Bug" continues to infect extremely wealthy sailors to this day, luring them with a prize that's not easy to win even when spending vast sums of money.

By the 1986-87 America's Cup in Fremantle, Australia, a central factor in the event was the fact that large portions of the teams' budget came from corporate sponsors. Dennis Conner, on his quest to reclaim the trophy, was maybe the most successful of all in the new financial landscape.

The 1992 defense in San Diego, California, saw what seemed to be countless commercial tie-ins for the teams and the event. Corporate support for the Cup was at a new peak. Yet the 1992 Cup was won by *America*[3], racing against Italy's Il Moro di Venezia. Co-skipper and primary patron of *America*[3] was Bill Koch, spending upward of $70 million USD against Il Moro backer Raul Gardini, who spent over $100 million USD. Just between the two teams, they built nine new boats for the event. Teams with lesser budgets felt priced out.

From the comparatively tiny nation in the Pacific came Team New Zealand, with a "family" of five corporate sponsors paying the team's way, not to mention funds raised by selling hundreds of thousands of pairs of signature red socks to fans back home. They had a modest budget, in relative terms, but in 1995 Team New Zealand swept the America's Cup match against a Defender who, like the other Challengers that year, was outclassed in speed.

BMW Oracle Racing's America's Cup-winning trimaran—the hard wingsail towered over 200 feet into the sky. (© 2010 Gilles Martin-Raget)

Team New Zealand was the exception, however, and would be the only team to race in the America's Cup match from 1992 through 2013 that was not primarily backed by one person's fortune. Team New Zealand hadn't won the Cup since 2000, but it had been on one side or another of the America's Cup match four of the last five times, except the 2010 Deed-of-Gift match. Only Team New Zealand had shown any long-term viability under corporate sponsorship. In fact, they would also be the only America's Cup team to survive that long—period.

The other top teams essentially relied on a single wealthy backer. And even a number of second- or third-tier teams were funded on that model. Conner's Stars & Stripes managed to make it into the Cup match in 1995, and lose 5-0 to Team New Zealand, but otherwise the teams that depended on corporate funding looked increasingly overmatched against teams that started out well financed more or less from Day 1 and could begin their Cup journey by signing talent instead of looking for patrons.

After the international economic crises that began in 2008, the pool of commercial sponsors, and more importantly the funding they could contribute, was shrinking in a time when the budgets for competitive Cup campaigns continued to rise.

Making the Cup Relevant

Aside from funding, the America's Cup was struggling just for relevance in the complicated twenty-first-century cultural and media landscape, trying to achieve some accessibility for the dedicated fans and enough visibility to attract new fans.

And there was a two-way dynamic linked to having more fans, which via making the event more attractive to corporate sponsors would then encourage the formation of a greater number of competitive teams. To get the attention of corporate decision makers, the event needed to do a better job of drawing spectators in person, of course, and importantly pull in new television and Internet viewers on a much larger scale.

The ability of the America's Cup to make the hosting venue a destination for global travelers was long proven; and the higher the level of cooperation from the host city, the easier it was to create an attractive visitor experience worthy of the historic regatta. Managed properly, it was possible for the America's Cup to get the local support needed to stage a successful regatta and leave a long-term legacy of waterfront redevelopment. Even Alan Bond's multiple America's Cup challenges in the 1970s were sometimes rationalized by him as promotion for his Western Australian real estate holdings.

In 2003, SNG and Alinghi had held a bidding process for the host city of the 2007 America's Cup that started with sixty interested European cities, and worked down to a four-city shortlist. Cascais, Portugal, long regarded as a favorite for sailing factors, lost out at the last minute to Valencia, Spain, a lively Mediterranean city on a redevelopment upswing, trying to keep pace with regional rivals like Barcelona and Madrid. Valencia's support extended to spending over 1.6 billion Euros on preparations for the event, a huge infrastructure project to reconfigure the harbor, an elaborate hospitality building along the new canal leading to the racecourses, including an estimated 500 million Euros in financial subsidies for the event itself. The 2007 America's Cup organizers used some of the funds to produce the television coverage and make it available to global broadcasters.

There was a careful line to walk, though, making proper use of the business potential of running yachting's most prestigious event, while still protecting the traditions that had made the sport meaningful since 1851, the true innovation, the constant elevation of performance and technology that stems from achievement in the design, construction, and sailing of advanced racing machines by talented sailors.

There was a countervailing point of view, questioning whether the America's Cup really could or should be trying to operate on a corporate sponsorship basis, and whether the more than a century of existence as the realm of wealthy sportsmen wasn't in fact a perfectly fine arrangement. Sailing is in some respects a nineteenth-century sport, from an era when wind and sail ruled the seas, and ruling the seas ruled the world. Remaking the event around a television audience evoked worries that something valuable, something essential about the America's Cup, would be traded away for the sake of some advertising dollars.

Did the America's Cup need to be an epic scale, multi-year quest for victory between the best sailors and designers in the world, or was it sufficiently successful as long as it hit corporate marketing return-on-investment calculations?

This was in fact one of the main concerns following the 2007 Cup. Alinghi's plans appeared to center on stocking the challenger fleet with teams from as many countries as possible in an attempt to gain media coverage in their home markets, and then leverage the potential marketing reach as a way to entice commercial sponsorships. To critics, it was a strategy that appeared to value quantity over quality, turning the historic regatta into a profitable annual circuit for some, but at the expense of the heights of excellence in sporting competition that made the America's Cup a great event in the first place.

Golden Gate Yacht Club's battles, first in court, and then finally on the water, were designed to stop plans that threatened a perpetually diminished Cup, and BMW Oracle's victory put Ellison, Coutts, and their colleagues in the driver's seat.

As their giant multihull crossed the finish line in 2010, Golden Gate Yacht Club accepted a Notice of Challenge from Club Nautico di Roma, represented by Mascalzone Latino, the Italian team that had competed in the 2003 and 2007 Louis Vuitton Cup. Mascalzone's (continued on page 36)

Visions of a New Cup

Tom Ehman, Vice Commodore of the Golden Gate Yacht Club, outlined some of the issues and how they fit into plans for the 2013 America's Cup in one of his CupDate talks in December 2010.

"If you draw a curve of the interest in the America's Cup," said Tom Ehman, "the interest from 1851 through the 1920s was huge, in some part because there really wasn't much else. But in 1930, they moved the Cup from New York City to Newport, Rhode Island. No, it wasn't because of the mansions; they could not run the races because of the sheer number of spectator boats and commercial traffic. They moved the Cup to Newport to get away from that—and Cup interest went downhill. So we're not taking the Cup to some media-centric era, we're taking the Cup back to the way the Cup was from 1851 until they moved to Newport.

"The balance of power changed in 1970," Ehman added, referring to the practice of multiple challenger candidates racing among themselves in order to face the Defender. "It did pique some interest initially, as did the little blips in 1983, when Dennis lost the Cup, and in 1987, with the great pictures from Australia. Otherwise, it's gone steadily downhill.

"We've got to do something or it's going to continue to decline—and when the interest declines, the sport declines as well. We've got to do something to regenerate and it's got to start with the kids. We've got to get kids interested in sailing. We've taken the Cup out to thank our constituents and a priority has been getting to the kids, to inspire them and get them interested in the technology of the sport.

"We don't want to lose our core audience, the life-long sailors," explained Ehman, "but we've got to bring the kids into this, so we've got to change the nature of the game. And that's what Larry and Russell are setting out to do."

To accomplish that objective, America's Cup organizers opted for the big multihulls—a decision that, good or bad, would indeed change the game.

"We're working really hard to get a second American Defender," said Ehman. "We—Russell, Larry, and I—think we're much better off having multiple defenders racing off for the right to represent Golden Gate Yacht Club."

The America's Cup World Series was created to help Cup teams transiton to multihull competition, and as a learning experience for organizers and fans alike.

"It's a much less expensive way to take the Cup and our sport to harbors all around the world. We want to sail close to shore, where people can see it. And the course won't be your usual windward/leeward. We'll test some of these new things with the AC45; different course types, having cameramen on board, everything.

"The current plan is to do the first regatta next summer in Europe," announced Ehman. "The most bang for the buck early on is there; there are more teams from Europe. Then, wherever the final venue is, there will be a dress rehearsal there. The last regatta of the World Series events will be there. If it is San Francisco, you'll see a lot of racing in California from September of 2012 to September of 2013. Once the teams are based here, if San Francisco is the venue, you'll see a lot of activity here, and maybe Auckland and Sydney as well, because they are so close.

"If the final venue is in Europe, we'll have to rethink that."

While Americans cannot accept a United States team defending the Cup anywhere else, picking a venue involves a lot more than just wind and dock space—it involves a host of logistical issues such as homes, schools, cars, taxes, and work visas, to name just a few.

"It's hard for us Americans to imagine, because we can go from California to, say, Maine on the same driver's license. You get a bunch of people coming to a venue like Spain—people in the Cup community have lived in Spain for six years, their children have only gone to school in Europe.

"So you've got to get the venue to help the families, because they're going to come live here

for a year," continued Ehman. "To get a driver's license in a foreign language is really difficult. I've got a German driver's license; it took me three bloody years to get it! So first you have to get all the regulations handled: and that means dealing with Sacramento (cue the sound of the entire crowd groaning). We have met with Governor Schwarzenegger. You have to get the state government interested, you've got to get these regulations sorted, so families can move there and live and operate. Sounds easy, doesn't it? It's not, it's quite hard. For example, how do you deal with health insurance for a thousand people coming into California? So that's the first thing, figuring out how to handle the logistics.

"Second, we have to have the financial support to do this. The problem is, you don't want your hard-earned tax dollars going to an event, even an event that brings a billion dollars into the local economy. We have asked—and the city of San Francisco has agreed—to help raise $270 million from corporate sponsors. We're meeting with a lot of companies up there to help raise that money, to get the financial support to run the television show, to run the pre-regattas, everything.

"The third thing is it really does come down to having a fantastic patch of water and a fantastic shore site. In Valencia, we did—they spent 380 million to create that harbor. We won't spend that here, or anywhere else, because in these economic times, it's just not possible. But the great advantage in San Francisco, provided we can sort all those other things out, is not just the wind, it's not just the velocity, it's the reliability. At 2:00 on most days between May and September, you can start a yacht race. Which means you can tell the sponsors that they can bring their guests and put them on the spectator boat. You can tell the public to come down and have a look because the boats are going to go out and go yacht racing and you'll be able to watch it along the city front. And you can tell the world-wide television audience when the yacht race will start, rather than losing most of your audience during a delay."

patron, Vincenzo Onorato, a Mediterranean shipping magnate, had been one of the most outspoken supporters of BMW Oracle during the legal struggles of 2007 to 2010 and one of the few existing Cup teams openly willing to criticize SNG/Alinghi. Though the specifics of the next America's Cup were far from decided, even if they didn't know precisely where AC34 would be conducted, Onorato and Ellison and Coutts certainly agreed on how it shouldn't be run.

To attract fans, sponsors, and broadcasters, they knew the event would need visuals that better translated to television. The racing needed to be intelligible to viewers who weren't expert sailors. The boats had to be something closer to the cutting edge. The gold standard for the America's Cup on TV in 2010 was still the coverage of the 1986-87 America's Cup in Fremantle, Australia. What was fondly remembered was wind, waves, and the adventure of watching the sailors battle the elements, Dennis Conner's *Stars & Stripes* '87 trying to take the America's Cup home against the Defender, Iain Murray on Australia's chosen defender *Kookaburra III*.

It wasn't hard to figure out what had gone missing in so many America's Cup matches since—namely, wind. San Diego averaged light winds, Auckland's Hauraki Gulf was shifty and difficult but usually light, and when it did blow hard, the ACCs didn't race. Valencia was hardly much different, breezes typically filling in at mid-afternoon, somewhat reliably once summer arrived but rarely enough to cause any excitement.

The America's Cup had historically cycled between higher and lower levels of interest, and by 2010 it was in trouble.

Trying to access the television broadcasters was becoming difficult after the endless delays that plagued the 2003 and 2007 regattas. Ratings were dismal for an international sporting event of such renown, and the 2007 coverage was offered free to many countries, an arrangement possible only through a generosity that Valencia residents likely now regret. Getting the America's Cup on U.S. television was in doubt entirely; the networks had become unwilling to air the feed at all because it had been performing so poorly for them. By some accounts, the broadcasters had never made money on any of their sailing coverage and were done trying.

And it wasn't just the America's Cup. Olympic sailing coverage in the United States was a couple minutes of highlights on secondary channels in the middle of the night. Olympic sailing coverage in Europe, by comparison, was actually substantial. The British Olympians were national figures, for example, and their Olympic and youth programs were ambitious, well funded, and nurturing a flock of upcoming talent as a result.

Sailing in the United States was all but undiscoverable to the public, and especially to young people. The future health of the sport was open to question. The status quo was not an option for success. New thinking for AC34 was needed on all sides.

THREE

Finalizing the Vision
for the 34th America's Cup
—Boats, Teams, and Venues

BOATS FOR 2013

A faster boat had been on everybody's menu, even after the 2003 America's Cup in Auckland. The America's Cup Class (ACC) monohull rule dated to 1989, when it was adopted under the name "International America's Cup Class" (IACC) for the 1992 defense in San Diego. First raced in 1991 in the IACC World Championships, the class was over 20 years old in concept by the time the Golden Gate Yacht Club won the Cup.

The IACC had been a compromise between two factions. One group, primarily composed of teams and sailors with experience in the International 12-Meter Class, favored making a Super-Twelve-Meter with a taller mast, greater sail area, and more exotic construction that would have improved performance, building on the body of knowledge about the 12-meters, and using existing boats as the stepping-off point. Another point of view, favored for example by 1983 America's Cup winner Alan Bond, an Australian millionaire who had backed teams for the better part of two decades, was that the America's Cup, as the most prestigious event in yachting, needed to be sailed in the largest, most extreme boats possible, something on the scale of the J-Class from the 1930s possibly. To this point of view, the scale of the yachts spoke directly to the importance of the event itself. Viewers should be awestruck by the yachts.

One participant in the deliberations, naval architect Britton Chance, Jr., wrote knowingly of the tensions in finding a class for the purpose. The goal of maximizing participation for multiple Challengers conflicted with the nature of the Cup as a test of skill in designing and building the fastest boats. Cost struggled against pushing the performance envelope. Having a development class ran contrary to having boats guaranteed to be good for close-match racing.

After several international open meetings, attended by sailors, team leaders, and a who's who of designers, a consensus was reached: a 75-foot monohull, the IACC was a 50,000-pound displacement yacht, with nearly 45,000 of those pounds in a giant bulb of lead ballast carried around the course at the end of the keel fin. It was large enough at the time to stand out, lighter than a 12-meter, and had a design rule with enough openness to give designers and engineers plenty of design space to explore in the search for speed.

The IACC served well in San Diego in 1992 and 1995, and with the class's name shortened just to "ACC," it remained the yacht class of choice in Auckland in 2000 and 2003.

The Class was aging though. New materials, more sophisticated design tools, and larger budgets were regularly creating larger and faster yachts for other events. No longer quite so exotic, despite all the attention that optimized and advanced the ACC in each cycle, by the new millennium the America's Cup yachts were being surpassed by new high-performance designs.

When SNG/Alinghi won the Cup in 2003, and chose Golden Gate YC/Oracle BMW Racing as the Challenger of Record, consideration was given to switching the regatta to a new design rule, or at least to boosting performance of the current class. There were several limitations. To give the boat more acceleration, the power-to-weight ratio would have to improve. Power comes from sail area and, in a displacement boat, waterline length. Weight was obvious: it was the keel. And the keel plays a vital role in stability, gravity acting on the thousands of pounds of lead in the keel counteracts the force of the wind on the sails, keeping the boat upright and moving forward.

Reducing the mass of lead while still being able to keep the boat upright was possible in one of two ways: a deeper keel, with more leverage to create more righting moment, or some technical change like a canting keel, pivoting the entire assembly to windward on each tack to increase the righting forces on the boat.

A deeper keel ran up against limitations of where the boats could sail, and which harbors were even capable of hosting the boats without dredging and other infrastructure that might not always be feasible.

The alternate of a canting keel for a short-course match racing boat required onboard hydraulics to pivot the keel against gravity, and an engine to provide enough hydraulic pressure so that tacking the keel would be possible without inordinate waits between maneuvers.

Organizers in 2007 felt that an engine on the ACC boats went against what seemed a wholesome tradition in yacht racing of man versus the natural elements.

From an event perspective, an overriding consideration was that with the move to Europe for the first time, they wanted to encourage teams to participate, and avoid a change to a new yacht design that would be unfamiliar.

For the 2007 event, America's Cup leaders had organized a series of preliminary regattas taking place in cities around Europe. The fleet racing and match racing gave new and existing teams a chance to adapt to ACC racing, while giving corporate sponsors more visibility and hospitality in return for their funding. Teams could compete in the preliminaries with used ACC boats, from the previous Cup cycle or even before, and with no nationality restrictions in yacht selection. A boat two generations old wouldn't win many races, but it was an affordable way to put a team on the water.

The design space for the 2007 version of the class rule, in fact, was narrowed greatly, with the range of waterline lengths, sail areas, and displacements tremendously reduced. The upshot in 2007 was that the differences among the yachts were more often differences in appearance rather than in performance. Disparities often came from sails, with boat speed dropping quickly as her sails aged. Mostly the boats were so similar that though they weren't far apart in time or distance, passing usually involved something going wrong on the other boat.

Two Attempts at a New AC Class Rule—AC90 and AC70

After Alinghi won the 2007 America's Cup, they had two aborted attempts to create a new America's Cup Class. First they announced a new 90-foot monohull with a lifting keel to replace the ACC, rather similar in shape though not in size to the TP52, a class that Alinghi designer Rolf Vrolijk had come to dominate. A year later, trying to increase the number of challenger entries, Alinghi tried to reboot the event in an AC70, similar in concept to the AC90 but now targeting a more affordable price point. Several political and public relations issues may have helped influence that change. In any case, Alinghi stirred substantial criticism from the challenger community by having their own design team create a Class rule without the consent even of the Challenger of Record, and even more since the rule seemed tailored to the strengths of their own designer.

In the end, Alinghi didn't prevail in court or on the water, and the AC90 and AC70 became footnotes.

Exploring the Potential Boat Concepts, Summer 2010

But the question remained: the ACCs had been passed by; what type of yacht would best replace them?

More speed and better acceleration needed some combination of more power and less weight. More power meant more sail area, but more sail area required stability to match. The canting keel was considered, possibly with a leading rudder, or canard, permitted. A lifting keel, lowered for racing and raised before docking, would at least bring some practicality, but it would still restrict the waters the boats could race within. A wider hull was another option, also increasing the stability, but extremes of beam ultimately ran into points of diminishing returns with handling the boat for ground and air transportation, and in some harbor facilities. For the America's Cup, some of the beam limitations were surmountable, but every solution brought its own set of problems to be solved.

Trials in Valencia, Spain, with RC44 monohulls. (© 2013 ACEA/ Photo: Gilles Martin-Raget)

From the event side, there was a desire to permit racing as close to shore as possible, making it possible for the largest number of spectators to be readily involved in person. The more spectators, the greater the financial rewards for organizers and host cities, too, increasing the ability to hold more events and provide the amenities to attract visitors. America's Cup races throughout recent history had been held miles offshore, visible only from excursion boats, and not easy to follow in person. Only in the early days of the defense in New York, when the match had been sailed on the "Inside Course"—that is, within New York Harbor—had the racing been watchable from shore.

Coutts considered the two options, monohull and multihull, in a manner befitting a development engineer. He didn't just study the decision; he held trials, match races between two RC44 monohulls outfitted with onboard high-definition cameras as they might be for racing, and a version of the whole broadcast setup including helicopters with 3D cameras filming the racing with a variety of onboard angles and audio, over four days of experimentation off Valencia, Spain, in July 2010. And they did the same with a pair of catamarans, Extreme40s, simultaneously. They also tested variations on racecourses and starting concepts.

On the technical side, they hired experts in each type of boat to look at options for a new class. The Royal Ocean Racing Club's (RORC) Seahorse Rating affiliate in England, along with Nick Nicholson and James Dadd, studied potential monohull configurations. On the other side of the pond, US Sailing, along with Morrelli & Melvin Design and Engineering, studied the multihulls.

"We've always said that the new design will be for the America's Cup community. The result with be a 'non-partisan yacht' rather than a 'defender's yacht,'" said Ian Burns of BMW Oracle Racing. "A great deal of input was sought from the America's Cup community, and the concept briefs given to the rule writers reflect that feedback."

Both yacht types shared some fundamental criteria.

"These boat concepts are all about similar performance between competing yachts throughout the wind range," said Burns. "Unique configurations are the expensive part of the America's Cup. We don't want a light-air boat taking on a heavy-air boat. The rule should ensure close racing while being able to sail in a wide range of conditions."

Restrictions on the number of hulls, masts, appendages, and sails were intended to help control costs.

RORC arrived at a 22m/72' monohull (scaled down from an 82' proposal), light displacement with a canting keel, optional forward rudder, and potentially two aft rudders. The keel would have a depth of 4.5m/14'9"and angle 50 degrees to each side. The canting movement would be powered by an engine, and the whole mechanism standardized across the boats. Most overall dimensions of the hull would be strictly controlled, as would sail area with the exception of the gennaker, which would be unlimited. A crew of thirteen would sail the boat at approximately 1.4 times true windspeed downwind, and at approximately 1.0 time the windspeed upwind, racing in a wind range estimated between 5 and 25 knots.

US Sailing studied a multihull. Morrelli & Melvin (M&M) was instructed to look at 65', 75', and 85' catamarans, determining performance, technical requirements, and expenses.

"We got a call in June asking us to start developing a rule for a multihull," Pete Melvin explained (see Melvin's full interview in this chapter's sidebar). "We're the leaders of the group, but we had consultants from all over the world. BMW Oracle didn't want just one person creating this rule; they wanted world-class input from everybody. We spent four months creating this rule and a lot of things changed along the way. For example, in a meeting back in May, when we were working on the initial study, we focused on a trimaran, as they are more forgiving and easy to sail and more high performance for the dollar. But there was a desire to have the boats easily shippable via air, and catamarans are more easily disassembled to go on a plane. Also, they wanted a wing instead of soft sails."

Gino Morrelli, a longtime multihull enthusiast, remembered after working on the 1988 *Stars & Stripes* 60-foot cat thinking that the America's Cup would never go back to multihulls.

Even after 2010's giant trimaran versus catamaran battle, it looked unlikely that multihulls would ever be let out of the bag again. Even with the multihull feasibility study announced, the weight of tradition behind monohulls seemed too great. It's a bias in the sailing community not unlike snowboarding versus skiing, or motorcycles versus four-wheeled sports cars.

There is a traditionalist group that suspiciously thinks multihulls just go too fast too easily, while the multihull group thinks that's exactly the point. Speed and performance are exciting, they say, so why sail slowly and drag all that lead around? The conflict has been going on at least since Nathanael Herreshoff's cat was banned from racing in 1876.

The America's Cup is one of the most entrenched traditions in one of the most tradition-bound sports, full of golden memories of classic yachts gliding by each other, circling for advantage at the start, wearing each other down in sustained tacking duels, and at least the image of dignified patricians in blazers and straw hats regarding the pastoral scene over cocktails from the afterdeck. That staid perception of events may have faded a bit since the summers of Newport, but the fact remained that the mainstream of sailing centered on monohulls. Even at the lowest levels of small beach cats, a multihull handles differently, with everything—good or bad—happening much faster. Switching from a mono to a multi requires relearning how to sail a boat in some regards, and probably getting wet in the process. The racing community is a bit segregated, with monos and multis off in their own events, and it's rare that the two realms meet.

A decision and public announcement of the rules and details of the next America's Cup was planned for September 2010 in Valencia.

M&M's Work on the AC72 Rule

Morrelli and his office broke into two halves, his design partner Pete Melvin leading a group writing drafts of the rule, and Morrelli working as the "ops team," trying to find loopholes that subverted the intentions of the rule. Yacht designers can make great names for themselves by finding those loopholes, and an America's Cup rule would be getting great scrutiny from the teams once it was published. M&M needed to close those doors.

M&M also had to find the balance between a rule that dictated a narrow almost one-design envelope for the Class and a totally wide-open rule with almost no limits. The design brief called for a boat that could reliably start a race in a wide range of conditions and then engage in compelling racing around the course upwind and downwind, and be exciting to watch even at the lower end of the wind range. For catamarans that was shorthanded to the ability to fly a hull in under 10 knots of wind, likely as little as 6 knots of wind.

"So we spent more time on the technical side, sizing the boat, how big the rig should be," Melvin said. "The desire was to be able to sail a race from 3 to 33 knots (wiggled down to 5 to 30) so we came up with a wingsail catamaran, with soft sails for downwind sailing. Carrying 11 crew members, it will do about three times true wind speed."

The boats would have to be disassembled and packed up for transport around the world by air cargo freighter, ready to ship in 24 hours, and able to be sailing again within 48 hours after arrival.

To sail dependably in the wide range of wind speeds, and keep the races on schedule, the boats would have two wingsails, one short and one tall, to calibrate power to sailing conditions.

The boats could use hydraulics to control the wings, but the fluid pressure in the system wouldn't come from an engine. Crew members would grind on their handles as before, but this time not turning mechanical winches; they instead would create hydraulic pressure in an accumulator, which the trimmers could release on command to move the wing surfaces.

This arrangement was a conscious decision, meant to make sure that the human aspect of the competition remained a central feature of the Match. Coutts even admitted to receiving calls from America's Cup crews asking that their role not be eliminated from the regatta.

The choice of the wingsail over the soft sail was partially to keep the boats at the cutting edge of technology, and to keep them powerful enough to fly a hull even when the wind was light. The wing was also partially a design feature that would distinguish the America's Cup from other multihull racing, which with only a few exceptions uses a conventional soft main sail.

A Box Rule

Class rules for racing yachts are the DNA of the boats. When asked, everybody will probably answer that what they seek from the rule is close and exciting racing. The path chosen to achieve that varies greatly. A strict one-design rule would try to make the boats as identical as possible, putting all the focus on the abilities of the sailors when it comes to winning. Strict one-design has its enthusiasts, and is probably best exemplified by the Olympics. The technology battle is reduced as close to nil as possible, and other than the day-to-day tuning and configuration of the boats done ashore and on the water, the boats are less a factor than the athletes.

At the other end of the spectrum are the development classes. Within the restrictions of the Class rule, design, engineering, and construction become critical parts of the competition. Some sailors shun development classes because of the financial and engineering arms race aspects, and the not-unrelated fact that the cutting edge moves inexorably forward, with spending keeping pace. Others are drawn to development classes for the same reasons, enjoying the test of ingenuity, a continual discovery of what's possible (and what isn't), continually challenging sailors and designers to get better, moving the sport of sailing forward.

With the enormous amount of resources brought to the task, both on and off the boats, the America's Cup has always been one of the highest orders of development.

M&M still had two possible approaches to a development class. One technique is a formula rule, however loose or tight the formula, that establishes a relationship between design parameters, most typically sail area, displacement, and waterline, but leaves it up to the designers to make the trade-offs they feel are best. There is a certain fairness to a formula rule in that all teams may make the allocations differently. In high-level-development events like the America's Cup, though, a tight formula doesn't necessary do much to control costs, and inordinate resources end up being spent on the tiniest details, looking to accumulate a large number of small advantages that might make one boat (continued on page 45)

Interview with Pete Melvin on the AC72 Rule

(Peter Melvin, from Morrelli & Melvin Design and Engineering, gave this interview in December 2010.)

"The rule is a box rule—maximum length of 22 meters, 14 meters wide, and some sail area max areas, with minimum and maximum weight limits and it has to be a catamaran—but everything else is pretty much open. You can have any hull shape you want. You're allowed to have two rudders and two foils, but they can be curved or canting. The soft sails, for downwind sailing primarily, can be made of anything but they have to be foldable. There's a height-and-area maximum for the wing, but aside from those restrictions, anything goes. And no computers on this boat—the wing will be controlled manually, by hydraulics or cables or whatever mechanical means the designers come up with."

A major concern voiced by participants and media alike has been budgets—and depending on who you believe, the budgets for the 34th America's Cup could be anywhere from $20 to $100 million dollars. Numbers aside, Melvin broke down where he thinks the bulk of the budget will go and from which direction the biggest design breakthroughs might come.

"The wing is a huge performance element and that's where I think a lot of the gains will be made. Hulls are fairly well understood—with a monohull, where the hull is very, very critical and a very key part of your design, you'll spend a lot of your resources developing the hull shape. Multihulls are all long and skinny things and whether you make one with a little more 'vee' or a little less rocker, it's not going to change the drag characteristic of the hull that much. So a lot of those resources that you might have put into design engineering will go into the wing or the foils and less on the hulls."

Speaking of foils, it's time for some new words in the vocabulary. We'll start with the curved foils. Melvin explains: "They're called daggerboards, but some people call them dagger foils. They not only prevent the boat from going sideways, they also lift the boat. I'm sure on some of the boats, they'll cant them, so you can angle them under the boat and increase or decrease the amount of lift you can get. The faster the boat goes, the more you'll want to lift it up on the foil and the more efficient it will be."

The initial plans had been for a one-design boat, but the more Melvin looked at it, the more loopholes he could see. The theory is that leaving the design open creates exciting possibilities for development.

faster than the other. The problem intensifies as a formula rule matures, with designs converging on similar shapes with fewer performance differences. Intense development happens, but it's concentrated on only certain aspects of the boats.

The other end of the spectrum for design rules is a box rule, setting out only basic minimum and maximum parameters for the boat, in the most extreme describing a box that the boat would have to fit inside and nothing else, though in practice there are usually additional rules and an unlimited box rule is uncommon.

Before 1930, the boats weren't even limited by a Class rule, just by a couple restrictions on overall length courtesy of the Deed of Gift, and when races were determined on a corrected time basis, the need not to run afoul of the handicap calculations. It was nearly a wide open design competition.

One intent of selecting the J-Class yachts for the America's Cup in 1930, bringing a class rule to the event for the first time, was to race in boats similar enough to be competitive, but different enough to be interesting.

ANNOUNCING THE NEW CUP

In Valencia, the plan for a twenty-first-century America's Cup was unveiled. The 34th Defense would be held in 2013; discussions were under way with San Francisco to host the racing, but nothing was final yet, and the venue would be selected by December 31, 2010.

It's Official: AC72s and AC45s

The big revelation was the boats, confirming that for the first time the America's Cup would be contested by two catamarans. Though three multihulls had now sailed for the America's Cup in the two no-holds-barred Deed-of-Gift matches, adopting a multihull class was unprecedented. The design rule was for a 72-foot-long catamaran class to be called the AC72, with hard wings 131 feet tall instead of soft mainsails. The boats would be 46 feet wide and weight was initially announced as about 15,000 pounds. Each team would be permitted to build two boats.

To aid the transition to multihulls for the sailors and shore crews, racing would begin in 2011 in a new one-design catamaran, 45 feet long, also with a wingsail. Called the AC45, all of the smaller boats would come from a single manufacturer, Core Builders Composites Ltd. in New Zealand, and be standardized except for the soft sails and some hardware components.

In 2011 and 2012, the teams would race the AC45s in events dubbed the America's Cup World Series (ACWS), both match racing and fleet racing, to be held in various cities around the world. The ACWS regattas would help publicize the America's Cup, increase public awareness of the new boats and format, bring visibility to the teams as they sought to secure sponsorships, and bring an additional return to commercial partners and sponsors. All entered teams, Defender and prospective Challengers alike, would be required to compete in the AC45 ACWS events.

The first generation of AC72s would begin racing in the ACWS in the summer of 2012, providing valuable experience to design teams, sailors, and race officials a year ahead of the America's Cup match and the Louis Vuitton Cup. The smaller AC45 yachts, no longer needed for the ACWS, would be transferred to a youth event. The second generation of AC72s would begin launching in January 2013, giving them six months of preparation before the Louis Vuitton Cup began.

Nationality rules would apply only to the construction of certain components, namely the hulls of the yachts, which were required to be fabricated in their home country. Other components could be manufactured anywhere.

Sailors and designers would have no nationality requirements to meet. Organizers said that they considered requiring that a certain percentage of sailors on each team reflect the nationality of the challenger, say 50 percent of the crew possibly, but ultimately felt that there would be enough burden on potential teams just to find the sailing, design, and management expertise in time to create a team without having to limit most of their recruiting to a single country. In some conversations, the possibility of adding a nationality requirement as a condition in a future America's Cup cycle was suggested.

Without revealing full details, organizers also said that the event and race oversight would be handled by independent entities with the goal of fair and neutral conduct of the regatta.

"I think that we need to acknowledge that the Defender has kept its word. The America's Cup is going to have fair rules and a truly independent management of the racing," said Vincenzo Onorato, president of Mascalzone Latino. "This change should've happened years ago in my opinion. I can see why this important development could last for many years in the future."

The agenda also included transforming the media presence of the America's Cup with ambitious upgrades to the broadcast technology and improved Internet accessibility. Races would be shorter and, with the new design of the boats, less vulnerable to wind delays.

"During our six months of planning we spoke to the teams, to commercial partners, to media and to the fans. A clear and compelling vision emerged—that to capture and communicate the excitement our sport can produce, we need the best sailors racing the fastest boat in the world," Russell Coutts said.

Limits on the number of boats, wings, rudders, and daggerboards that could be built were intended to help prevent runaway costs, as were restrictions on the number of support boats and the institution of no-sail periods. The onboard crew was reduced from seventeen people in the 2007 America's Cup down to eleven people. No-sailing periods and staggered launch dates for each team's new boats were meant to level the playing field by putting a cap on expensive two-boat testing programs, capable of burning $1 million to $2 million per month just in constant sailing of the boats.

Though all of these measures were promoted as cost control, and they would help deter the sorts of virtually infinite spending that some teams had been able to pursue in the past, there were no expectations that such steps were going to make the 2013 America's Cup a low-budget proposition. The aim was to keep it from getting out of reach too quickly.

Curiously, in light of the path that events eventually took, a few proposals for managing the boats were still being floated that did not come to fruition. One was the ability to depower the wing by removing upper trailing-flap panels. Another was a cost control measure that would have mandated a one-design daggerboard shared among all boats. Either might have changed the course of the 2013 America's Cup.

Not Quite Final

The AC72 Class rule was still being drafted, and at the time of the Valencia announcement was not due to be published for another three weeks, so the presentation wasn't able to commit to all of the aspects of the boat. But they repeated the goals that it be interesting to watch for spectators, physically demanding to sail for the competitors, and technologically advanced to ensure that the America's Cup remained the pinnacle of yachting competition.

The Valencia announcement left plenty still undecided: the location of the defense, the number and location of the World Series regattas, and the specifics of the AC72 Class rule. But seven months after the GGYC and BMW Oracle had won, the Cup world now had some decisions made and could begin to move forward.

In the world of the America's Cup, this was a lot of change to be thrown at participants and fans alike. Multihulls, wingsails, a great deal more speed, and the ambition that most new Defenders bring to the table: improving the event in every aspect, reshaping the Cup in the way they thought best, fixing what they thought was wrong.

Ellison had been trying to win the event for nearly 10 years, at first sharing some of his vision as a Challenger of Record from 2003 to 2007 and then being completely opposed to the ideas of the Defender following 2007. Coutts had won the America's Cup first for RNZYS/Team New Zealand and then for SNG/Alinghi, winning with both organizations only to run into friction with the senior leadership over the subsequent direction of the team and the control of the regatta—and not just minor conflicts, but enough disagreement that it led to his departure from the team both times.

Other senior BMW Oracle Racing figures had spent similar portions of their America's Cup careers involved in the America's Cup, picking up plenty of ideas of what should be done, but unable to set the priorities and make their own ideas a reality. Now there was the chance to reinvent the Cup for the modern era, adapting to the technological possibilities and responding to the commercial opportunities that they had been studying at close hand for years.

The efforts for the next Cup centered on improving the sporting competition, making sure the event stayed the pinnacle of the sport, upgrading the spectator and media experience, conducting a fair regatta, and making competing in the event as accessible as possible for interested teams.

TEAM FORMATION FOR 2013

The 2013 Protocol set a few requirements for teams to enter, primarily that they represent a yacht club eligible under the Deed of Gift, and that they be prepared to meet certain financial hurdles.

Twenty-four teams sent representatives to a meeting held in Paris, France, on October 22, 2010. Their actual identities were kept confidential, but thirteen countries were represented, with Italy, Spain, Greece, Australia, New Zealand, South Africa, South Korea, and Switzerland said by some reports to be among the teams. ACEA (America's Cup Event Authority)/ACRM (America's Cup Regatta Management) officials provided the prospective teams with background on the event plans, and looked for ways to support formative teams.

The hopeful teams had several big tasks to accomplish. In addition to recruiting sailing talent, they needed to create an organization capable of designing and building a boat and managing the campaign. And, most importantly, they needed money to put their plans in motion and to meet entry requirements. In addition to the funding needed to run the team, each entrant needed to pay $25,000 when they filed their Notice of Challenge, post two $1.5 million performance bonds by the end of July 2011, and pay a 1 million euro entry fee in April 2012.

It was expected that the AC45 regattas would begin in summer 2011, less than 12 months away, and prospective teams would have to acquire an AC45 yacht, at a reported $1.4 million US dollars, and maintain enough sailors to man the five-person sailing crew and enough shoreside resources to launch and maintain the boats, in addition to public relations operations and internal team logistics. The AC45 regattas were intended to help generate interest in the event and create a return on sponsorship dollars, but the regattas also created responsibilities and expenses for the teams.

Debated in the wake of the 2013 Protocol unveiling was whether moving the planned date of the 2013 match forward or back by a year would make it easier for the teams. Even if it sounded like a good idea, ETNZ CEO Grant Dalton admitted that an added year past 2013 probably just drove up costs. Another year in some ways became just more time to spend more money, and the money would end up being spent. Moving up the race to 2012 looked difficult or nearly impossible in light of the technical and design unknowns that would be involved.

Racing to Challenge

From September 2010, when the timeline for the 2013 event was announced, there were 33 months until the Louis Vuitton Cup began in July
2013, but only 15 months until the first AC72s could be launched and 22
months until they would start racing in the World Series San Francisco in
2012. With an estimated 4 to 6 months to build one of the big cats, that
left barely somewhere between 9 and 15 months to raise funds, recruit a
design team for a boat that no one had ever seen before, and design the
first boat. The location of the 2013 regatta had not yet been finalized.

And where to get the design and engineering expertise? There was
precious little experience with the yacht type on a large scale anyplace in
the world, and the only large wingsail multihull in recent memory was
the Defender's giant trimaran. The Defender already had a design team in
place, already had funding in place, and had the benefit of everything they
had learned from beating Alinghi's giant cat earlier in the year.

Additional challenge entries would be accepted beginning November
1, 2010, with the early entry window closing at the end of March 2011.
Who would come?

Grant Dalton would not confirm until April 2011, when the NZ Government approved funding, that his team would officially be a Challenger
for the 2013 Cup. By then the Kiwi team had recruited a design group
of about thirty-five members, signed commercial sponsorships, and begun a training program to gain multihull experience for skipper Dean
Barker and crew. The Royal New Zealand Yacht Squadron entry, though,
had been sent in on the first date that additional challenges were being
accepted.

Actually, the New Zealand challenge notice arrived too early, via email
on October 31, just one second before midnight, according to GGYC's
mail server. Before ETNZ resubmitted close to an hour later, an entry
from Artemis Racing also arrived, 15 seconds after midnight, making the
Swedish team the first of the multiple Challengers to file their notice. The
competition had already begun, and Team New Zealand was behind by
49 minutes. That tiny margin would come to loom large as time went by.

Optimisim reigned, and Coutts' initial prediction was for a dozen
Challengers.

Eleven teams would apply and be accepted as official Challengers
for the 2013 America's Cup before the early challenge deadline closed on
March 31, 2011. Late challenges, if any, would be accepted only at the
discretion of the GGYC.

The identities of the Challengers were not all publicly revealed, at
least as they came in. GGYC left it up to the individual teams to reveal
themselves with whatever level of media production they preferred.

A French team, Aleph, challenged in December, as did the Multihull
Yacht Club of Queensland. January brought the Peyron brothers, Loïck
and Bruno, a second French team. The Peyrons were some of the most

experienced people in the world with large multihulls, though like everyone else in the type their racing was nearly always offshore, in the open
ocean and often around the world. Sailing giant cats around the buoys on
a tight inshore course, let alone match racing them, was something that
had almost zero history. But the Peyrons had been among those at the
forefront of developing the big multis, and Loïck had been at the helm of
the Alinghi cat for parts of the 2010 America's Cup match against BMW
Oracle Racing.

March brought entries from China, Korea, and an unnamed team.
Three more notices of challenge slipped in as the March 31 deadline approached, including another Italian, Venezia Challenge. Identities of all
were due to be revealed in mid-June.

The Australian team had been seen test-sailing an AC45 in Auckland,
and announced they were working on an agreement for ACEA to stage an
ACWS regatta in Sydney, so it was a surprise when they were not included
in the June announcements, apparently over funding issues that had not
been resolved.

But the big news ahead of June was that the Challenger of Record
(COR) was gone. Mascalzone Latino, representing Club Nautico di Roma,
had resigned on May 11. Team patron Vincenzo Onorato had earlier expressed concerns about finding enough funding for his team to be competitive, and although two sponsors had been signed, he had decided that
Mascalzone Latino was not going to be prepared to win.

From Onorato's public statement:

> As Challenger of Record, we have worked with humility next to
> Oracle and I am satisfied of the result we have reached: a new Cup,
> spectacular, with new boats, the catamarans, that will launch on the
> international scene a new generation of sailors.
>
> With Russell we have discussed for long time the most difficult
> challenge that the next Cup must face: an international situation
> with big economic crisis and therefore huge difficulties to find spon-
> sor. This is the only, true, real enemy of the next Cup. We have then
> thought of the idea to create the class AC45, a concrete way to make
> [a] lot of teams get involved in the event, reducing costs, at least in
> the delicate period of the start-up.
>
> On our side, I must thank the two Italian sponsors that believed
> and confirmed us their trust. We are not able, however, to reach a
> budget that allows us to be a competitive team.
>
> In our sport, men in blazers have overcome by now those in
> oilskins. I'm a man in oilskin and when I go in the sea, I want to
> win. I'm not interested in a hopeless challenge, I would lie to the
> sponsors, to our fans, and last but not least, also to myself.

It was a heartfelt letter that said a lot about his regard for the Cup,
but the resignation was a surprise since Mascalzone had been one of the

architects of the new America's Cup format, agreeing to the new boats and all the other conditions. It wasn't the first time a COR had resigned—the Royal Thames YC had pulled out of the competition before racing began in 1974, but it was a surprise.

Aside from the loss of Mascalzone from the 34th America's Cup, the COR's resignation changed the political landscape of the challenger field. Per the 2013 Protocol, the role of COR then fell to the Challenger who was next, chronologically, in submitting their original Notice of Challenge. That was Artemis, whose email had arrived 15 seconds after midnight on the first possible day, and not Emirates Team New Zealand, whose messages had arrived either 1 second too early or else 49 minutes too late. Being COR under the 2013 Protocol mattered, since the rules for this cycle had been written to give the COR veto power over changes to the Protocol, even if a majority of the rest of the Challengers agreed. Whether making the COR rank first among equals was the proper separation of powers was an issue that would arise later, regardless of who it was that held the title, but the Protocol governed, Artemis became COR, and the challenger field was down one major player.

June 15, 2011, in the restored Ferry Building on the San Francisco waterfront, saw the official announcement of eight Challengers, seven of them now revealed, plus the Defender.

GreenComm would not be publicly announced until the next week. Eight challenging teams would have been a great showing given the circumstances. Organizers had hoped for more, but fund-raising in the economic environment of the time was not easy. Even BMW Oracle Racing had parted with their automotive sponsor, reverting temporarily to their original name, and would later adopt ORACLE TEAM USA to emphasize the patriotic role they played as the Defender.

Australia was still working to satisfy financial terms, but ultimately could not, bowing out along with teams from Canada, Italy, France, and

CHALLENGERS FOR THE 34TH AMERICA'S CUP AS OF 6/15/2011

China	China Team	Mei Fan Yacht Club
France	Aleph-Équipe De France	Aleph Yacht Club
France	Energy Team	Yacht Club de France
Italy	Venezia Challenge	Club Canottieri Roggero di Lauria
New Zealand	Emirates Team New Zealand	Royal New Zealand YS
Republic of Korea	Team Korea	Sail Korea Yacht Club
Spain	GreenComm	Real Club Nautico de Valencia
Sweden	Artemis Racing	Kungliga Svenska Segel Sallskapet
United States	OTUSA Racing	Golden Gate Yacht Club

Russia who had been publicly working toward submitting challenges and trying to raise funds.

America's Cup organizers had been trying to work with teams to make it less difficult to participate. In early June, the competitors had agreed to move the earliest AC72 launch dates back six months, from January 2012 to July 2012. The $1.5 million performance bonds no longer needed to be posted, nor the 1 million euro entry fee; they were replaced by a straight $100,000 entry fee. This biggest initial hurdle was the requirement to purchase an AC45 and race it in the ACWS, which would be a commitment of about $1.5 million for the boat, plus the personnel to campaign several times a year in various countries.

Financially, historical arrangements for past Cup entries had cycled between very low fees intended to give everyone as much chance as possible until the last minute, and steep early requirements intended to keep the pretenders and the unprepared from becoming distractions. Since the 1980s, the math had usually been that up to half of the paper Challengers would withdraw before the racing actually started.

In dropping the fees and eliminating the performance bonds, there was some recognition that participating in the ACWS itself was already its own substantial threshold.

But the real task in order to be a viable challenger was to put in place a design team and manage a boat-building program in time to be able to have an AC72 yacht to race.

Pushing back the launch deadline would level the playing field somewhat, and pushing the racing debut of the boats from 2012 to 2013 would backload a lot of spending into the schedule, giving just a little more breathing room for teams trying to raise funds. The well-funded teams enjoyed a first-mover advantage—they were already up and running—and that was hard to avoid. Early sailing time would have been a huge advantage for them, especially with the ability to refine the second boat, putting a late launching team a generation behind in every regard. As it was, the big teams with their budgets already in place were going to get more time for design, and they had the resources to get gains from that as well.

But pushing the deadlines back and lowering the financial barriers to remain in the picture might help some teams secure funding in time to make it to the Louis Vuitton Cup two years off from the challenger announcements made in the Ferry Building that day.

Other changes had already been implemented to help control costs, too. Rather than two wingsail sizes, tall and short, for the AC72, the Class rule had been amended in February 2011, leaving only the tall 40m wing, and the number of wings that may be built per team had been cut from eight to six. The short wings didn't necessarily double the design problem, but they added numerous complications. The two wing sizes would have needed their own suits of soft sails, too, and likely for each rig the yachts would have been optimized around different appendage configurations. Components that didn't swap out from wing to wing would have to be optimized to balance performance under both rigs. Design teams had plenty on their hands with just one of the scenarios, let alone both, and the change to a single wing size was welcomed.

The Shared Design Program

In April, ACEA had announced another idea to help the teams: the "Shared Design Program." The platform would be designed by VPLP (Van Peteghem Lauriot Prévost) of France and the wingsail and soft sails by North Technology Group (NTG). VPLP was one of the top multihull design offices in the world, and North and their affiliates were one of the global leaders in sail, mast, and rigging technology.

Any of the currently entered teams, fourteen Challengers and the Defender, could participate in the common study of hull platform, wingsail, and appendage designs that would produce a baseline AC72 that all could use as the starting point for their 2013 yachts. The resulting "ACRM" boat as designed might be sufficient for start-up teams with limited resources, though the top teams were likely to move well beyond the shared design in many respects.

The rules already permitted designers, plans, and performance data to be shared among teams until June 1, 2012. For a brand-new racing class with so many unique aspects, the Shared Design Program would at least provide a floor in performance for all the teams, a common starting point, and take some of the pressure off the teams who were still fund-raising.

The shared program would draw upon industry experts across several yacht design and construction disciplines to create the jumping-off point for the first batch of 72-foot multihulls. The idea of sharing design data in this manner for the America's Cup, which at its core has always been a contest of yachting technology just as much as sailing ability, was unprecedented and would have been against the rules in many years. Regatta organizers were allowing (and encouraging) the practice within limitations as a means of getting the new and technically advanced yacht class up to speed, literally, in a shortened time frame.

Golden Gate YC and OTUSA leaders also were reported to have considered a more radical plan at one point, too, changing the 2013 America's Cup to the smaller AC45 yachts entirely, and not racing AC72s at all. The plan would have certainly raised the number of participants, though it threatened to run afoul of the Deed of Gift requirement that competing yachts be constructed in their own countries.

The plan to switch to AC45s was not met with acceptance by the teams that had entered, and who would have had to agree to the new direction. They had already committed to building AC72s and had funding in place, and the prospect of facing a large field of nearly one-design opponents while abandoning substantial work already under way wasn't in their interest. Grant Dalton, of ETNZ, had been a vocal critic of the cost and complexity in the AC72 program, but it was one thing to have to beat Artemis Racing, the most imposing Challenger on the radar, when the New Zealanders were building their own boat. It would have been a different proposition altogether to face say a dozen or more competitors with nearly identical boats, ETNZ perhaps ceding nearly all their technological advantage.

Attrition would continue to take a toll on the Challenger community, though. As GreenComm, the Spanish Challenger, was being publicly announced, Venezia joined Australia in being excused from the regatta, for not meeting required commitments by a deadline that had been agreed on with ACEA.

AC World Series Kicks Off—August 2011 —and Challenger Withdrawals

The ACWS kicked off in August in Cascais, with eight teams participating, including the Defender.

The challenger picture brightened considerably in October. The Golden Gate YC accepted a late challenger. Patrizio Bertelli, the head of the Prada fashion empire, decided to come back to the America's Cup. After making it all the way to the America's Cup match in 2000 against ETNZ, the Italian boats had been a fixture of the Louis Vuitton Cup ever since, very high-spirited representatives of their country. Given their late arrival on the scene, they would have been nearly a year behind everyone else in designing and building a boat.

With the rules permitting shared design, though, they had negotiated an agreement to contract the design and some of the construction of a boat to ETNZ, a duplicate of the first AC72 that ETNZ was building. This arrangement was acceptable under the rules provided that the yacht's hulls were still constructed in Italy, and that sharing of design information, and testing results, be restricted in certain ways, and not permitted at all after a certain date. ETNZ would offset some of their costs, and at least three Challengers now appeared to have confirmed funding in place.

From a racing standpoint, an ideal turnout for the Louis Vuitton Cup would be to have at least four teams competing, since that would open up the schedule significantly, allowing each team to race every day against a different opponent. If there were only three teams, one would always have to sit out. In the end, the boats weren't able to race quite that often anyway, but four boats would have meant twice the competition in the early stages compared to three.

Fund-raising wasn't getting any easier to come by, though. The spring of 2012 saw more losses.

Aleph signaled in March 2012 that they weren't meeting funding goals and expressed hope that they could instead continue as an ACWS team with an eye toward fielding a full challenge for the 35th Defense of the America's Cup in possibly 2015 or 2016. Unfortunately, the next month Aleph withdrew from the 2013 America's Cup and the ACWS.

AC45 yachts fleet racing in Plymouth, England, September, 2011. (© 2013 ACEA/Photo: Gilles Martin-Raget)

Aleph team leadership cited difficulty in fund-raising, but praised the new format of the regattas. "Although this new circuit is starting to fulfill its promises and in spite of very promising sporting results against the best teams," said Hugues Lepic, chairman, "the economic environment does not allow us to go all the way to San Francisco in 2013."

"We fought hard," said Philippe Ligot, CEO, "with all our drive and enthusiasm, to find a budget allowing us to participate in the final phase of the 34th America's Cup. We did not want to compete with resources that would not allow us to credibly challenge the best teams. France has, without a doubt, all the sporting, technical and managerial talent to win the Cup, but the current economic environment makes funding a commercial team extremely difficult."

Also in March, GreenComm denied reports they were out, reiterating their plans to build an AC72, but in mid-April they, too, withdrew.

China competed all the way to the end of the ACWS schedule, skipping only Newport, but was unable to put a real budget in place, either, and it became clear in August 2012, when they had not paid their 2013 entry fee, that they would remain an ACWS-only team this cycle.

Though Team Korea did announce that they had paid their entry fee for the 2013 America's Cup, no construction on an AC72 yacht was detected, and as 2012 and 2013 progressed, with the other teams sailing their new AC72s but no Korean boat in sight, Team Korea officially confirmed in March 2013 what had been apparent for a while—that they were not going to be a Challenger for 2013. Korea also withdrew from remaining America's Cup World Series activities, namely the April 2013 regatta in Naples, but expressed their intent to make another try for the next America's Cup.

Hope for a sorely-needed fourth Challenger had rested with Energy Team. There was great respect for the proven capabilities of the French multihull experts, and a lot of curiosity about what they would bring

Ten thousand spectators per day lined the shore at Ft. Adams in Newport, Rhode Island, to watch America's Cup World Series racing in the AC45s in the summer of 2012. (© 2013 ACEA/Photo: Gilles Martin-Raget)

to an AC72. The Peyrons had tried to set a schedule to build at least one boat, as late as possible in the process but giving them maximum time to put the funding in place. It had not come to pass. On August 1, 2012, the team announced that they did not have the funding necessary to build their new yacht as intended, but would continue to compete in the America's Cup World Series, and enter a Youth Series team as well, with the goal of becoming an America's Cup Challenger for the next defense of the America's Cup instead. Loïck would soon become a part of Artemis Racing's program.

Seven AC72s would be built: one for the Luna Rossa Challenge, and two apiece by Artemis Racing, Emirates Team New Zealand, and ORACLE TEAM USA. The three Challengers would meet in the Louis Vuitton Cup in July and August 2013, while the Defender would try to get ready on their own for the America's Cup match starting in September 2013. *(continued on page 63)*

Making the Multihull Decision:
Pete Melvin

Pete Melvin is a die-hard multihull guy.

For that reason, he pretty much figured that the pinnacle of sailing, the America's Cup, was out of his reach. But an improbable Deed-of-Gift match led to the chance of a lifetime—bringing Melvin and his team to the forefront of plans to bring multihulls to the venerable Cup.

The team at Morrelli & Melvin Design and Engineering, the Newport Beach, California, yacht design firm, helped design the wing and other features of BMW Oracle Racing's *USA17* trimaran that sailed in AC33. When America's Cup 33 ended in February 2010, Melvin celebrated the victory and thought his time with the Cup had come to an end. However, it turned out that a seed had been planted.

"During the Cup, I honestly don't think anyone was thinking that far ahead," Melvin said. "It was all new to most of the Oracle guys. I mean, you can count the number of guys who had been involved with multihulls—especially multihulls with wings—on two hands. It's a very small community. They weren't sure how that was going to turn out, so no one was thinking about how the next Cup was going to look.

"Around a month after the America's Cup ended, everyone realized it was time to get serious about the next one. A lot of opinions were being formed over the course of the match and even within Oracle a lot of people thought it would go back to monohulls the next time, that this was just an aberration, that they'd built the fastest boat within the Deed and that was it. That was the general feeling—and Larry Ellison had even stated that several times—that if they won, they'd go back to monohulls.

"But you could see, working with the design and sailing team, most of them said, 'Gosh, this is so exciting and so much fun, we really hope it stays in multihulls!' And among the sailors, they were used to two-boat testing where they'd be out there grinding away for hours on end, just changing one little inch on some rope, and it was really tedious, but this was all just wild open development. We're not just dialing the knobs in, this was all totally new thinking, clean sheet of paper and a lot more exciting intellectually.

"That had been percolating for a while, so after Larry sailed on the boat in the last race, he really started getting a buzz for the whole multihull thing, as did Russell."

So much so that when it became time to start thinking about the next Defense, BMW Oracle leaders took a serious look at the possibility that the future of the America's Cup could lay in multihulls. In March 2010 they dialed-up Morrelli & Melvin again.

"We were elated to get that call in March, to ask if we could help develop a concept for a multihull for the America's Cup," said Melvin, with a smile. "We worked with the Oracle guys on the concept for a couple of months, culminating at a designers' meeting in Valencia with everyone in attendance. We went in with no pre-conceived ideas of what it should be, our thought was just 'Let's open up the envelope of multihulls.' We looked at the matrix of boats from 60 to 80 feet long, catamarans and trimarans, and looked at all the options—what each of those options might cost, how difficult the boat would be to handle, what kind of loads, logistics, all of that. So we narrowed our ideas down to a 70-foot trimaran with standard sails.

"We'd looked at an 80-foot trimaran, which is a much bigger and more powerful boat, but it had an engine and I don't think anyone wanted to see that move forward. But we wanted to show a couple of options and see what kind of comments we got back. And it was fairly unanimous between the designers that they didn't want an engine. So we knew the 72 footer—similar in power to, say, an ORMA 60' trimaran, where you could sheet loads and power the thing with humans pretty aggressively, and sail around a course—was a pretty good size."

Melvin believes that, in the end, the rampant sentiment against using onboard power on America's Cup yachts was the downfall of the monohull.

"I think in the end a big driver against the monohull was the engine. In the meeting, Bruce Nelson did a really good job of laying out different monohulls in that size range with deep-draft fixed keels, retracting keels, canting keels—it was clear that you either had to have a retracting keel or a canting keel. The canting keel was the preferred choice, because the performance was better. But the downside was that you'd really need an engine to match race the thing."

Melvin realized the potential was there for fallout from traditionalists worried that multihulls are not the America's Cup, but the chance to be involved in the most high-profile event in sailing overrode any fear of backlash. Especially since Melvin was only proposing the idea, not making the decision.

"We're not really the front line on receiving criticism for the choice of vessel," said Melvin, "so we're a little bit insulated from that. It wasn't our choice, it was Larry Ellison's and Russell Coutts' choice."

Following the proposals in May, 2010, Melvin and the multihull contingent had to wait through an extensive series of on-the-water studies off Valencia in the summer that took hard looks at both the multihull and monohull options in practical situations. Despite the fact that the best choice of yachts was being debated, deadlines for a public fall announcement required moving forward on design development and writing class rules, even though that meant advancing both classes in parallel until a decision was set. The logical process made it clear that engineering minds were shaping the regatta, trying to be methodical in considering the questions as agnostically as possible based on some real-world evaluation.

Still, even with the engine proposition working against the monohulls, it would have been easy to believe the deck was stacked against multis.

"After the May meeting, the idea was that they would make a decision about the type of boat based on the information presented at the meeting, so we were all waiting to hear. They contacted us a few weeks later, saying they still hadn't made up their minds, that they wanted to do more research, but they realized that time was getting short, that they needed to start working on a rule. A rule takes time. So they had us continue forward creating a rule, but they also had a team in the UK overseeing writing a monohull rule. In the meantime, they were doing trials in Valencia, with the Extreme 40 and the RC44, getting input from different areas to figure out the big puzzle of what they thought would be better for the America's Cup as a whole. I thought that was a great way to go about it, getting opinions from all these different experts, like engineers, designers, media people, event organizers, teams.

"When they first asked us to start working on a concept . . . even at that designer's meeting it was extremely one-sided. Most of the people in the room were monohull people—most of the community is. There were only two or three of us who were dyed-in-the-wool multihull designers. It was extremely clear along party lines with most everyone wanting monohulls and us multihull guys saying 'We're open minded, but we see more benefits in the multihull than you guys are seeing.' But it comes down to match racing. The biggest criticism from the monohull guys was 'You can't match race these boats.' There are very few people who have really match raced a multihull. I was fortunate enough to have been involved with the Oracle guys in their match racing development and knew how exciting it could be, but it's hard to tell the monohull people 'Wait and see, it really will be great!' "

By the time September 2010 came, and with it the Valencia announcement bringing official word that the new boat would be the 72' catamaran, Melvin and his crew were knee-deep in what would become the AC72 Rule for the 34th America's Cup.

"We embarked on writing a rule and had four months to do it, so it was a fairly fast time pace. I think last time, they took a year to write the rule—but we didn't know that! We put a lot of resources into it, with four or five people from our office working on it plus a bunch of outside consultants. That was another good thing the Oracle guys did; they wanted to be removed from the rule writing part of it completely. They wanted to make sure we got a balanced, even approach and that we had checks and balances to ensure that everyone agreed with it, that this was the right way to go. Teams are going to be spending millions on these boats and hopefully for a period of years, so it was super important to get the rule right. So there was definitely some pressure on us.

"At first, we worked mostly on the technical aspect of it, what the boat should look like, catamaran versus trimaran, wings or sails. At the end of the day, it came down to someone saying 'Let's move forward' and it was Russell in the end who decided to go with a catamaran with a wingsail. The biggest reason for a catamaran was transportation. When we first started working on this, there was very little reason to have to transport these boats via aircraft, but it became more desirable as the studies went on and they started thinking about the events and how they might be run. So that was one of the main reasons for a catamaran."

Speaking of transportation: AC72 Class Rule 5.12 stipulates that each yacht, hull, and cross structure shall be capable of being disassembled and packed in shipping boxes within 24 hours and capable of being reassembled within 48 hours. That's a bloody tight schedule. But that's the deal, says Melvin.

"You have to be able to put them on a ship. Most of the time, the boat will stay together. The idea is that there's a schedule and the next event, you have to be able to pack the boats up and send them off to the next port. I can't tell you if the schedule will be that tight, but you'd better be prepared to do that, or you might miss the boat! (laughs)."

Pete Melvin also explained a few other bits, looking ahead to what these large new yachts might be like: where technology development is likely to focus for the AC72, why the America's Cup cats ended up with two wing sizes, and the role of the sailors in what looks like an increasingly computer-driven fast-tracked development environment.

The wingsail, brought forward from BMW Oracle Racing's successful America's Cup 33 challenge, might just be the area of greatest design advancement for the 34th Defense of the America's Cup in 2013, he said, speaking in January, 2011. There was noticeable excitement in his voice when discussing the possibilities of a Class Rule left wide open—and left that way for a reason.

"I think the wing and the underwater foils will be two huge areas of development. The wing needs to be a certain height and area, but how you get there, how many elements or slots or what your structure is or what your controls are, that's up in the air. There's been some good development on the wing in the past, but budgets have been pretty small, so we're hoping to see development in that area."

What sort of advancements?

"You never know, things that work better and are simpler and less expensive. . . . There's a lot of promise for wings on boats, so I think this will be one of those areas that will be a good trickle down. We think there is some area for improvement in wing design, so we didn't want to limit it to geometries that have been used in the past. We looked at a rule that's more restrictive, such as the wings that are being used in the C-Class, but it was very difficult to write a rule around a 3D object with moving parts. Whenever we wrote a rule to limit something, we would find five ways around it. By writing very restrictive rules, you actually increase complexity and cost, so by leaving things open, things turn out to be much simpler, elegantly efficient.

"For instance, the Oracle trimaran originally had six foils," Melvin points out. "It ended up with four—the center daggerboard and rudder were removed in the end. The wing could have been any design. But it actually ended up with a fairly simple wing, geometrically, and the appendages were as simple as you could get. If you look at the very successful racing classes around the world, such as the Open 60, they have very few rules. They're a box rule and they've ended up very elegantly simple. Every year, there are incremental performance gains, but the boats don't cost any more, it's just different geometry and configurations. If you're going to spend time and money on something, you might as well leave it a little bit open and let true development happen."

"The parameters of the boat we have restricted to small ranges are really the key elements: beam, weight, sail area, waterline length. Those are the main restrictions.

"The hull shape can be anything you want. You're allowed to have two rudders and two daggerboards, but they can be any shape you want. We'll probably see wider variations at first, but as everyone tests designs, they'll probably all start to look alike as we go forward, and performance will be closer. A bigger performance difference will be the actual sailors. These are new boats, so there will be differences in the learning curve."

Depending upon what you read during America's Cup 33, what with hydraulically-canted masts, thousands of data points processed per second, and real-time heads-up display of structural loads and alarms, it's easy to believe that software was running USA17, not a real live crew, and that computers will win the day for AC34. But as an experienced designer of some of the most advanced multihulls in the sport, Melvin has every confidence in the ability of top sailors to figure out this new design, and he knows that sailing talent is a key ingredient in creating a fast boat in the first place, let alone winning with one.

"The best sailors, sailing either an Optimist or an AC72, the cream will always rise to the top. Some people may not be able to get their heads around a totally different concept, but if you're a world-class sailor and you have an open mind, there's no reason you can't become a world-class multihull sailor as well.

"The design teams should be able to give the sailors a very good idea of how to set the boat up and sail it initially, but like any other new boat, it will have to be developed on the water. It's impossible to model the real world in a computer, there are too many variables. It will be a development process; most of the teams will be sailing similar boats as they ramp up, like the AC45s, and I would think you'll see most of the teams sailing other multihulls, getting some smaller boats, designing and testing smaller wings for those boats, testing some concepts and tuning up the sailing team and the design team."

If one actually reads the Class Rule, it is instructive to see just how much leeway Melvin and the organizers have incorporated.

"What is interesting about the rule, and the event planning, is that organizers are leaving quite a bit up in the air so they can discard concepts that don't work and change plans midstream. The size and the type of racecourse, for example, is still being debated and several ideas will likely be tried during the next year of America's Cup World Series events."

The practical implications of bringing wingsail technology to the America's Cup illustrate the sort of complexities that arise in adapting to the new class rule.

"When we were sizing the wing, the end requirement was that the boat would be able to race in 5 to 30 knots. That's a pretty wide range. But that was one of our challenges, the mandate from the media that 'the show must go on,' that there couldn't be the delays we'd seen previously. The TV crews are there from around the world, so even if it's not perfect conditions, we have to race."

Although the demand to be able to start races on time in most wind conditions was essential for the 2013 Defense, the America's Cup is about both advanced technology and high-intensity match racing, and even if the starting sequence is on schedule, the racing itself has to be America's Cup-level competition. Bringing the sporting side along in the move to the cutting edge required some creative solutions.

"That was one of the more challenging technical aspects of the rule, to come up with something that could fly a hull in five or six knots, but also race effectively in 28. We ended up with a wing that was a moderate size and some large headsails so you could vary your sail plan area by quite a bit through the range of conditions. We thought that you could still survive in 30 knots, but for anyone who's raced around the buoys in 30 knots, it is pretty much survival at that point."

Rather than compromise excessively on the new boat, several options for adapting wingsails to the conditions were considered, and the resulting AC72 Class Rule now provides for two wing sizes. [Note: Based on the results of initial AC45 testing, the AC72 Class Rule was modified to eliminate the short wingsail option that is discussed here.]

A tall wing can be used in lighter breeze, with the shorter wing employed in the types of higher winds that kept the old ACC boats at the dock.

"The short wing came in toward the end—the feedback we were getting was that guys would rather be able to race hard in 25 or 30 knots, so we looked at the concept of removable tips at the top of the wing, above the forestay, but the more we researched it we didn't think it would be effective. So we thought a short wing would be preferable solution.

"It's not something you have to have in 2012, but in 2013 you have to show up at events with a short wing," Melvin says. "All that is a protocol issue, so I would imagine the call for a short wing would come the night before a race."

The two wing sizes each have corresponding jibs, code zeros, and gennakers, which shall not be intermixed—bringing up still more questions that Melvin and his team could not answer in the four months they had to write the Class Rule.

"We thought about whether we should do more research into logistics for this rule, but we decided that the task of writing a rule in four months was big enough—to design a logistical program was asking too much. We were a pretty small team, so we knew that all the good ideas were not going to originate with our team. Once the rule was out, incredibly bright people from all these teams would start to figure it out. So the logistical team goes from 10 people to 100-plus people. We thought that was a better way to let it naturally evolve."

In absence of hands-on experience with the AC72 in a regatta setting, how the teams and race organizers handle the big cats will indeed be a learning experience.

"Also under discussion is whether or not to take the masts out at night and how quickly teams should expect to have to change from the tall wing to the short wing," says Melvin.

Knowledge gained from BMW Oracle's wingsail experience is only of limited help, but Melvin believes the America's Cup community will progress readily up the AC72 learning curve and gain confidence in how to deal with them.

"BOR90 [the trimaran raced in AC33] developed ways to handle the wing, which was over 200 feet tall. It was scary taking that thing up and down, because of its sheer size and all the unknowns involved, so it was very stressful. These boats are quite a bit smaller. The Stars and Stripes boat from 1988 is closer in size to the AC72, at 60', and the owners down in Mexico keep it on a mooring. That seems to work very well most of the time, so, unless you have some extreme weather coming in, the easiest way to park the boats would be in a mooring. As the teams get more comfortable with the boats, all these perceived issues will go away."

What did get written into the rule was a large amount of media-specific design, courtesy of Stan Honey (see sidebar page 65), chair of the media development group. Melvin believes it's a good move on the part of organizers to focus on the media presentation, to put viewers right on the trampoline of the boat as it screams across San Francisco Bay. The AC72 Rule requires provisions for no fewer than seven high-definition agile mounted cameras, three platforms for camera operators with handheld high-definition cameras, and 18 microphones for surround-sound, plus two media bays for cases, cabling, batteries, etc. This equipment is provided by the America's Cup Regatta Management and, unlike past America's Cups, none of it can be turned off by the competitors to escape scrutiny.

With the AC72 Rule officially adopted, these days Melvin has taken off his writing hat and replaced it with his designing hat, working with challenger Emirates Team New Zealand on their first new boat. Leaving so much up in the air is great for the rule writer, but for the designer? Not so much. Some might wonder about a conflict of interest when a Class Rule author becomes a designer of that very same class, but for Melvin the design task is no easier because of it. He faces the same questions everyone else does. It's difficult to know for sure which paths to pursue with the new boat.

"The courses have not been developed. I know with the AC45s, they're planning some innovative courses and will do some experimentation there. It is a little bit tough, now that we're working on designing one of these boats, we'd like to know what the course looks like, whether we'll have reaches or not, whether you want to design the boat so it's faster downwind or upwind, or what the right blend there is."

In the current Protocol for 2013, the courses are due to be announced in December 2011, but the designs of the first AC72s will already be committed at that point, with the boats far along in the construction process and nearing launch.

"There's no time to understand what the courses are before you design your boat. I really hope they revise that and move that date closer so that when you're designing your boat, you know. But I'm not sure if that will happen, so it's a little bit of a guessing game. In some of the meetings, they have showed some prospective courses to some of the challengers, and they involve reaches and even downwind starts, things like that. So it's all up for grabs right now."

How do you proceed with a boat design amid that degree of uncertainty?

"Right now, I think you'd better be designing a boat that can do everything well, being able to switch gears and have some ideas on how you might model your boat for different kinds of courses.

"The fun part for us is doing all the 'what ifs,' just getting our heads around the rule as it exists, thinking of what the boat might look like and coming up with conceptual ideas, investigating different ideas.

"One neat thing about it is it's as much a management competition as it is a sailing or design contest. If you just hire a group of designers, put them in a room and say 'design this boat,' you could have people going off in all sorts of directions and looking at all sorts of cool stuff, but in the end there's a budget. And most important is time. This conceptual phase is extremely important. You realize there are some things that we think could be interesting, but we're not going to have time to look at that. When it's all new, there are so many things going around everyone's heads, so many things you could look at and investigate, but you've really got to quickly boil those down to the things that are really promising and will give you the best return and get you across the finish line first."

If only because definitive proof will take until 2013, one question that will linger is what will a full-bore Louis Vuitton Cup and America's Cup be like in a multihull class?

"I think that after the match in February [2010], there was a lot of opposition to having multihulls in the America's Cup. But over the course of time between February and the release of the rule in October, more people had become open-minded about it. If you can change a person from being a monohull fan to multihulls, I don't know. But I think people are willing to have an open mind, let this process play out and see what happens."

Melvin knows how much is at stake here—including a lifelong reputation as a guru of multihulls. He also knows that many America's Cup fans and participants alike have a way to go until they are convinced that a multihull will do justice to the event in which they are so invested. All Melvin asks is "Give this a chance."

SELECTING THE VENUE

Leading Up to Selecting San Francisco—Cities for 2013

At the May 6, 2010, Rome press conference, Coutts revealed little regarding the venue other than that consultants were studying the feasibility issues, and it was believed that detailed discussions were taking place with the city of San Francisco at that time as well.

BMW Oracle leaders in early July 2010 also referred to two other unnamed European cities under consideration. Only one was ever named, though, with an offer made in private by the Italian government offering a $500 million package to host the event near Rome. Rumors persisted that a Middle Eastern country could be a potential host, too, willing to pay similar sums for the America's Cup to be staged on their shores. Neither of those options appeared to have come very close to being selected, though.

What the America's Cup needed was exposure in the United States, something that had dwindled down to almost nothing. Another overseas regatta wasn't going to accomplish that.

What the America's Cup needed onshore was a place to house the teams and their boats, some administrative offices, and ideally a good location for an America's Cup village, the center of activity for fans coming to see the event. Hospitality for the guests of sponsors needed to be considered, and the regatta has historically attracted visitors on giant luxury yachts of all descriptions, so-called superyachts, that are a spectacle in their own right just tied to the dock.

The natural starting point was San Francisco. On the sailing and spectating side of the equation, the Bay Area was well suited for exactly what organizers had in mind: windy conditions with racing in sight of shore, plenty of places to view a race from, and a sophisticated major city that would provide hospitality and entertainment for fans from all over the world.

As a backup to San Francisco, GGYC maintained a running dialogue with the State of Rhode Island and related parties about holding the 2013 America's Cup in Newport, which had been the home of the event from 1930 to 1983, and been a home to Defender trials even before that. The state was willing to help fund improvements at Fort Adams and in other areas of Newport Harbor to help attract the America's Cup back to the home it enjoyed for 53 years. Newport wasn't the wind machine that San Francisco Bay was, but it was a feasible U.S. option if they were willing to support the event.

Several other cities tried to throw their hats into the ring, ranging from San Diego, California, to New London, Connecticut. America's Cup officials always emphasized, though, that San Francisco was their first choice, if it could be accomplished.

Agreement with the City of San Francisco was simple. GGYC would bring the America's Cup, hold two preliminary regattas, and in 2013 the Louis Vuitton Cup and the America's Cup Match itself.

The city would get a world famous sporting event, drawing tens of thousands of visitors per day, and, depending on the number of teams, an economic benefit projected in one independent study at $1.4 billion for the region, creating 8,000 jobs in the midst of a recession.

The deadline for a venue announcement was December 31, 2010.

After agreeing in principle with GGYC on the form of the agreement over the summer, San Francisco held hearings throughout the fall of 2010 regarding using the waterfront south of the Oakland Bay Bridge with a Cup Village on Piers 30 to 32 (the southern option). The city held more hearings, changed the proposal, and moved the Cup Village to Piers 27 to 29 (the northern option). Following yet more hearings, the San Francisco Board of Supervisors unanimously approved the northern option in mid-December, subject to further negotiations in private between GGYC/ACEA and the city.

On New Year's Eve, the city and GGYC were finally able to shake hands on a deal, and San Francisco was announced as the host of the 2013 America's Cup. Piers 27 to 29 would host the main America's Cup spaces for the public. Marina Green and other locations along the northern waterfront would be prime viewing areas, and Piers 30 to 32 would host the team bases.

There followed a six-month 2,500-page Environmental Impact Report; more rounds of hearings, comments, and revisions to the report; the adoption of the report by the city; a lawsuit by local community groups disputing the adoption of the report, potentially delaying construction; and a settlement of $225,000 with the community groups in exchange for which they withdrew the lawsuit.

Various permutations of an intricate deal for Larry Ellison to pay to refurbish the piers, let them be used by the event, and then be leased back to Ellison as compensation for the cost of the repairs came to naught. Ultimately the time lost in negotiations also sank plans to improve anything except Piers 27 to 29, where the city built a long-planned cruise-ship terminal, letting the America's Cup use it for the America's Cup Park, and then took it back following the 2013 regatta. OTUSA ended up staying in their huge Pier 80 base, farther south, inaccessible to the public. Artemis rented a seaplane hanger in Alameda, across the bay. For their bases, ETNZ and Luna Rossa ended up using the portions (continued on page 67)

Stan Honey — Sailing on TV

Sailor Stan Honey was recruited to help make sailing the America's Cup more understandable to spectators.

Sailing on TV isn't always the easiest thing even for sailors to keep track of, the appearance of who is ahead changing with the perspective of the camera, and the leader not always known until they cross close to each other or round the marks.

The AC broadcast began using computer animations in the 1990s to show viewers a visualization of where the boats were relative to each other and the racecourse, and starting in 2000 in Auckland, serious fans could even watch the virtual races live on their computers, tracking speeds and lead changes in real time. For a few thousand dedicated America's Cup fans around the globe, this was an immersive multi-screen experience of live TV, virtual boats, and international chat rooms that could teach volumes about sailing. But it wasn't going to help the America's Cup reach out to the casual fan trying to understand what was going on.

When the helicopter mounted TV cameras pulled back far enough to show both boats and the mark, the scene was tiny and the boats looked like they were sitting still. When the cameras zoomed in and gave a sense of speed, there was no useful orientation to the racecourse or the competition. Queen Victoria's famous question "Who is Second?" allegedly asked back in 1851 is actually quite natural for a yacht racing spectator with a high-definition screen in front of them, too. Providing an easy visual answer would open up the sport for viewers.

Stan Honey was the right person to help solve the problem for AC34, his résumé an ongoing intersection of sailboat racing, computers, navigation, and broadcasting. He is a competitive sailor, an experienced ocean navigator with a Volvo Ocean Race win to his credit, plus Transatlantic, Transpac, and Around-the-World records. Honey is also an electrical engineer with a high-tech pedigree, a founder of mapping and navigation company Etak, Inc. and, with Ken Milnes, broadcast graphic company SportVision, Inc.

Honey already had some notable achievements bringing sports visualization to television. He was behind bringing the first-down line to National Football League broadcasts, a resounding success in the presentation of the sport. At the request of Fox Sports, he also came up with the glowing hockey puck seen for a short while in the National Hockey League. That was not well received by viewers and eventually dropped by the broadcasters, but a technical accomplishment nonetheless. And then Honey brought along the ability to identify and highlight the individual NASCAR competitors onscreen as they rounded the track at over 200 mph. He also put the strike zone on TV for Major League Baseball. With Stan Honey and Ken

Milnes, what could be done for the America's Cup?

First there was the need to accurately track the locations and movements of the boats. GPS units were used, with their accuracy improved using dual-frequency Real Time Kinematic receivers so that the positions and orientations of the boats could be established within 2 cm, updated 10 times per second. Inertial navigation units backstopped the GPS units, approximating the yacht positions in case GPS signals were interrupted.

The first-down line in football works by calculating the appearance of the virtual line from the point of view of the real-world camera, and then superimposing the computer-generated line in proper perspective over the live image. With a little additional processing to obscure the line when players walk "in front" of it, augmented reality starts to look convincing.

For sailing, the plan was to show the racecourse, the start and finish lines, laylines, course boundaries, and other features overlaid with the live television image. A particularly effective graphic turned out to be "course ladders," lines drawn perpendicularly across the course in the style of the yard lines on a football field every few hundred meters, making it instantly obvious where the boats were trying to go and who was ahead.

All of the tricks from the older computer programs could be overlaid, too—the yacht names, flags of the boats, instantaneous speeds, or other telemetry information as needed—and by the time of the America's Cup matches, even animations of disturbed wind coming off the wingsails, or the ebbing and flooding currents of the San Francisco Bay tides were used to illustrate critical effects on the racing.

The system, dubbed "LiveLine," was essentially a more sophisticated version of the football technology, complicated by the issue that not only does the yacht racing course move around depending on conditions, unlike a football field, but also the cameras are flying around the course mounted on helicopters. Rendering the graphics required the precise location and orientation of the helicam be known, plus the marks and the Race Committee boat, too.

LiveLine and the Racing Rules for the AC34

With the racecourse outlined, and the locations of the marks included in the system, it was a natural progression to make the system available to the umpires, too. The Racing Rules of Sailing for the America's Cup were enforced by a combination of umpires in powerboats on the water, following the racers around the course, and additional review back onshore in front of a screen. Relying on the precision of LiveLine, the umpires could view incidents as they unfolded, play them backward and forward, and after a quick conference among themselves, issue penalties. Critical questions for applying the rules, such as whether a boat was over the starting line early, or which boat had an overlap, and countless other potential incidents where the exact position of the boat affected penalties, could be reviewed within seconds of the occurrence with a high degree of confidence. Knowing the locations of the boat in endless detail still couldn't solve questions about whether a right-of-way boat had allowed the other the proper chance to keep clear, often a pivotal question in a rules incident, so the element of judgment wasn't removed completely from the equation.

Protests were signaled to the umpires by pushing a "Yankee" button onboard the yacht, in place of the traditional flag used to get attention. Penalties received were also signaled electronically. A system of bright flashing LEDs in various places on the boat were used to make visible whether a protest had been raised and whether the penalty had been given. LiveLine also drove a warning system to help alert the crew as they approached a boundary, though in the heat of battle, this was at times overlooked by a busy crew.

And when a team was penalized, LiveLine was employed to apply the penalties. Where once a rules infraction on the water was an automatic disqualification, the Racing Rules of Sailing for years had been modernized to allow a penalized boat to perform a sequence of turns to clear their penalty. The exact combination has varied depending on the class and the amount of disadvantage the turns inflict on the competitor. The America's Cup in 2007 typically required a 360-dgree turn to clear a penalty, which in an ACC yacht usually amounted to 25-30 seconds compared to sailing full speed. For the 2013 America's Cup, the system allowed the penalty to be assigned in terms of boat lengths.

When a penalty had been issued, the system calculated a line two boat lengths astern of the penalized boat, moving toward the next mark at the expected speed of the boat for the wind conditions and point of sail. Clearing the penalty required the crew having to slow the boat to lose speed until the requisite distance had been lost, and then resuming racing. A penalty not taken after ten seconds, however, caused the two-length distance to increase with time. Referred to as "Slow and Go," the new penalty process was proven out in the America's Cup World Series, which served as a test bed for integrating the LiveLine system into race operations.

Trickle Down of LiveLine to Other Sailboat Races

The ability to conclusively determine boats that start too early, for example, could be helpful to race committees in many other kinds of sailing, too. LiveLine uses commercially available technology that is probably still too expensive for all but the most well-sponsored regattas, but Stan Honey has estimated that the current $5,000–$7,000 per boat hardware cost could be reduced as adoption increased. Standard GPS receivers don't have the accuracy to be used for Racing Rules situations, but it's not hard to imagine that a similar technology may assist other race committees in some form in coming years.

The technology to launch LiveLine was not too far out of reach. Like many innovations, it just required properly framing the problem and then setting the right people to work on it with sufficient resources. The LiveLine system won a technical Emmy award for contributions to broadcast technology. As a basis for making so many racing aspects of the America's Cup visually obvious, the recognition was well deserved. LiveLine is also a publicly visible example of the sort of inventiveness that the America's Cup more typically spurs behind closed doors.

of the unrefurbished Piers 30 to 32 that were not structurally deficient. Not all of this was optimal, but time and money had not permitted all the plans to come to fruition.

Efforts for the public were concentrated at the America's Cup Park, and at the America's Cup Village on Marina Green. The AC Park featured a visitors' center, Cup exhibits, restaurants, shops, VIP clubs, superyacht mooring, and the media center. The Cup Village was similar on a smaller scale, full of visitor activities, concessions, and bleachers that overlooked the racecourse. Additional locations along the waterfront, including historic ships and a parking garage, were the site of more VIP viewing, though there was plenty of breakwater and park space that could be accessed for free.

The reduced expectation for the total number of teams did not play well on the stage of local politics in San Francisco, though. In the end, however, many of the city's expenses scaled down accordingly and actual problems for the city were minimal. Although the city of San Francisco would be hosting fewer teams than had been promised, the Louis Vuitton Cup and America's Cup regatta would still deliver a lot to fans and to the city.

FOUR America's Cup World Series —Sailing the AC45s

The America's Cup World Series kicked off in August 2011 in Cascais, Portugal, just west of Lisbon. Cascais is a charming beachfront town. Plymouth, England, followed in September, the first venue that really approached the stadium sailing concept, and many thousands of spectators came out, especially on the weekend dates, to sit on hills ringing three sides of the historic English harbor. A few days of high winds taught the AC45 crews how to capsize the boats, with bearaways working best, but just about any direction doing in a pinch. San Diego followed, with the United States debut of the wingsail cats in the harbor of the laid-back Southern California town. Racing right off the piers downtown drew enough crowds to require bleachers. The most popular portion of the event was an out-and-back fleet race that managed to culminate in a chaotic finish.

In 2012 ACWS regattas resumed in Europe. Well-timed with the late entry of Italian challenger Luna Rossa, two events in their home country confirmed the passion that the Italian public has for their teams. Luna Rossa debuted two AC45 yachts in Naples, treating their fans to top finishes their first time out. Venice followed the next month, with the incredible sight of wingsail cats racing to a finish line on the Grand Canal, lined with fans on land and afloat.

Newport, Rhode Island, the traditional home of the Cup, and the yachting capital of the East Coast, got their turn to host in late June, and it was a bit of a lovefest: 10,000 people per day were paying to get into the park at Fort Adams to watch the racing just offshore. The Sunday championship races saw national TV coverage on NBC in the United States, the first live Cup racing on a major network in 20 years. Sailors and organizers were getting their acts down. Not just good experience for the sailors, but also for the event organizers, it was an ongoing real-world experiment

(continued on page 71)

Emirates Team New Zealand Works Up to Sailing the AC72s

(This report from November 2011 in San Diego at the ACWS provides insights into the New Zealand lead-up to the 2013 Cup.)

Dean Barker has made quite a name for himself in the America's Cup, winning his first-ever race in the Cup in 2000 when Team New Zealand skipper Russell Coutts handed the helm to his then young trial horse driver in the fifth and final race of the 30th Defense. And it was Barker and his Emirates Team New Zealand crew on the Challenger who gave Defender Alinghi all they could handle in the 2007 America's Cup final.

So perhaps Barker and ETNZ had the most to lose when Cup organizers sent the America's Cup Class monohulls into the history books and forged a new path for the Cup, staking their collective reputations on the excitement and risks of a 72-foot catamaran, and on top of that, holding two seasons of regattas racing 45-foot versions of the winged cats.

Some veterans were skeptical of the new boats, fearing that their futures with the Cup would be lost as decades of monohull experience would somehow became irrelevant, but Barker wasn't one to worry over it. The team wasted no time looking backward. Instead, they bought an A-class catamaran to learn the ins and outs of cat sailing, embarked on an Extreme 40 campaign in the ultra competitive Extreme Sailing Series, and picked up two SL33 cats to be used for crew training and as design guinea pigs to explore options for the AC72. And all of that in addition to the ETNZ AC45 that was delivered last April.

To say that it's been a lightning-fast course in "Catamarans 101" is an understatement.

"It's been an incredibly steep learning curve for us," said Barker. "The biggest challenge for us initially was making the transition, to understand what cat sailing is all about. We thought we had a pretty good grasp on monohull sailing, so to transition across has taken quite a bit of time and a lot of effort. Slowly but surely we're getting there and I hope we can continue improving at a really good rate."

Barker and ETNZ have clearly been quick studies, judging from the lead in the match racing and fleet racing standings of the America's Cup World Series that they carried heading into San Diego. In fact, ETNZ had equal match and fleet racing points after the Cascais, Portugal, and Plymouth, England, events. They won the fleet racing in Cascais and finished second after Oracle Racing's Spithill in Plymouth. In match racing, ETNZ scored a second place in Cascais, then beating Team Korea for the match race title in Plymouth. ETNZ was beaten in the ACWS San Diego match racing semi-finals by Jimmy Spithill's entry, and finished third.

"The most difficult thing has been to understand the boundaries and the limits of what these boats can and can't do, and boat positioning. You know what you want to do most of the time, but actually being able to do it is a completely different thing. Whereas you could place an old version five boat on a dime, in these boats it's much more difficult to understand what the boat will do—how quickly it will accelerate or slow down, how will it tack and gybe. That part has been very difficult. And they accelerate fast—they're light and they have enough sail area when there's breeze, so it's amazing how quickly you can go from a dead stop to accelerating quickly."

One of the biggest hills to climb on the AC45 involves the new hard wingsails. But Barker is typically matter-of-fact regarding mastering the new design element, which will, by its very nature, be a much different proposition on the AC72 than it is on the AC45.

"The 45's wingsail is actually quite a basic wing. It's very simple, it's very robust, so it's a very good tool for us to learn with. The 72-foot wings will be much more complicated, I'm sure, and probably a lot more fragile. But these have been fantastic. We learn little bits every time we go sailing on how we can handle them better and what effect they have on the maneuverability. They're much nicer to sail with than a soft sail, particularly in these reaching courses."

The latest news for ETNZ involves their training arrangement with Luna Rossa, a late entry accepted for the 34th America's Cup. The two challenger candidates will trial in New Zealand on AC45s and share information as they design and build their first AC72s in cooperation.

"The relationship with Luna Rossa is going to be good for us, once we get the 72s into the water. It will certainly accelerate the learning curve with those boats. We have a limited number of days, so we have to be pretty quick to learn and develop." The NZ team's AC72 will not splash until July 2012, and the Protocol for the 34th Defense limits the teams

to 30 AC72 sailing days before January 31, 2013.

Design work runs apace as teams learn more about what they do want and don't want based on their experience in the AC45. Barker and his sailing team work closely with Morrelli & Melvin partner Pete Melvin, the author of the AC72 Rule and now a designer for ETNZ. Few people know as much about a multihull as Melvin, and with three multihull world championships to his credit, he knows what sailors want.

"The sailing team is actively involved in the design process and we've got a really strong design group back in Auckland, with Pete Melvin and a couple other guys from his office. The input is valuable—different ideas, different concepts—so hopefully it's pushing us in the right direction. It's been great working with these guys because of their multihull experience and everything they can add back into the design process."

Typical of ETNZ's way has been bringing in multi-faceted talent, so to speak, like Glenn Ashby, who was the 2008 Tornado catamaran World Champion with teammate Darren Bundock (himself now helming Oracle5). Ashby serves with the Kiwis as an AC45 wing trimmer and participates as a design team member.

"Glenn Ashby has also been really valuable with his experience, so we're learning more and more," says Barker. "A year ago, we couldn't have made any input, because we just didn't know what the boats were and how to manage them. We feel like now we have a much better understanding, but still we have a lot to learn."

Barker knows that the clock is moving, with barely 20 months to go between now and the start of the Louis Vuitton Cup in San Francisco in July 2013. Plans for the next few months involve training, designing, and more training.

"It sounds as though there will not be an [AC45] event in January, so we'll take our boat back to New Zealand and sail with the Luna Rossa guys there. There are other design projects we need to carry on with ourselves, so time is ticking very quickly. It won't be long before we'll be putting our AC72 into the water!"

in learning how to run races, get the action across on TV, and make it work for spectators on site, too. Newport wrapped up the first season of ACWS racing, and now it was time to test everything in the new home of the Cup: San Francisco Bay.

GGYC had promised the city of San Francisco two preliminary events before 2013 began. Originally, plans had been for a regatta in August 2012 that would be the premiere of AC72 racing, giving everybody a chance to find out how the boats would adapt to their new habitat, and vice versa. But with concessions to the reality of developing the new cats, the AC72s wouldn't even be launching until mid-summer at the earliest. The ACWS would remain in the AC45 yachts for the duration, and the AC72 wouldn't see action until the Louis Vuitton Cup began. So the AC45s came to San Francisco for two regattas. The August arrival of the regatta drew a great reaction from fans—some serious sailors, and others curious after all the attention the event had re- *(continued on page 75)*

AC45s Help Shore Crews Prepare for 72s

(This interview from September 2012 describes the on-shore support critical to racing the AC45s and the AC72s.)

"I'll tell you right now, we've got the best shore team. There's no question in my mind. They're the first guys down there and the last guys to leave. They really put everything into it and it really allows us to just concentrate on the racing."

That's how skipper Jimmy Spithill describes his OTUSA shore team—the ten guys behind the scenes who make sure that his AC45 stays in top shape, no matter how hard the day's racing.

One of the primary cogs in the ORACLE TEAM USA wheel is Australian Andrew Henderson, the head of rigging and part of the reserve crew.

"Hendo" has been with OTUSA since just before the catamaran-versus-trimaran America's Cup showdown in February 2010, bringing an extensive ocean racing background to the program, including his experience in 15 Sydney-Hobart races. He takes us on a tour of the ORACLE TEAM USA compound, talks about the mountain of work involved in dealing with two AC45 catamarans during the America's Cup World Series events—and how one little mistake on the racecourse can ruin the evening for the shore crew.

The ACWS is a road show, but instead of touring the country they cross the globe, with America's Cup Regatta Management (ACRM) taking the show from Europe to America and back again multiple times.

Jimmy Spithill's AC45 at the America's Cup World Series in San Francisco, August, 2012. Late in the summer of 2013 ORACLE TEAM USA was penalized for illegal adjustments to weight at the forward kingposts on their AC45s. (© 2013 ACEA/Photo: Gilles Martin-Raget)

"Everything we have packs into the four shipping containers that make up the compound," explained Henderson. Arrival in a new venue follows a practiced sequence. "First ACRM places the containers, then we put up the tent—we have to wait to unload the wing until the tent is set up, because any wind across the wing could be catastrophic.

"We get here on a Monday morning at 9 am, and by 3 pm this whole thing is up and ready to go. From putting the containers on the ground until we're ready to go, sailing is three or four days.

"The more you do it, the less daunting it becomes. The guys who made the rule understood how long it would take—they asked us, Artemis, Team New Zealand. We all gave an opinion, so there was a consensus as to the timing."

Once empty of the main components of the disassembled AC45s, the OTUSA containers then become the workshops for the different departments. "One container is for sail storage—all the racks fold up when not in use. The sails sometimes get stored inside the wings for transport, otherwise one wing goes into the rack in two parts and the sails go on the side. One 40-foot container can hold the whole wing and all its associated parts, which is quite a few boxes. It's amazing how much we can fit into such a small space. Another container is for boat building—anything that has to do with the building or repairing of the boats is done in one container. And we have our rigging container, where we have a test bed so we can test all the strops that go on the boat. They are pulled to the load they'll see before they go on, so that we know that any given part can deal with the load.

"The wing elements have their own stand, or splash, that they go into. They go into the splashes and get anchored to the floor of the container. It all happens pretty quickly, since everywhere they go is marked. Once they're in the splashes, they're pretty secure, with all the straps. All the shore team guys are designated into teams and we work pretty efficiently.

"Because we've been sailing these boats more than anyone, the set-up and the pack-up—the details of how we put everything together—is pretty well straight on."

While the sailors and designers love having two boats to learn on, for the shore crew it means twice as much work—and then some.

Because ORACLE TEAM USA adopted a two-boat program ahead of everyone else, plus a San Francisco-based training program, they quickly built up a lot of experience with lifting and dropping the boats in and out of the water, along with the pre-sail preparation and post-race care needed to maintain an exotic multihull racing yacht. They estimate that even in the first six months they had probably done about 1,000 lifts and drops. That much repeated motion naturally inspired efforts to streamline the process, save time and effort for the crew, and minimize risk of damage to the boats. And having multiple boats on the water naturally bred some internal competition, too.

"The development sort of chases each other, so we're always catching up with that—one boat has one thing and the other boat wants to do it," Henderson said. "But it's good, because our boats are quite obviously fast. The guys have done nice work, we just need to point them in the right direction!

"We do a thousand little things to make the boats perfect—after a round, we bring them inside, put leaf blowers inside them. We dehumidify the wings to take ounces of weight off them. We do all the really small things—then the guys miss one tack or a gybe or get a wrong windshift and all that work means nothing. It can be a little bit frustrating, but it's all part of the game. That's why we enjoy being the shore team, because the joy for us is in those little small things, in tinkering with the little things.

"The wing frames are super lightweight; they're made with honeycomb on Nomex. They have a tendency to suck up water—so if you tip them over, they'll absorb water quite quickly. And it weighs nothing, you can twist it or break it or snap it over your knee. On its own, it's a very fragile piece of equipment, but all together, it provides the frame for the film we put on, so we really look after it.

"So when they guys sail, if they're tight in a race and forget to let off a line, the wing will come across and hit the line and break all the frames along the edge. So we have to cut holes in the Clysar film, clamp it, and repair it. There's a lot that goes on after a small mistake on the water—it makes a big job list in here."

Not that Henderson is complaining—the shore crew is equally as proud of the sailing team as the sailing team is of the team that gets them out onto the water every day.

"We have extreme confidence in our sailing team. They're really good guys and they've brought home some really good results. So the effort is worthwhile. And they're very appreciative of our work so that makes the job easy."

Admittedly, as a one-design class, innovation with the AC45 is limited by the rules. Much of the cat's technology is predetermined—but teams are finding ways to improve the product by tweaking rigging, soft sails, the bowsprit, and the furling systems.

Among the myriad new terms introduced in the America's Cup lexicon this cycle is Clysar, the film used to cover the ribs of the hard wing, though a competing product, with the trade name Cryovac, is the material actually being employed. It is a flexible packaging film that seals in products via a shrink tunnel, specially engineered for strength and clarity. All of the teams have had to learn how to deal with this new material.

"The big issue we have with the transportation of the wing is the temperature variation, from where we start to where we end up, and how it fluctuates in between. Once you close one of these containers up and it gets hot in there, we have issues with shrinkage of the Clysar film that covers the wings. Often we get to an event, with a tight setup time, and we've got a new Clysar job to do, because it split or pulled away—sometimes, we've even had the adhesive on the tape melt, it gets so hot in the container."

ORACLE TEAM USA added another variable into the equation by coloring their wing black, giving Henderson and the rest of the shore team another large problem to stay on top of.

Black objects absorb a wider spectrum of sunlight than clear film or other colors, transferring more heat. The shore team has to keep an eye out during the regattas since even a bright sunny day can be problematic for the delicate film.

"On a day with little wind and with the sun directly on the wing, we can have an issue with it shrinking and breaking in spots. So while it's a terrific marketing tool, logistically it's a nightmare!

"The black just attracts so much more temperature. When you set the wing up, you put double-sided tape along all the frames and along the trailing edge and then you apply the Clysar across it. You stick the film across the double-sided tape to apply it, trim off the edges, then use a heat gun to shrink it up. Then you iron the whole thing. We've had to do more taping than any of the other teams—one wing takes two guys about two days. So if you've had an issue, that's four days gone for two guys. So it can be a bit of an interruption to our setting-up process!

"But we've had to make patches every regatta, so we're getting good at dealing with it. And it doesn't seem as though the other teams have had this issue at all! So while marketing's important, is it important enough to cost you races—I suppose that's the question. But we're dealing with it. In Cascais, we hosed down the wings (to keep them cool). We'd leave them in the shed for as long as possible and bring them out half an hour before the race."

One of the primary areas of innovation for the teams has been the soft sails—the inventory of gennakers and genoas that complement the hard wing.

"We feel we're pretty strong downwind," said Henderson. "The boys have done a lot of work with the gennaker, with the size and shape. There is some good footage of Jimmy and the guys deeper and with a lower angle, but with the same speed as the other guys. A lot of that is technique—steering and how they sail the boat—but the gennaker doesn't hurt!"

Henderson admits that the team probably has a bit of an edge with the catamarans, given their experience with the 90-footer in 2010. But a surprisingly small percentage of information translated directly from the trimaran to the AC45s.

"I'd say we brought maybe 15 percent of the stuff we learned from the 90-footer to these boats. The knowledge base is out there and it's easy to find out about this stuff, but the familiarity with it and being with a design or a concept—it all rings a little more true since we worked on the 90-footer with the big wing. So we're ready to take the next step and develop it further, rather than having to come to grips with a new concept. Most of the other teams are working with a new concept—the wing with the way it cambers and twists—whereas our guys have already done it, so the concept is familiar. So straightaway we're into developing it or tweaking other areas. So we can invest our time better because we already have a grasp of the key concept."

The stakes are going exponentially higher with the new AC72s. OTUSA launched their first catamaran at the end of August 2012, and to date has sailed it for four of the allotted 30 days permitted before the end of next January. The development process for the 72-footer places an even higher set of demands on the team.

"A new class in itself is intimidating because there are a whole lot of bad traps that you might not have seen before. And the design team is always trying to push the limits—we've tried to get fittings smaller, lashings smaller, rigging smaller. With everything you do, there's a weight cost, especially with these boats. So it meant a new round of testing—and none of what we learned about the 90-footer is really relevant once we go to the AC72. We'll need to be on top of our testing for every specific component, because each component should be just strong enough and last just long enough to do the job. It should be 'just there,' with a big enough safety factor so in case there's a strange load case, it survives. Everything is going to be right on the edge once again for this new class—there will be some action.

"But I think the 45 has been good—we've done a lot of testing with different configurations that hopefully will scale up to the 72. And we've got a pretty talented design team that are very inclusive of guys like myself, who actually operate on the ground, in regards to what we're seeing with the 45 and making sure it gels with the 72," says Henderson.

Getting a 72-foot wingsail catamaran ready to not just hotdog around the bay, but making it both bulletproof enough and fast enough to face a Challenger when the America's Cup is on the line, is the ultimate goal. Incidents while testing, like losing a daggerboard during the shake-down cruise, though unwelcome, aren't unexpected, and are indeed why the teams test so hard, but racing to defend or challenge the Cup is an utterly unforgiving task.

"I think we're fairly confident it will be a good product, but there will be a hell of a lot of hours between now and then—not only in testing, design, and development, but just in getting the boat out there and thrashing around, making sure it's a reliable product. The America's Cup is only a few races and a whole lot of time prior to make sure everything's perfect. We're a very well-funded team, so we have no excuses at all. There's no excuse for any sort of failure, be it rigging, sails, we should have every base covered. That's why we're working so hard now, to put on a good show and to not have any failures. It's going to need to be the same in the AC72."

ceived in the local media after the city had been selected to host the 2013 defense. October included some great racing, although it was harder for fans to navigate, with the ACWS forming part of what local lore was calling San-a-geddon: the confluence of the ACWS, the U.S. Navy Fleet Week, the 60,000 visitors for the Oracle Corporation's annual Oracle Open World, and the start of post-season baseball play with the San Francisco Giants on their way to a World Series sweep.

ACWS racing on the AC45s wrapped up with one more event, again in Naples, Italy, in April 2013. The event ran well enough, but the teams were already getting anxious about preparations for the summer with the AC72s. As beautiful a regatta backdrop as the Bay of Naples could be, the teams had their minds on the other city by the bay.

Of course the sailors and shore teams benefited from the time spent sailing a smaller cousin of an AC72 in various race environments. But for the event as a whole, too, the ACWS regattas came through, serving as a test bed for working out the rules of racing fast (continued on page 77)

ETNZ's Chase 1 — Upgrading Their Chase Boat to Keep Up with the AC72s

(This interview is from August, 2012.)

With the 34th Defense, Emirates Team New Zealand's Chris Salthouse notches his sixth America's Cup with the storied racing team. Salthouse was a mainsail trimmer for most of those campaigns, but the AC45 and new AC72 wingsail multihulls have changed the ballgame considerably. Salthouse now drives the team's chase boat and handles logistics—and in typical Kiwi fashion, he doesn't mince words when explaining what prompted the switch from sailing on the boat to working on the shore crew.

"Age!" he says, smiling. "It's a new game. The level has changed a lot—it's a young man's sport and I'm 43 years old now. I used to trim the mainsail, and for trimming the wing and maneuvering in these boats, I think you need to be younger and a bit stronger. But I really enjoy this side of things—it's my responsibility to get the big boat off the dock and into the water. Over here, I look after the wing, so I'm enjoying the change.

"Sometimes, it is hard to watch, because these new boats are pretty cool, but if you want to stay in this sport, you have to adapt and roll with it. And it's cool to be able to follow along behind the AC72—I'm looking at the wing, at the sails. I've got the coaches and the sailmakers with me, and it all becomes rather collaborative. We can watch them trim the sails and we can all look at the differences. So we're a bit removed, but not really."

Salthouse has carved out another niche with the team, putting him in charge of a pretty cool new toy—he worked with Pete Melvin of Melvin & Morrelli Design and Engineering, one of ETNZ's AC72 designers, to come up with a state-of-the-art catamaran chase boat that meets the daunting task of keeping up with the team's America's Cup boat. "We started with a blank piece of paper, and a budget," explains Salthouse. "The old Protector boats were great for working with Version 5 boats; they could go all day at 12 or 13 knots. With these big boats, it's one thing to be able to go fast, but you've got to be able to go fast for long periods of time. With the 30-day rule between now and February, the days on the water are going to be long, 12 or 14 hours. If you're doing 30 knots all the time, you have to have something that's efficient and fast, with a range capable of being out there all day to support the boat.

"You've also got to have a boat big enough to carry all the spares to keep the boat on the water. We can't keep coming back to the dock, so we have to carry sailmakers, hydraulic guys, winch guys, engineers, designers—all these guys and all the spare parts, like boatbuilding parts, sailmaking parts, wing repair parts, rigging, all that stuff. That's what drove us to design a catamaran, the need for something fuel efficient and light, something that would go quicker than what we had and could carry more gear.

"I put a concept together and sat down with Pete Melvin and told him what I wanted. He drew the hulls up and we worked together pretty closely on all the rest of the stuff, like the cabin and what needed to fit in where."

With little time or budget to spare, Salthouse and the team turned to a boat builder that they knew would understand the parameters involved: Salthouse Boat Builders, started by Chris's father, now run by his younger brother Greg. Needless to say, the brothers communicated well during the entire build process, with no family tussles to report, as the 14m chase boat came off the line.

"I knew I had a budget to work to and quite

a tight time frame, so I thought we could trust Greg to deliver it on time, be on budget, and be what I wanted. I ended up working pretty closely with him at the yard and they did a really good job.

"To be honest, it was really nice to have someone that I could really ask 'what do you think?' He was a great sounding board—if he didn't agree with something, he'd tell me. And he knew that if it wasn't right, he'd be in trouble!

"The boat performs even better than we had hoped. It has a top speed of around 58 knots, but I'm sure we could get it over 60 knots if we wanted to. But with all the fuel and things on board, it will do 58 knots, which I can tell you is plenty quick enough. You're going about 100km an hour, and things come at you pretty quickly. The biggest thing is to watch for stuff in the water, but you do get used to it. But most of the day is spent doing 25 to 30 knots and that's where the boat is most efficient."

Powering the new boat are four 300hp Yamaha F300B V6 four-stroke engines. Why four engines? Because that's how many engines it takes to right a capsized AC72—something no one hopes to see but a possibility that everyone must plan for.

"We put four engines on the back of it for a couple of reasons—if we ever have a capsize, two engines would not be enough to right one of these big boats. We thought we needed the extra power. Also, with the wings, if you break something, you can't just turn and go home, because the wing loads everything up. You've got to be able to tow faster than the wind speed home, which we can do now.

"At 30 knots, with all four engines, we use 100 liters of fuel an hour. That's better than the other chase boats that have two engines. Because they're not working as hard—we're cruising along at 3,000 revs—the engines aren't as loaded. The boat holds 1,700 liters of fuel, which means I've got a range of 510 nautical miles at a consistent 30 knots of speed, or 17 hours. That's pretty good."

As Salthouse notes, alongside the spares and equipment also ride all the personnel who need to monitor the AC72 as it tests in the Hauraki Gulf. Finding the balance between comfort and practicality called for more innovations on board the new chaser, so Salthouse returned to that blank sheet of paper.

"We designed and manufactured our own suspension seats for the boat. It used to be that if you were traveling along at 12 knots it was fairly comfortable, but long days at 30 knots mean we're going to get more of a pounding some days than the cat will. So we have suspension seats that work really well. It's a lot more functional than it is comfortable, but the ride of the boat is fantastic. We've been in some really rough stuff and it handles well.

"And we're lighter than the old boats. This boat is five and a half tons, while the Protectors were seven and a half tons. So we can go alongside the 72 without being right next to it—they're pretty fragile boats, so you don't want to risk damaging them. So the 72 can be rolling along at 30 knots and we can be rolling along with it. After a while, the speed starts to feel normal, you have to look at the speeds to realize you're both doing 30 knots."

With the first week of testing with the first of their two AC72s behind them, Emirates Team New Zealand is pleased with where they stand as the lead in to the 34th America's Cup begins.

"We did a good job of estimating what we needed, like realizing we needed weighted trolleys to help lift the wing onto the boat. We've also bought little tugboats from Rayglass with a little engine in the middle that swings around, so you can turn the AC72 in any direction.

"But it's 'so far, so good.' We've lifted the wing in 20 knots, in 25 knots. But it's the day that you're starting to get comfortable with the whole thing that it will bite you. We know a day will come that it will be blowing 30 knots and we'll have to get the wing out—and it will remind us pretty quickly how big it is."

wingsail catamarans on tight courses, proving the best ways to apply the LiveLine technology, how to engage with crowds in person and via online and broadcast technology. Importantly, they re-set everybody's horizons, providing some advance notice of how fast the 34th America's Cup action would unfold, and what it would take to keep up.

The number of ACWS regattas had been much more ambitious at the outset, with talk of eight events per year. Constraints of logistics and finances were a limiting factor, with only a short period of time to make arrangements for sponsorships, which brought that number down quickly. Australian, New Zealand, Asian, or Middle Eastern hosts had been considered as additional stops, and even New York City was weighed as a possibility later in the process, all of which might have been of interest for fans, and good media exposure for the teams and sponsors. Despite their limits, the ACWS had served well as training ground for the new concepts of the 2013 Louis Vuitton Cup and America's Cup.

FIVE ORACLE TEAM USA's AC72s

OTUSA PREPARES FOR THE AC72

OTUSA Racing operated out of a base south of AT&T Park in San Francisco that can be described at best as spartan. Identified as Pier 80 only if you know what you're looking for, for a long time there were few indications at first that this base was occupied by the Defender of the America's Cup—no billboard signage, no flags. Only a healthy array of razor wire gave the uninitiated visitor a clue that something serious was going on behind the gates.

On a foggy Tuesday in February, 2012, OTUSA hosted local media at their base for tours, a press conference, and a ride aboard the historic USS *Potomac*, President Franklin Delano Roosevelt's "floating White House."

Guests were taken first through the lair where the next generation of America's Cup boats was being built. Behind a shed-wide curtain declaring the area "Top Secret" sat the molds in which the Defender's two AC72 catamarans were taking shape, literally before visitors' eyes. Long layers of carbon fiber were being placed into the molds by OTUSA crew members wearing white cotton gloves to avoid contaminating the materials with oils from their skin. The only problem? Cameras were forbidden, though our guide, design team coordinator Ian "Fresh" Burns, was happy to answer nearly any and all questions, along with rig designer Scott Ferguson, structural engineer Kurt Jordan, and design engineer Aaron Perry.

A press conference followed, with OTUSA CEO Russell Coutts, helmsman James Spithill, tactician John Kostecki, and designer Dirk Kramers sharing their views about racing for the historic trophy in San Francisco, the dangers of the AC72, and how quickly the rest of their America's Cup competitors might get up to speed on the nuances of the 2013 Cup venue.

Four-time America's Cup winner Russell Coutts asserted that the new Cup boats and the new venue would showcase all that was right with the America's Cup world.

"I think the Cup here on San Francisco Bay will be just spectacular," Coutts said. "We've seen the AC45, and the AC72 wings will be twice as high as those boats and will go somewhere between two and three times the wind speed."

Coutts didn't miss the chance to lobby the City of San Francisco, reminding them of the impact the America's Cup made on the city and port areas of Fremantle, Auckland, and Valencia—just in case there were still a couple of members of the SF Board of Supervisors who needed any more convincing. "Fremantle was a quiet, sort of rundown fishing port before the America's Cup went there. The same thing happened in Auckland, but on an even bigger scale. I even look back on my past life as an Olympian," says Coutts. Today it's hard to imagine all that Barcelona gained as a legacy of hosting the Olympics, but, said Coutts: "It really transformed the city into one of the most popular destinations in the world. It reconnected the waterfront with the old city. So this is much more than a sailing event.

"Once you picture the spectacular boats, racing in a summer of activity in San Francisco, it's going to be a really cool event."

One of the easiest knocks on the Cup during the press conference was the number of challenging teams—only Sweden's Artemis Racing, Emirates Team New Zealand, and their training partner Italy's Luna Rossa, had paid the entry fee due by June 1, 2012. Aside from having the millions in financing in place for their AC72s, and hence the confidence to put down the $200,000 fee early, these three are among the stronger of the eight challenger entries. The difficult international economic climate certainly loomed over this edition of the Cup—so the question remained: Was quality going to trump quantity?

"The situation in Europe obviously affects things. There are four teams out there building two AC72s, three other syndicates that are going to be two-boat programs," said Coutts. "For the one-boat programs, you don't actually have to announce that you are building a boat until June 1. There is at least one other single-boat [challenger] that will be or might have already started building a boat. So I think we will see other teams before the so-called Big Four teams. But even eight of these AC72s out on San Francisco Bay? I think that will be a pretty cool thing to see." Coutts also threw one very large bone to the home crowd: the image of two defender yachts hosting exhibition-style races against each other simultaneous with the Louis Vuitton Cup, the challenger selection series. With the prospect of a second OTUSA AC72 helmed by British Olympian Ben Ainslie competing head-to-head with the "A" team driven by Spithill, could the undercard outdraw the challenger event? Coutts didn't think so.

"In terms of the four teams that currently have the two-boat programs under way, I think all of them are very competitive," he remarked. "So in a competitive sense, at the end of the day, the America's Cup is going to be about the best challenging team racing the team from the U.S. I think that race will be as competitive as any I've seen in my America's Cup experience. I think the Louis Vuitton Cup, because of the (continued on page 82)
(continued on page 82)

AC72 — Big Data Goes Sailing

One of the keys to going fast is to consistently optimize the boat for a range of conditions during a race. First is to find out what makes the boat go fast, and second is to be able to shift into the right configuration for the current conditions. Especially valuable is understanding the boat well enough to be able to change gears for close-in tactical situations—for example, sailing slightly closer to the wind for short periods, trading a little bit of top speed to gain a better position relative to the opponent, or being able to lay the mark without an extra tack and loss of distance.

Optimizing the boats was once strictly the province of experienced sailors and designers—with keen eyes, a pencil, and notebook—who studied the yacht's sails, angle of heel, rigging, and other elements that drive a boat. Today, the human eye is supplemented with high-tech sensors. After all, the eye alone cannot detect how the wind flows over the inflexible surface of an AC72's wingsail.

Tuning up an America's Cup yacht has not only gone high-tech but has entered the age of big data.

Optimizing an AC72 involved the use of hundreds of sensors mounted throughout the boat. These sensors include load cells in the rigging to measure tension. Diffraction sensors, built into the carbon-fiber structure, using the properties of fiber optics, measured stress as they deformed under load, while others monitored the loads on winches, the positions of wing components, and the pressures in the hydraulic systems. Emirates Team New Zealand designer Nick Holroyd admitted to 50 such sensors in the platform of their first boat alone, and 25 more in the wing. Still other sensors tracked the speed, heading, heel angle, pitch, and acceleration, as well as the helm and the wind conditions, which were all logged electronically dozens of times per second. ORACLE TEAM USA had 300 onboard sensors recording 3,000 variables running ten times per second (an astonishing 30,000 variables per second). Measuring stresses in real time, a network of sensors could also trip warnings and alarms as loads on the boat increased; this allowed the crew to push the boat to the edge when needed.

All this data was collected by computers for detailed analysis and made available at multiple locations. The first was on board the yacht, where the crew could observe the boat's current configuration and then compare the actual performance to the target performance. Being able to quickly and consistently repeat optimal configurations in a variety of situations was a key goal. It's hard to use intuition, the feel developed in traditional boats, aboard a hydrofoiling AC72 powered by a hard wing. Just being able to keep the boat stable required knowing the precise information from second to second.

Asim Khan, performance database programmer and Defender ORACLE TEAM USA's Director of Information Technology, explained the data flow during an interview in the New Zealand *Herald*, saying, "Big data definitely helped us turn our fortunes around because without it [helmsman] Jimmy [Spithill] would have just been going on intuition."

While sailing, the crew could access the information on tablets, wristwatches, or forearm displays, and for skipper Jimmy Spithill, in a pair of heads-up display glasses. During ORACLE TEAM USA's two-boat testing, the sailors toggled between what they were doing and what their opposite number on the other yacht was doing to compare the wing's trim, for example, in real time.

The data was also analyzed aboard chase boats by engineers and technicians who shadowed the yacht. During practice, the data could be shared live via a two-way wireless connection. Real-time info was relayed from the AC72 to the chase boat, which acted as an on-the-water analytical hub. From there, the performance team would test changes and suggest setup modifications for further testing. During an actual race, the connectivity to/from the hub was shut down since the sailors were not allowed to receive outside assistance; but the chase boat's onboard systems collected a stream of information, including weather conditions (wind, apparent wind, tidal predictions), platform, wing and appendage strain, boat settings, and relative speed. Some components of the AC72 could even be adjusted remotely from the chase boat, though not during actual races.

The team sourced rugged tablet devices that were up to the harsh environment on board, including the jarring vibration and instability of the AC72 platform, meeting essential high-speed wi-fi connectivity/refresh requirements, and the marine elements that go with sailing yachts, like moisture, salt water, and variable light conditions.

The tablets were removable to be repositioned when updated for the day's expected conditions or, while training before the Match, to reflect the intended test regimen to be conducted on a given day. On race days, tablets, being portable, would permit last-minute loading of customizable data sets, so they were preferable to a fixed device embedded in the wing whose data set might be hours older.

Gilberto Nobili was a dual-tasking member of both the sailing crew (being a grinder on the racing crew) and also liaison and software developer/co-ordinator on the performance team to integrate the technology systems on board the race yachts.

ORACLE TEAM USA used an Oracle Exadata Database Machine combined with a Ruckus Wireless multidirectional wi-fi system on board the AC72s as well as the chase boat hubs that interacted with the onshore "design center."

Ashore, the crew and coaches could pull together metrics to study crew work and maneuvers, and compare the performance of one combination of techniques and technical setup to another.

The design team looked for broad patterns that would improve performance, and to identify which inputs and settings were most important in improving top speed. A simple form of these calculations was a regression analysis to identify the most important variable to control. More sophisticated tools included techniques like neural networks, capable of taking a large number of variables and discerning the relationships between them as they changed.

The collected data could be used as a guide to future designs, letting the engineers know whether structures were seeing the loads expected and responding as predicted, and building a finer picture of what the loads would be under new design concepts. With only two boats allowed per team, and limited time to build the second before the first was really very far along, the influence of the collected data was limited from boat to boat on the major hull and cross structure elements, but studying the actual loads and stresses helped confirm that design intent was being achieved.

The data acquired could also be used to shed light on extreme incidents. ORACLE TEAM USA relied on their data acquisition program in analyzing the capsize of their first boat, though for competitive reasons the team was tight-lipped on exactly what they did wrong, or how they responded. Likewise, the data from the Artemis Racing accident may have been instructive, though the team has declined to provide specifics about what factors might have contributed to the capsize and how they were able to investigate the incident.

ORACLE TEAM USA's crew train aboard their second AC72 in May, 2013. OTUSA's AC72s each sported a pod that may have served three purposes: it extended the wingsail to restrict airflow beneath the wing; to produce additional lift when sailing upwind; and to enclose structural members to reduce aerodynamic drag. (© 2013 ACEA/Photo: Gilles Martin-Raget)

From any metric one might choose to measure, the 34th America's Cup was easily the most technologically advanced regatta in history.

The degree of technical innovation, permeating nearly every aspect of the 2013 event, is barely approached by most other sports. The America's Cup continues to be a contest of technology, producing the fastest sailing in ways that the original winners never could have imagined, but still might have appreciated.

quality of the teams, will be as competitive as the previous Louis Vuitton Cups. So yes, frankly, it would be nice to have more teams, but if we don't, this will still be a spectacular event.

"But there is a tentative schedule laid out, in the program of racing, where we'll be racing our two boats at the same time as the Louis Vuitton Cup. We're scheduled to race first on most of those days, and then the Challengers will race."

How would Ainslie fit into the OTUSA picture? Coutts hinted that the line-up was pretty much set.

"We have a pretty good idea of who our sailing team will be now, and we're gearing everything toward supporting that. But in my experience, you really need to have that competitive series leading up to the America's Cup series of matches. Because if you don't, imagine going out and racing the best Challenger cold. So one of our challenges is to develop an internal race program that prepares our team even better. It's a tough thing to do, but we have the capability to do that."

Helmsman James Spithill knew what lay ahead, having won back the

America's Cup for the United States two years prior in Valencia, Spain. Spithill was happy to turn the clock forward to 2012 and look at an America's Cup happening 2013, and stare the challenges of the somewhat daunting AC72 square in the eye. "We're very, very close to the launch of our new boat, which will be in July," said Spithill. "So for the sailing team, it's great to be back out on the water, back out on that racetrack, getting used to what it will be like in a very short amount of time."

Spithill looked forward to the launch of the AC72, knowing that the designers had taken into consideration much of what the sailing team had learned from the AC45.

"The sailing team is the end user, the customer. So we've had to have a big influence in the boat. It's exciting for the sailing team as well as the design team, because it's a blank sheet of paper. With the old class, we went through a few iterations, but we knew what it would be like. But now, we've got a few challenges—we've got two hulls, a trampoline, trying to figure out the deck layout. How we're going to get through these maneuvers and doing all this in a very short race is going to be very challenging. It's something that goes on on a daily basis, with the design team and the build team."

There had been a great deal of conversation regarding safety with the gargantuan AC72. Russell Coutts wanted a racing series that compared to NASCAR, but even a race car driver knows what happens when something goes wrong at high speed. So does Spithill.

"On the sailing side, there is a great deal more risk now. People are excited when they see Russell go through the wing, but at the end of the day, if there's more risk, it's more challenging for the athletes. In a race car,

Recruiting Talent to the AC

(These interviews—on pages 85 and 91—conducted just after the summer Olympics in 2012, provide insights into the life of professional sailors.)

When you ask America's Cup sailors Ben Ainslie and Nathan Outteridge to sum up their feelings following gold medal performances at the London Olympics, you get one simple answer: "Tired."

Neither has had the chance to take a breath and process their Olympic experiences. Ainslie was sailing his Finn *Rita* along the Thames in London just last Thursday before boarding a flight to San Francisco. Outteridge's route took him even farther afield, with one night at home in Sydney to re-pack before the long flight to California. Both sailors took time at the start of the America's Cup World Series San Francisco to reflect briefly on their recent Olympic efforts and to look toward their America's Cup futures.

the harder you push, the faster you go. In the past, with the old boats, there wasn't a real risk; maybe you would bump the boats together or tear a sail. But now, on the AC72, there are some serious consequences. But if you push, you're rewarded for it. And I think, for the Everest of sailing, the America's Cup, it needs to be like that. It's not for the average person. This is right on the edge, and the team that pushes the hardest will be rewarded. And that's exactly the way it should be."

Structures designer Dirk Kramers, who has seen more than his share of change in the America's Cup, felt that the exotic boats that would contest the 2013 Cup gave the venerable event a "much-needed, um, aft lift vector."

"What's happening now with the Cup is the biggest kick in the a— that the Cup has seen in years," said Kramers. "And you're going to see it, front and center, right here on the Bay. That's going to be fantastic."

Kramers also acknowledged the work the design team was doing with the sailing team, to make sure that the final product, the AC72 that would race for the 34th America's Cup, was optimized for the sailors' needs.

"We're trying to figure out how to make deck layouts work, how to power these boats. These boats will be very demanding on the crews, so we'll have to develop systems to help these guys sail the boats."

As for Kostecki, the kid who grew up on San Francisco Bay earning championships that started with a Sunfish title in 1982, a certain amount of local knowledge goes a long way. Or at least until everyone else gets here.

"The strong sea breeze during the summertime is pretty spectacular, with tricky currents," said Kostecki. "San Francisco is a natural amphitheatre, so it will be awesome for what we're doing with the America's Cup. It's a difficult place to race sailboats, but, when you get it right, it's quite rewarding.

"Being a local, I'd like to think that we have an advantage, but I know we'll see the other teams arrive here this summer, sailing the AC45s out on the same racecourse, and they'll all get used to these conditions. It is tricky and it does take a little bit more time than a normal racetrack, but they'll figure it out."

OTUSA'S AC72 CAPSIZE

The AC72 yachts had barely started sailing when an accident put the spotlight on the risks of the new high-technology development class.

After Team New Zealand launched their first AC72 in July 2012, OR-ACLE TEAM USA followed with their first boat on the water in late August. By mid-October 2012, Luna Rossa was preparing to launch their own boat in Auckland, and Artemis Racing's AC72 was being assembled in San Francisco and was nearly ready to sail. All the teams were up against a limit that permitted a total of 30 sailing days each until the end of January 2013. That restriction on AC72 sailing was intended to help control costs and level the playing field, but in a brand-new yacht class, both designers and sailors had an enormous amount to learn and not much time to learn it.

An agreement among the teams had already pushed the launching dates back by six months. The window of time for figuring out how to sail these boats, and to sail them fast, was becoming compressed, and for OTUSA, that time frame was about to be cut even shorter.

Recovering from breaking a daggerboard on the first day of sailing in August, ORACLE TEAM USA adapted a temporary replacement board from their 2010 trimaran and by mid-September the yacht, 17, was back on San Francisco Bay testing again. On October 1, Day 4 of sailing, they started getting the boat flying, up on her foils at times.

On October 16, 2012, OTUSA was out training on 17 in a building breeze, with winds reported in the mid-20-knot range with gusts into the 30s, and a strong ebb tide. Completing a fast upwind sprint, the crew put the helm down and started to bear away for the downwind work. Bearing away in high wind is one of the more precarious maneuvers in a multihull, changing the balance of forces on the boat. As OTUSA changed course, they were caught by more wind than expected, in steeper seas than they

Ben Ainslie, BAR (Ben Ainslie Racing)

(This interview from August, 2012.)

Ainslie carried the psychological weight of an entire country, serving as a sailing poster boy for the London Olympics, with actually winning a gold medal in the Finn class being something approaching a national expectation. But last January [2012], he had already revealed the direction for his post-Olympic future, announcing a partnership with ORACLE TEAM USA that has him forming his own America's Cup World Series team, J.P. Morgan/ Ben Ainslie Racing, for the AC45 regattas and serving as the other half of the Defender trials against OTUSA stalwart Jimmy Spithill.

Ainslie had a rather full plate from January until the July 29 beginning of the Finn portion of the Olympic regatta. Delegation was the order of the day.

"I had to just compartmentalize the whole thing, really, and just put the America's Cup stuff to one side so I could focus on the Olympics and the job I needed to do," Ainslie explained. "Thankfully, I've got a great team around me, so they got on with the job of preparing the boat and the sponsors. I was able to just focus on the Games—and thankfully, I got that job done—but I tried to keep an eye on things, on the general direction of the Cup team, and have input on that. And now it's completely about 'turn and focus on the America's Cup,' which is really exciting, for the next twelve months.

"But it's been crazy. It would have been nice to go away for a couple of weeks and just have some rest and take it all in, but it's been *(continues)*

a complete rush. I'm pretty tired, but at the same time it's quite a buzz to be here and sailing in these boats, so I am pretty excited about being here."

Ainslie's comments regarding the move away from monohulls two years ago—and the demise of the British Team Origin—were rather critical—words he remembers somewhat ruefully.

"I suppose I was a bit of a traditionalist. I preferred the monohulls; that's what a lot of us had been developing our skills in. But then I watched the AC45 racing on TV and was impressed by the program, the boats, and the competition, and I wanted to be a part of it. So that's how I got involved with Russell and ORACLE TEAM USA, and started my own team."

Once the America's Cup gets under way next summer [2013] in San Francisco, the Challengers will compete in the Louis Vuitton Cup for the right to take on ORACLE TEAM USA representing Golden Gate Yacht Club in the America's Cup Match. But OTUSA won't be just waiting quietly in the wings. Ainslie and Spithill will be out on the bay sharing courses with the challenger selection series, racing their two AC72s in a Defender trial—of sorts.

"It's not really about Jimmy or [me], it's about the team and getting the team in the best place to defend," says Ainslie, with praise for the job Spithill has been doing. "It's not about me trying to take his role, it's about me trying to support him and the whole team."

had yet experienced, and, worse yet, they were caught a bit slow in the turn with the 131-foot-tall wingsail up there like a barn door. Bearing away puts a lot of downforce on the forward sections of the hulls, and eventually, even on a yacht as big as an AC72, the bows were forced under. Unable to readily de-power by easing the hard wing, the boat pitchpoled, essentially tripping over her bows and suddenly capsizing forward.

Floating at first on her mast and the bows of both hulls, *17* was eventually turned on her side, mast still in the water. The crew members were accounted for and recovered with no major injuries, but the main spar of the wing eventually snapped, breaking the wing in two. The "platform" of the hulls and crossbeams was damaged; the development schedule was in shambles; and the entire team appeared a bit stunned after seeing their new boat quickly reduced to wreckage despite their best efforts to save her.

Safety issues with the America's Cup 72-foot-long catamarans had been a topic when the new design was first unveiled. In concept the boats were exciting, but match racing them around an inshore course was uncharted territory. Capsizing an AC72 yacht to informed observers wasn't an "if" but a "when"—and "when" had arrived in San Francisco Bay for OTUSA after only their eighth day of sailing, soon enough to leave some people wondering about the feasibility of racing these extreme boats. Not to mention the wisdom of doing so.

Watching the incident unfold was Dirk Kramers, engineering director of ORACLE TEAM USA, who with his design and building teams had spent the better part of the last two years creating *17*. As one of the multihull experts behind the only two catamarans to previously race in America's Cup matches, the 60-foot *Stars & Stripes* wingsail cat in 1988, and the soft sail 115-foot *Alinghi 5* in 2010, plus the monohull-based campaigns of Alinghi and Young America, Kramers was one of the most experienced active players in the event.

When first interviewed on the topic, before the capsize took place, Kramers believed that many of the safety systems as initially designed into the 17 program were fairly straightforward: personal safety equipment, rescue personnel, chase boats, righting lines—but it wasn't expected that all those safety systems would see much active practice.

"There are a lot of different safety aspects, most of which are common sense, like wearing life preservers and helmets," Kramers said, touring the team's Pier 80 base earlier that month. "It's also important to always have a knife on you in case you get stuck or caught somewhere, like a diver you can cut yourself free."

"The boat is set up with righting lines, in case we have to right the boat. We also have buddy-breather cartridges, so if you have to dive, you can go under longer. But it's also an organizational issue; we have three to four boats out there supporting us, and there's a whole set of response maneuvers that we've practiced to make sure that we do the right thing at the right time. For example, if someone falls off and gets hurt, that's the first priority. The next priority is getting the boat head-to-wind. So there's a whole series of events that have different response maneuvers."

The design of OTUSA's first boat included a large pod under the hard wing, covering some of the structure and acting as something of a wing extension to provide more power closer to the waterline. Possibly the pod was an advantage for speed, but not for rescues. "One of the aspects that's difficult about this kind of boat is that once it's capsized, you can't really climb up or climb down," said Kramers. "So you're sort of stuck. With the AC45, you can climb up and down, but this boat has the big pod in the middle. And you can imagine falling off, if the boat is at 90 degrees. If you fall down into something hard, that's not going to be good. We've had a lot of guys falling off the AC45s, but we've been lucky that no one has hit something hard yet—like what happened to Russell [Coutts, thrown through the wingsail in an AC45 capsize], it was inches away from it being a big problem. And it's happened to other guys. That is the biggest thing, making sure the guys have something to hang onto.

"When we sailed the big boat event [in the 2010 America's Cup], there was a lot of talk about whether you were better to jump or to hang on. But you're hanging 90 feet in the air—that's a long way to fall. At that point it was better to hang on and dangle, and wait for someone to come get you, rather than trying to save yourself.

"During that campaign, [Alinghi] capsized one of the 60-footers and it was a real eye opener," said Kramers, referring to the Swiss team's practice on an ORMA (Ocean Racing Multihull Association) trimaran. "Some guys got caught underneath the boat, which really brought to light that you need a knife. But this boat [the AC72] floats fairly high because of the pod if it's upside down, so hopefully that won't be as big of a problem. But in the trimaran it was an issue. Some of the guys were holding the net up so the guys underneath could breathe."

Once a 72-foot catamaran is capsized, turning it back upright is not a simple proposition either. Righting lines are run to both sides of the OTUSA AC72, since after the boat has gone over, there's no guarantee that anyone would be able to rig the lines in a timely fashion.

"The biggest thing is keeping the boat head-to-wind so you don't start going dead downwind, and do it fairly quickly," Kramers said. "The problem Team New Zealand had in Newport [when they capsized their AC45] was the wing extension filled up with water and they couldn't get the boat up quickly. But the French team was able to right themselves, since they were quick enough. So you have to be quick and you have to plan exactly what you're doing.

"There are righting lines led to both sides, so even if the boat is on its side with no one up high, you can get to the righting line. But the righting process is not something we're going to practice!"

The obvious new features on the AC72s are the foils, which can lift the entire yacht off the water when sailing. The foils were intended to make the boat faster around the racecourse, but the safety question is whether the foils make the boat more or less stable. The answer appears to be "It depends."

"The foils actually help you," said Kramers during the early days of the team's AC72 testing. "Our hull is quite small, much smaller than Team New Zealand's, so we are reliant on the foils to keep it from pitchpoling in a bearaway. But on the other hand, when you're flying, if you have a mishap with the foils, it can bring you to a stop very quickly and you can pitchpole that way, if you make a wrong maneuver with the foils. It will be interesting to see how much we'll actually be foiling. There's no guarantee that once you're up on foils, you're faster."

Once a boat has gone over, the teams know they must be prepared with rescue equipment and personnel. And during testing, safety is the team's responsibility, not that of the official America's Cup organizations. America's Cup Regatta Management (ACRM) will take care of all rescue requirements during the regattas, but Regatta director Iain Murray noted that when the teams are testing, they are on their own.

"We're not involved in setting the procedures within the teams," said Murray in early October 2012, before the capsize. "They'll have their own safety drills and procedures within their support staff, safety manuals with the crews, how they'll deal with capsizes, righting moment, possible injuries, all of that.

"We bring all that to the table when they come to the racecourse. We have all our plans in place now, including safety paramedics in wetsuits in jet boats with stretchers in case there is an accident. That will obviously get bigger with the bigger boat next year, with more craft and more people because the incidents could be bigger and the danger is probably more.

"So we'll take care of them during regattas and official practices, but when they're trialing, they have to make their own arrangements. We're happy to help and work with them and we do, as the teams are adopting a lot of the same principles in how we go about things, so it's consistent all the time."

America's Cup Regatta Management put together an AC72 crisis-preparedness manual, detailing the types of responses for anticipated scenarios. The manual's creation was overseen by a security company made up of personnel well schooled in dealing with critical situations.

"We have a plan that's about a hundred pages that covers the event," said Murray. "We have a security company made up of former military people that manages all of it. It's a very thorough document and it combines the police, the fire department, homeland security, and Coast Guard. It's been a work in progress for the past six months so that everyone is brought into the same safety policy."

Preparation can anticipate only so much, though. OTUSA's Dirk Kramers thought he had seen it all in his five America's Cup campaigns, but that was before the drama that played out in San Francisco Bay as he watched the team's first AC72 catamaran capsize in big wind and drift out to sea, breaking into pieces along the way.

Many who watched the incident play out, aired live on local television news and streamed across the Internet, questioned ORACLE TEAM USA's decision to take the new AC72 out in difficult conditions on only its eighth day of testing. Hindsight is always 20/20, especially when wind gusts of 25 to 30 knots or higher and an ebb tide kicking up seas of more than seven feet are involved.

"What made life a lot worse for us is that we capsized in the second biggest tide of the year and we got swept out," Kramers said. "At first, when we capsized, we looked around and thought, 'Okay, we'll wash up on Alcatraz.' The next thing, you look up and realize you're going the other way. Within an hour, we were outside the Gate. The wave action outside the Gate is what did in the wing."

17 ended up in an area known as the "Potato Patch"—a shoal on Four Fathom Bank outside the Golden Gate. The Patch made short work of the cat's giant hard wing and sent the team on a scavenger hunt trying to bring home as many pieces as possible. Just where some of those pieces ended up will undoubtedly become local legend.

"The next day, we went out to try and retrieve all the little bits and pieces that were still floating around out there, just to clean up after ourselves the best we could," Kramers said. "Someone picked up a three-foot section on a beach somewhere, but they were associated with Artemis, so now it's in the Artemis compound—we didn't get that one back!"

Despite the extent of damage, the Defender couldn't just write off the loss of the first boat.

Being the representative of the America's Cup Defender, ORACLE TEAM USA wouldn't participate in the Louis Vuitton Cup regatta, which tests the mettle of the challenger candidates and selects the best of them to become OTUSA's opponent in the America's Cup match.

OTUSA's plans for 2013 relied on having both of their boats sailing against each other for testing, training, and in-house racing in order to be ready to defend the trophy.

Kramers and his team had to salvage, re-engineer, and rebuild the injured 17 while at the same time completing the build process on the team's second boat.

Lessons Learned from the OTUSA Capsize

Until it happened, no one knew exactly how a rescue operation of this magnitude would unfold—after all, no sane person would capsize a brand-new 72-foot catamaran just to test righting procedures. But once the crew was safe, the team now had facts where they previously had only theory. "We obviously learned a lot about what to do and what not to do with this little exercise—and these are things we will share with the other teams, because it's a question of safety," Kramers said after the incident.

"First and foremost, you have to take care of the people. Second is how to deal with the righting, and making sure you have actions and methods to deal with every version of the capsize—you can capsize and lose your wing right away and that's a whole different recovery situation than capsizing with the wing staying intact. And there's a different scenario, with both bows in, which is the way we ended up, or just on your side. So you need to develop recovery schemes for each of these scenarios. In the aftermath of this incident, we're working on those and we'll be sharing our recommendations and lessons with the other teams."

When OTUSA pitchpoled their first AC72, Emirates Team New Zealand had already been trialing their new AC72 in the Hauraki Gulf, near Auckland, New Zealand, and accumulating more days on the water with an AC72 than any other team to date.

Kevin Shoebridge, chief operating officer of ETNZ, said his team tried to learn from the Defender's experience, too, closely watching the video of the OTUSA capsize.

"Once there's water in the wing, the chances of righting the boat are limited," said Shoebridge. "We are looking at ways of preventing that. Keep the boat floating and the wing from sinking and there's a good chance of righting it."

"We have concentrated on the people . . . knowing what to expect and how to deal with any given situation. Each crew member has a breathing apparatus strapped to their back. If they are ever caught, tangled, or trapped under the trampoline, they have quite a few minutes of air, and they each have a knife strapped on their shoulder to cut their way out." ETNZ began training in a deep dive pool, including using the reserve air, to help sailors and rescue crews prepare. *(continued on page 92)*

Nathan Outteridge, Team Korea

Australia's Nathan Outteridge was putting all his focus into his 49er Olympic campaign in the years leading up to the 2012 Games. He saw heartbreak four years earlier after losing a gold medal within sight of the finish line, and he wasn't about to let that happen again. He was all-in with his Olympic preparations when a bit of a wrench was thrown into the works in February 2012. Team Korea had just lost skipper and former 49er sailor Chris Draper and was searching for a replacement.

"I got a phone call from the team at the start of the year," remembers Outteridge. "They said that Chris had left and they were looking for someone to drive the boat for the season. I had big commitments with the Olympics and the 49er was the priority, so they asked if I could fit it in. They gave me the dates for the Europe races and Newport, and it worked out perfectly. I went from Naples to two 49er events in Europe, then straight to Venice, off to Weymouth for the Olympic test event, then to Newport. So I was going between the two. It was a bit tiring and time consuming, but I was confident it wasn't going to affect the Olympics in any way.

"But I told the team that as soon as I left the AC45 event, I would shift. The 49er was my job—the team kept ticking over and I was being informed on what was happening, but the focus shifted to the next class. I left Newport and went home to Australia for a few days—I hadn't had a break since March. I needed some time to relax and not live out of a suitcase. But then it was on to Weymouth, some training, then the Opening Ceremonies, so we could get involved in the Olympic atmosphere. Then the regatta."

Outteridge and crew Iain Jensen blew the competition away in Weymouth, winning five races and securing the gold medal before the medal race even began. For Outteridge, it was the culmination of four years of effort toward a concentrated goal—but a win that gave little time to celebrate his victory.

"We were the most prepared team and we just went out and did our job. By the time the medal race came along, we had enough of a point lead that it didn't matter. It was a really nice week for us. I went to the Closing Ceremonies, then hopped on a plane home to Sydney and had one night at home. I dropped off my Olympic kit, picked up my Team Korea kit, got on a plane and came straight here last Thursday, and was on the water within an hour. I'm still jet-lagged and recovering from the gold medal party! I do have to say I'm looking forward to a break at home after this.

"It is hard mentally to have been preparing for one event for four years and then go straight to the next job. You miss being able to thank all your family and friends, everyone who supported you. Luckily [on the 49er], I sail on a two-person crew, so Iain is taking care of all that—I'm sure he'll have plenty on my behalf!" (continues)

Outteridge considers it a plus that he's been able to race so many different kind of boats and gain knowledge from many different sailing arenas while avoiding the dreaded sailing burnout.

"For the past four or five years, I've been sailing multiple kinds of boats—if I was just fully focused totally on the 49er, it could have gotten a little bit tough, like a full-time job. It's nice to have a break, do some other sailing, where you're learning—and whatever you learn, you can bring back to the 49er. I was going back and forth between the 49er and the AC45 and taking what I learned with each boat to the other program, which complemented each other very nicely. And now that there's not much to do on the 49er, I'm focused on this now—it's nice to really have some time to spend in the 45."

This iteration of Team Korea first hit the water at the America's Cup World Series event in Naples, giving the team a limited amount of preparation to get to know each other and streamline boat maneuvers. The team has gotten off to a slow start, but looks forward to starting anew—with next year's [2013] America's Cup in their sights. Much of the reason Outteridge made such an extreme effort to get to San Francisco was to make sure that the seat in the back of the team's AC72 remained his.

"I had five days' training before the regatta in Naples—and most of it was really light, under 10 knots of breeze. So it was great, but it wasn't like the speeds I was expecting from the boat. Since arriving here and sailing in some proper wind, I can see that they're impressive boats, and very powerful.

"The plan is for me to stay on through the America's Cup—that's why I'm here! I could have easily told the guys that I needed this event off and they could have found someone else to drive the boat and I could have missed my chance for the next year. So I'm looking forward to experiencing everything over the next year!"

"We are also instituting a buddy system so that in event of a capsize if you're okay—find your buddy and check that he's okay. And every sailing day, two paramedics are on the main chase boat. They are trained divers and are ready to go into the water and get to the platform as a first response.

"We have developed a comprehensive management plan that is run from Chase 1," Shoebridge said, referring to their custom-built 1200hp support boat. "That's where decisions will be made about the rescue and recovery operation."

Rod Davis, ETNZ afterguard coach, in blogging about the OTUSA capsize, noted that every second counts when trying to minimize damage to the boat.

"Once the people are under control, the focus changes to the boat," wrote Davis. "Oracle's wing survived the initial impact, but the boat was sitting nose down, making it hard to right. Somehow they got the boat on its side and attempted to right it. We think there is a window of about ten minutes after a capsize when there's a good chance to right the boat. After that, the chance of righting falls dramatically."

Kramers agreed, but he also saw firsthand that nothing is as simple as it sounds. "Righting it immediately is one thing, but you have to be very careful when you right it to make sure there are no people on the boat that could be in danger. You have to be quite well orchestrated when you right the boat, so you don't get into even more trouble. For example, you could right the boat and all of a sudden the boat takes off on its own and capsizes again. We've seen that quite a bit on little boats.

"There are lots of little things we learned, like if you don't wear gloves it's very difficult to climb down the netting. But then again, it seems the safest part was being inside the cockpits—the guys that were inside the cockpits said they felt quite safe and in control, while the guys who were on the nets ended up having the biggest troubles."

There were plenty of opinions among America's Cup watchers regarding the exact cause of the big multihull's pitchpole—did the foils add to the cat's instability? Nick Holroyd, technical director for Emirates Team New Zealand, interviewed at *Sailing World*, highlighted the interaction between hull volume and foil lift during a bearaway, lending some credence to a point of view in some quarters that the hulls of OTUSA's first boat might have been too narrow upfront.

OTUSA as a team was keener than anyone to make sure the right knowledge was gained from the incident. There was a vast data stream generated by the AC72 for the team to crunch in their analysis, thousands of points per second examining velocities, sailing conditions, control inputs, and loads and stresses via dozens of onboard sensors in the moments before, during, and after capsizing.

"Obviously, we learned a lot about pitchpoling," Kramers said. "We have a lot of good data, so we're studying that, but there are a lot of the aspects of pitchpoling—the foil behavior, the boat behavior, the dynamic pressures, the hydrostatic loads and so on. The hull volume is just one aspect of that. I wouldn't say it was the dominant one, but it's just one more aspect. You need to choose how much you need and want, and that's driven by the conditions you intend to sail in as much as anything."

Critics at the time were quick to latch onto the foiling aspects of the large multihulls, though the answer may just be that with enough wind any multihull is at risk in certain maneuvers. Catamaran sailors know that bearaways in strong winds are a prime vulnerability even for much smaller and more conventional beach cats.

"A bearaway is often the scariest maneuver you can do," Kramers said. "It's getting into the 'death zone,' as some people call it. But we were pretty much through that 'death zone' before we started to go over and you get this acceleration phase. The level of control you have or do not have with the foils is a contributor to that. So you cannot really bear away in really high winds without foils, or it's much more difficult without foils. But on the other hand, you really need to maintain a certain amount of control over your flying when you do fly. It's a tightrope."

For OTUSA's part, analysis of what happened was only the start of the process. After drawing as many lessons as possible from the eight days they spent with boat number one (less than one third of the 30 days they had expected to have before the end of the first restricted period on January 31, 2013), the design team then had to decide on changes and plow that new understanding back into boat number two while there was still time to reap benefits. The aftermath of the capsize put the ORACLE TEAM USA boatbuilding and shore teams on double duty, repairing the hulls of *17* and building a new wing while construction on the team's second AC72 continued with minimal interruption.

"Boat number two was well on its way, so only a small amount of the early days we got with this boat had a significant impact on what we did with boat number two," said Kramers. "It's mostly a question of getting the wing ready to put into it, as obviously the biggest damage was to the wing, which was in lots and lots of pieces. The hull mostly got damaged on the tow-in, with loose bits of wing banging into it, so there are a bunch of dents and bumps to fix up.

"Then we'll take the opportunity to make a few changes we wanted to make anyway. We'll take on as many modifications as we can afford to do until the wing is ready, such as changes to the platform layout. Then we'll be ready to start sailing again, hopefully by the end of January or the beginning of February."

With the benefit of experience, the design team also made a few tweaks to the safety systems on the AC72, the obvious goal to make sure what went wrong in October didn't go wrong again.

"One thing that became more difficult than we thought it would be was keeping the boat head to wind," Kramers said. "It was really difficult to attach lines to the boat and effectively maneuver the boat relative to the wind. We were never able to get lines to the top of the wing, which I think would have been helpful to maneuver the boat in the right direction."

The team adapted some features and techniques to get lines and flotation to the top of the wing as quickly and easily as possible after a capsize.

Kramers was pretty matter-of-fact about how the experience stretched the team's resources and personnel, as ORACLE TEAM USA scrambled to get both boats ready for action in early 2013.

"The second boat is continuing on as planned; this is just an additional build job that appeared on the floor here," he said.

The start of Louis Vuitton Cup racing in July 2013 was less than nine months off, and the second-generation boats weren't due to begin launching until February 2013 at the earliest.

As ORACLE TEAM USA recovered from the capsize and near loss of their boat, all the teams and the America's Cup organization tried to learn from the incident. By all measures, it appeared that the risks of sailing these very new, very fast multihulls were being seriously and thoroughly addressed. In noting that the boat had been damaged but the crew was safe, though, it was easy for outside observers to take away the wrong lessons from the OTUSA capsize. Across all the organizations, some very smart and experienced people had put preparations in place, and were now elevating those efforts based on experience. Yet tragedy, and a great deal of turmoil, still lay ahead.

SIX Artemis Capsize and the Loss of Andrew Simpson

rtemis Racing's first-generation AC72, *Artemis Red*, was alone among the seven AC72 yachts to be built as a non-foiling yacht. The team had considered the possibility of foiling, but chose to press ahead without that capability.

Artemis's preference for a non-foiling design was apparently based on the designers' assessment of the balance between upwind and downwind sailing. Foiling was clearly fast, much faster, when sailing off the wind if the boat could be controlled. Upwind, sailing the slightly lower angles that would get the boat out of the water on foils just didn't make the boat move to windward more efficiently than sailing it conventionally and pointing higher. A non-foiling boat could also carry a much smaller daggerboard, resisting only leeway, not having to lift the boat, and therefore would generate much less underwater drag. Most boats are faster downwind than upwind, and on a windward-leeward racecourse, that means yachts spend much more time on the upwind legs, and as a consequence it's more important to be faster than an opponent on upwind legs than the reverse. If that was conventional thinking, it was a principle that had been proven correct time and again in yacht racing, and particularly in the America's Cup

Artemis Red was the last of the first-generation AC72 boats to hit the water. She arrived in San Francisco in August 2012, her platform already assembled in Valencia, Spain, and shipped on the deck of a freighter to the venue. On October 19, the morning of the boat's planned naming ceremony, just before sailing for the first time, her platform was damaged during a towing test on the bay. Artemis did not publicly reveal details of what had gone wrong, but it took another 26 days to examine the boat and make repairs before she was launched. The big red boat finally sailed under her own power for the first time on November 14.

Artemis had worked out an agreement to train alongside ORACLE

TEAM USA, both of them planning to have their first-generation boats worked up during the first AC72 sailing period. ETNZ and Luna Rossa had adopted a similar plan to sail together in Auckland. While there were limits on what sort of data could be exchanged between the teams without running afoul of the Protocol rules that limited acquiring a second boat or obtaining a surrogate boat, in a class of yachts with zero history there was a lot to learn just by sailing in the company of another.

Through the end of the first AC72 sailing period, Artemis clocked seventeen sailing days, gaining experience with the big boat, but alone in San Francisco Bay while OTUSA worked double-time to get their old boat repaired post-capsize and their new boat built. Artemis boat two was under construction, too, with a 2013 arrival date. The late launch of all the AC72s, especially compared to the original schedule, limited the ability of all the teams to apply lessons from the first boats in time to have a major influence on the designs of their second AC72s. The second-generation AC72s were permitted to launch beginning February 1, 2013. Only ETNZ would come close to that date. OTUSA would relaunch their first boat on February 5, but not unveil their second boat until April 24th.

But when her competitors began foiling to one degree or another, questions were raised about Artemis Racing's direction with a non-foiling cat.

Development of an America's Cup boat is about balancing an equation. On one side, the more time designers and engineers have to work on the boat, the greater the performance potential of the boat. On the other side of the equation, the more time the sailors have to sail, test, and tune a boat, the greater a percentage of the yacht's potential can be achieved. Launch a slow boat early and the sailors can have it highly optimized, but it maybe not be fast enough in the long run to win. Launch a fast design too late, and it may never come close to achieving its full capabilities to achieve victory in time. (In 2003, the One World Challenge launched their boat ahead of other teams at the expense of a longer design gestation. The strategy paid off in the beginning, as One World's sailors had the benefit of accruing more hours of training on their boat; as a result, they dominated the early stages of the challenger selection series, winning 13 of 16 races. However, the other teams eventually caught up and passed One World as the other sailors began to take advantage of the full potential of their boats.)

By February 2013 Artemis had clocked 23 sailing days. They were into the second AC sailing period, each boat being permitted 45 days of sailing. On February 13, ORACLE TEAM USA's boat one, a foiler, and Artemis Racing's red boat, a non-foiler, sailed together for the first time. It didn't take 30,000 data points per second and 300GB of data to provide the verdict. The foiling boat was leagues ahead of the non-foiler in speed. Reports suggested that OTUSA was faster than Artemis off the wind, as expected, and was also faster than Artemis going to weather. OTUSA's large foils for hydro-foiling did not seem to be a disadvantage going up-wind, as Artemis had suspected. A non-foiler wasn't going to be competitive. Artemis pulled their red boat from the water and embraced the wisdom of foiling.

Artemis soon had a pair of foils attached to an AC45 cat and had her sailors begin learning how to hydrofoil a multihull. The red boat received a number of upgrades, foils not among them, but boat number two, still in construction, took a new direction. She would become a foiling cat. Adapting to a foiling design would push her launch date back further still, but without the change there was little chance to be competitive.

Artemis Racing number one (the red boat) came back out on March 22, still not a foiler, but sailing continued so that tactics, tuning, boat handling, and crew work all could be worked up. They tested soft sail shapes, hard wing trim, and on and on as they tried to climb a learning curve all described as nearly vertical. Artemis Racing boat two would miss the second AC72 period completely, and none of the teams would approach their maximum 45 days with even one of the two boats permitted, but sailing days starting May 1 were not capped by any restrictions. Admittedly, there were only 66 days in May, June, and early July before the Louis Vuitton Cup Race began, so the opportunities were getting very limited, but the restrictions were no longer artificial.

Artemis planned to launch boat two in May. OTUSA had just launched their second boat. ETNZ and Luna Rossa had several weeks of downtime shipping their boats from New Zealand to San Francisco, and were both in the process of setting up and getting out on the water. San Francisco Bay was about to become a hotbed of sailing activity as the few remaining weeks of preparation before the start of the LVC ticked down.

On May 9, Artemis Racing was sailing in moderate to strong breezes. Winds were in the low to mid 20s, with gusts sometimes into the 30s. Nathan Outteridge was at the helm, soaking up all he could from multihull veteran Loïck Peyron.

Word soon snapped across the VHF radios that Artemis had capsized. Worse, images and reports from the scene revealed a broken boat, the port hull snapped into two pieces near the stern, the wingmast broken and limp in the water. Support boats rushed to the scene, pulling people from the water. Not just Artemis support boats, but from all the America's Cup teams. The question of any concerned observer in a yachting accident is always whether everyone was safe. And the "yes" answer was not coming. Minutes went by. A rescue boat was seen apparently hauling a crew member to shore, meeting an ambulance on the breakwater near the Golden Gate Yacht Club. Emergency responders were working to save somebody. The answer soon came that it was too late; there was nothing more they could do.

All but one crew member had been rescued. Andrew Simpson, a 36-year-old husband and father of two young boys, had died. Simpson, nicknamed "Bart," was well-liked and was a memorable personality around the America's Cup community. Sailing together in the Star class with Artemis Racing's Iain Percy, Simpson had won the Olympic Gold medal in 2008, and the Silver medal in 2012.

The sequence of events that led to Simpson's death was uncertain. The sequence even of the capsize was not clear. Had the boat broken up while sailing or broken up as a result of the capsize? How had the many safety precautions failed: the chase boats, the rescue divers, the training, and the buddy system?

Little was certain other than someone's life was gone. A fair bit of shock ran through the America's Cup community at the loss of life, a personal blow to the many who knew Simpson and stunning news to fans of the sport.

Once the initial news registered, the questions reeled off. Many knew that the boats weren't without risk, but a loss of life wasn't supposed to happen. So many precautions had been put in place. So many talented minds had been engineering the boats, planning for contingencies, and expecting that the worst case could be avoided. There was of course going to be risk, but the risks seemed known, and the risks seemed to be accounted for.

With the Louis Vuitton Cup eight weeks away, a second boat had capsized, and someone had died. How dangerous were these boats? Had some aspect been miscalculated? Were they safe enough to race? All was in doubt.

The reaction outside the America's Cup world was a maelstrom rapidly spinning out of control. Few or no facts were no barrier to endless pronouncements of what was wrong, who was at fault, and what sort of dire future it meant for the event.

Monohull sailors were quoted on television news adamant that the accident proved that multihulls were too dangerous. Multihull sailors were sure it was because of the wingsail. Some on the Internet were quick to blame hydrofoils, not aware that the boat lost was the single non-foiling AC72. Non-sailors blamed organizers for sailing boats that were fast, or seemingly for sailing boats at all.

Every bit of unfortunate news related to the America's Cup was pulled up and piled into stories questioning the event's very existence. One print magazine had a story on their website within hours of the accident, declaring the cause in definitive terms. A few stories reported some sensational versions of the incident, said to come from insiders. Some were later retracted.

Tragedy rightly brought scrutiny. It was hard to object to some aspects of the examination being conducted in the press, and concern for the loss of any innocent life naturally raised the questions of what could and should be done to prevent such a horrible occurrence. To those who had followed the evolution of the event, and the development of the new boats, and knew the regard that the teams and the organizers had for the risks, the pillorying that the event was taking in the public eye was upsetting in its own right.

Few details have been released by the team as to exactly what took place when *Artemis Red*, their non-foiling cat, capsized. People had died on America's Cup boats before, in training as in the Artemis Racing incident, but not while racing. This is the second time in the modern era that a crew member has been killed in training on an America's Cup boat. In 1999 Martin Wizner died after being struck in the head when a block failed on the Spanish yacht *ESP-56*, a more conventional America's Cup Class monohull sailed at the time. One other recorded death was a sailor swept overboard and drowned in 1903 after *Shamrock III* was dismasted during training in the UK.

Here in the 34th America's Cup, two AC72s had capsized so far, and one of those accidents had killed a crew member. It wasn't unlikely that another cat could go over. Were the boats too dangerous? And if they were, then could the America's Cup be held? Could the AC72s be made safer? And how safe was safe enough?

ARTEMIS RESILIENCE

Artemis Racing had already set themselves up for a steep climb by changing their program midstream from a non-foiling boat to a foiler. The new direction would pour the resources of the design and building staff into remaking a design before it had even sailed, and would give the Swedish sailors just weeks between a mid-May launch and the early July beginning of the Louis Vuitton Cup to evolve their skills for a foiling multihull, while the other teams had had months to become familiar with their boat. Artemis tried to jump-start their sailors by having them sail AC45s modified with lifting foils, and sailing them in San Francisco Bay, not the gentlest of venues. Ashore, the team had adapted the hulls of the new AC72 yacht to enable hydrofoiling daggerboards. While they were able to build two pairs of the new boards, and the rudders, they were going to come into the foiling fraternity seven to nine months behind everyone else.

It would have been a rush just to be ready to race at all, and internally they had been planning to use their participation in the Louis Vuitton Cup Round Robin period throughout July to further their development, racing against the other teams and learning from them, and expecting to be at a competitive peak level by the start of the semi-finals in August.

Following the accident, the team, and the America's Cup community, first had to deal with the human aspects of the tragedy. For friends and teammates, there was mourning and personal loss, and for many others just the processing and acceptance of what had taken place and their relationship to the tragedy. And soon, for the Artemis Racing members, the question of how to respond as a team.

It was a level of emotion that nobody was used to mixing into a sailboat racing effort, let alone a demanding America's Cup campaign that was already testing their limits. The Artemis team—sailors, shore crews, technicians, and engineering staff—believed that they owed it to themselves, each other, and to Andrew Simpson to finish what they had started—to race in the Louis Vuitton Cup—if they could.

It was one immense commitment. In the wake of the accident, the new boat would need additional investigation, and structural testing under load to verify the strength of components and the assembled platform, too. It meant weeks of tests onshore to validate the design after yet more modifications to platform and wing were complete. The program would proceed full speed, with all the time and money that implied, but even then just launching the boat would be a mid to late July proposition, and Artemis would not be ready to compete in the Louis Vuitton Cup Round Robin. Not racing in those rounds would mean zero points, and a third-place standing, but not elimination. But they might just make it in time for the semi-finals. Winning the America's Cup was now beside the point—Artemis had something different to accomplish.

ACCIDENT AFTERMATH

On May 14, 2013, America's Cup organizers held a press conference to begin the process of responding to the tragedy. Iain Murray (Regatta Director and CEO of ACRM) and Tom Ehman (Vice Commodore of GGYC) met the press, the strain of the last few days unmistakable on their faces.

Together they described the way forward.

A review panel was to be formed, with Murray as chair and five international yachting experts, including Sally Lindsay Honey (USA, deputy chair), John Craig (USA), Chuck Hawley (USA), Vincent Lauriot-Prévost (FRA), and Jim Farmer QC (NZL). The goal of the review panel was to evaluate the policies and procedures planned for the Louis Vuitton Cup and America's Cup races, and determine what changes should be made in the interest of a safe competition. But the panel was not formed to take on the responsibility of investigating the Artemis design and why it might have failed.

A meeting of all four America's Cup teams was held that morning, attended by senior representatives including Paul Cayard for Artemis, and the tone was described as supportive of the appointment of the panel, with the competitors intending to learn from the review and adopt any recommendations. The teams were characterized as looking forward at this point in time to the upcoming summer's racing.

It was informally requested that all teams hold off on sailing activities for a week's grace period out of respect, not sailing their AC72s and AC45s.

The review panel, though serving on behalf of the teams and the event, lacked powers of enforcement. The pause in sailing ran contrary to the teams' need for practice. Despite the safety panel's request, Luna Rossa started sailing their boat on May 18 to begin load testing and other tests.

Safety Recommendations

On May 22, the review panel issued a list of 37 AC72 safety recommendations. The list touched on many topics. There would be third-party structural reviews of the AC72 platforms and wings, performed confidentially. There would be a significant lowering of the maximum wind limit to 20 knots during the Round Robin, to 21 knots in the Louis Vuitton Cup Semi-Finals, to 23 knots in the America's Cup Match, down from the previous 33-knot top end.

The number of Round Robin races per boat would be reduced from seven to five to allow more time to maintain and repair the boats in proportion to racing them.

If a yacht did capsize during racing, it would be disqualified, to allow immediate rescues without hesitation on the part of chase boats.

Safety provisions would be increased for the sailing crews. Crew locator technology was to be implemented, which later was specified to be a personal strobe locator device for visibility to rescuers, plus a "keychain" device that each crew member would click to send a signal that they were safe and permit electronic headcounts by rescuers. Requirements were upgraded for hands-free underwater breathing apparatus and high-visibility markings on crew helmets and uniforms.

Other recommendations included the requirement for additional emergency response measures to be available while training or racing that included divers/swimmers ready to aid crew, and paramedics and AED defibrillator devices to be on rescue boats.

The wing cladding film to be used on the lower sections of the wings was to be made clear to avoid obstructing visibility in the water near where crew members were likely to be found.

Race Management abandoned plans to set the course with mark boats, and instead switched to soft inflatable buoys.

The plan to bring guests on board during races, as had taken place on the AC45s and the ACCs before them, was dropped.

Two changes would have particular impacts on the Louis Vuitton Cup and America's Cup.

One, there was no longer a penalty for failing to sail during a scheduled race. On the surface this was to avoid pushing a crew to sail in conditions where they did not feel safe enough. It also made it easier for Artemis to skip the Round Robin portion of the Louis Vuitton Cup.

Two, the reduced wind limits would cause some racing to be scrubbed, altering the schedule obviously but also changing the wind range in which the yachts would compete, with the upper third of the original range no longer relevant.

The list was initially met with general agreement and expressions of appreciation by the teams.

Conflict Concerning the Proposed Rule Changes

It was impossible to make changes to some of the rules without affecting the competitive balance of the teams, however. ACRM believed that given the severity of the accident, precautions had to be put in place. Wrecking another boat might put an end to the regatta. In some circumstances, without a Challenger or Defender able to sail, the entire event could be called off or awarded by default. And that says nothing of negative implications for the sport's reputation if the organizers failed to put in place prudent safety measures. Any reasonable steps to avoid a preventable tragedy were required.

However, in the ensuing weeks, each team began to consider how certain recommendations could give an advantage or a disadvantage to another competitor. When it came time to adopt the recommendations, the teams could not agree on making all the changes to the AC72 Class rule. This was a serious roadblock because changes to the rule required unanimous consent by all the teams. Unanimous consent was necessary in the sport to prevent a group of competitors that embraced a common design theme from tilting the rules in their favor.

The objections ostensibly centered on two issues. The first and most complicated involved changes to the rudder. The second was an increase in sailing weights to allow for structural reinforcements.

The rudders were to be made deeper, with larger wings permitted on them to increase the stability of the boats. ETNZ objected to this change at such a late date. Their perception was that they had made design choices to ensure a stable boat within the original rudder specifications and in some respects had traded performance for stability, but had also achieved the most stable AC72 design. They believed that the other boats, with other systems, might not be as proficient at foiling. Artemis was less of a concern, but all the teams would be able to mount the larger rudder wings, and it was apparently ETNZ's belief that the Defender might be benefiting from the rudder change to a greater degree.

A jury member attempted to act as a mediator, but the situation could not be solved by consensus.

ACRM's position was that every one of the recommendations needed to be adopted; the teams could not pick and choose on the issue.

The AC72 Class rule and the Protocol did not explicitly give the Regatta director the power to make modifications to the Class rule. ACRM stated that the requirements were in the best interest of the regatta, and that the operative mechanism for enacting the rules would be the incorporation of the changes by attachment into the United States Coast Guard Marine Event Permit (MEP) issued for the event. Article 16 of the Protocol required compliance with laws and regulations of authorities with jurisdiction, and the Protocol took precedence over the Class rule. ACRM took the position that the terms outlined in the MEP were thus binding on the teams. The safety recommendations were included as part of the MEP application, and on June 28, 2013, the USCG issued the permit.

ETNZ and Luna Rossa argued that Murray had no right to make what were effectively Class rule changes absent their approval. The teams submitted protests to the America's Cup Jury.

Artemis Racing, working all-out to prepare their second AC72 for late entry into the Louis Vuitton Cup, needed concessions. The Swedes had rudders that complied with the original rule and also had built to a new design that would comply with all the requirements of the safety list released in May. But Artemis had no time to change to a configuration that would meet only the portions of the safety list that everyone agreed on.

Artemis Racing's new AC72 also had received structural reinforcements, and was overweight by Class rule. A 100kg variance would be needed. Artemis needed agreement from their fellow Challengers on those issues in order to compete at all.

Elements of brinksmanship were displayed by the various factions of Challengers, the Defender, and ACRM, suggesting that the consequences of one jury ruling or another would prevent someone from racing.

The protests were filed in late June. The jury held hearings on July 8, after the scheduled start of racing, and issued their ruling on July 11. The method of ACRM's changes to the racing rules via the Marine Event Permit was rejected. In the end, Artemis was granted dispensation by her competitors, given a waiver to use their existing rudders and maintain their modified weight.

Racing could resume.

SEVEN Louis Vuitton Cup Racing Begins

ROUND ROBINS: JULY 4 TO AUGUST 1

The three challenger candidates, Emirates Team New Zealand, Luna Rossa Challenge, and Artemis Racing, were scheduled to race in five Round Robins, 10 races per boat, 15 races total.

But Artemis Racing announced prior to the start that they did not expect to be ready to race until the semi-final round, which meant that they would take last place in the Round Robin. That left a three-team Round Robin to be held with only two teams able to sail.

Whether zero, one, or two boats crossed the starting line, there were points at stake in the Louis Vuitton Cup. Each Round Robin race win was worth one point. The team that finished with the highest total of Round Robin points would earn the right to choose how the teams advanced into the semi-final and final rounds, and what the pairings in those rounds would be. The semi-final and final would separate the men from the boys, eliminating the loser of each match from further competition. No team could be eliminated during the Round Robin Series.

Among the changes adopted in the name of safety, the 2013 Protocol no longer penalized teams for not starting races. Artemis Racing would simply score zero points and technically be scored Did-Not-Start (DNS). But for ETNZ or Luna Rossa to earn a point for a win, under the Racing Rules of Sailing for the America's Cup (RRSAC), they had to start the race and complete the course.

As logical as that might be, more than two-thirds of the Round Robin races somewhat absurdly featured a single boat sailing around the course unopposed. It wasn't ideal, but if the teams couldn't agree on how to change the rules, they still had to follow them.

Sunday, July 7, was to have been the long-anticipated debut of a match between two AC72s. Instead it was the debut of just one boat, ETNZ's *Aotearoa*. Luna Rossa did not race because its protest over the en-

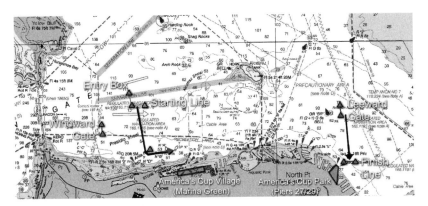

San Francisco America's Cup course location superpimposed on the NOAA chart of the Bay. (© 2013 CupInfo.com)

forcement of the safety recommendations had not been heard yet by the America's Cup jury. ETNZ had filed a similar protest, but they were willing to race, citing commitments to sponsors.

On flat water in 14 to 16 knots of wind, ETNZ sailed the seven-leg course in 46 minutes, alone except for the chase boats and spectators. ETNZ went up one point, but for the fans and media it was a disappointment, especially since one team had intentionally chosen to sit out over a protest issue.

July 9 was scheduled to be a race between ETNZ and Artemis. With Artemis still working to launch their boat, ETNZ completed the course alone to add a second point.

Luna Rossa finally went out on July 11 with Artemis again DNS, picking up their first point, and the first cycle of the Round Robin was complete, with no boats having yet raced against each other.

On Saturday, July 13, Round Robin, Round Two was set, with ETNZ and Luna Rossa in the first official race between AC72s to ever take place. (The AC72s were supposed to debut in the summer of 2012 in San Francisco, but the teams pushed for longer launch deadlines to spend more time to design and develop their new boats.) Fans had been watching the big cats foiling, looking faster and faster, but they had not had the satisfaction of seeing them race against each other in earnest until July 13.

AC72 racing was unknown territory.

Who would have the speed? What would the tactics be? Would they engage each other or sprint to the buoys? Would there be a dial-up, a time-on-distance start, or something else at the gun? Many people had ideas, and there had been plenty of experts talking about a boat race they've never seen, but everyone would finally learn what AC72 racing was actually like. This moment had been building for nearly three years.

Race 1: Winds were 17 to 18 knots on course at race time.

Dean Barker on ETNZ boxed out Chris Draper and Luna Rossa, holding them deep in the starting box and away from the line at the gun. ETNZ headed for the line late, with a good jump on Luna Rossa, and rounded Mark 1 eight seconds ahead. On the first downwind leg, they traded gybes, sailing in the mid 30-knot range, ETNZ getting the better eventually, and extending to a 29-second lead at the downwind gate. Both boats turned left, and headed offshore to start the first upwind leg.

ETNZ stretched to about a 500m lead halfway up, continuing to pull away from the Italians, and the delta more than doubled to 2:02.

The margin continued to grow on every leg, and ETNZ won the first head-to-head AC72 match.

Luna Rossa crossed the line 5:23 behind, unofficially, and DNF (Did Not Finish) officially. Per the Racing Rules of Sailing for the America's Cup, the principal race officer terminated the match race five minutes after the first boat finished.

Round Robin Two continued, with ETNZ picking up their unopposed point against an absent Artemis on July 14. Luna Rossa in turn sailed their course against a still absent Artemis for their free point on the 16th.

So it continued. Of the 15 planned races over the month of July, only one race per round did not involve a sail-over by Luna Rossa or ETNZ. And since Luna Rossa had sat out the first Round Robin, that left only four real races.

The outcomes of the Luna Rossa versus ETNZ Round Robin meetings themselves were never in much doubt, since the Italians were sailing a boat largely identical to ETNZ's first-generation boat while the New Zealanders had their second-generation boat. If a first-generation boat was seriously competitive against a second-generation boat, something would have been terribly wrong with the ETNZ program.

In their second meeting, on July 21, Luna Rossa was only 2 minutes, 18 seconds behind ETNZ at the finish, cutting the losing margin in half.

On July 23, the two met again, the fourth of five meetings, ETNZ winning again. This time it was another DNF for Luna Rossa, after the five-minute time limit expired. Unofficially, the delta was 7:13. The win was the mathematical clincher for ETNZ's first-place finish in the Round Robins.

The Round Robins ultimately served as a proving ground for crew work and tactics, and provided a glimpse of performance to come. Both teams had upgrades taking shape back in the work sheds, looking ahead to the Louis Vuitton semis, and finals, and ultimately the America's Cup Match. Most prominently, Luna Rossa had a new wing on its way, and ETNZ many tweaks, kept confidential.

ETNZ's sailors would have told you they were sailing flat out, although they were usually hiding their true potential in the early rounds. The telemetry from the boats during races was available to the public, making possible some informed analysis of exactly what the boats were doing.

In Round Robin 3, July 18, ETNZ recorded a top speed of 44.1 knots (more than 50 miles per hour) on a reach while sailing unopposed against a DNS Artemis. All the more remarkable, the wind was recorded as 15 to 17 knots throughout the race and the boat still averaged over 34 knots/39 mph on the downwind leg and 22 knots/25 mph on the upwind leg. Still, 50 mph was worth just one point. Concern was also rising about the wisdom of risking the AC72 boats in stronger (continued on page 109)

New Crewing Opportunities

In the 1970s and '80s America's Cup crews were largely composed of young sailors under 30 years old, often even as skippers. In the 20 to 25 years since, a professional rank emerged, and a number of sailors stuck around the event, becoming familiar faces and in the process raising the average age of the competitors. Many of the skills needed to make 2013 America's Cup boats go fast, however, came out of a different sailing tradition, and opened the door for a whole flock of young talented sailors who never expected that their résumés would lead to an America's Cup career. In the following interview, Nathan Outteridge talks about transitioning from a small Olympic dinghy to a big AC45 to a huge AC72, becoming a leader at Artemis, and learning to race a foiling wingsail multihull in eight days.

Artemis Racing helmsman Nathan Outteridge. (© 2013 ACEA/Photo: Gilles Martin-Raget)

Australian Nathan Outteridge was among the most prominent of the new generation of sailors, the "Young Guns" who found unexpected opportunities when radical catamarans became the next generation America's Cup boat. As the required skill sets for sailing the AC45 and AC72 became apparent to the 2013 America's Cup teams, suddenly younger, athletic sailors with experience on high-performance boats were in demand. After winning a Gold medal in the two-person, 94 kg-hull-weight 49er dinghy the previous summer, Outteridge ended up at the wheel of a 72-foot 40-plus-knot Louis Vuitton Cup Challenger in 2013.

"I can say, guaranteed, that if the America's Cup stayed in keelboat, if they'd stayed with the Version Five boats or something similar, I'd still be sailing my 49er back in Australia," Outteridge confirmed. "The opportunity to get involved in the America's Cup this time has been completely different—suddenly we were sailing [AC]45 cats that sail like dinghies."

Outteridge started his Cup career with the smaller Team Korea (see page 95), an America's Cup World Series competitor that was ultimately unable to field an AC72 campaign. He was following in the footsteps of Chris Draper, who also broke in with Team Korea and then jumped to Luna Rossa Challenge. Other rising stars in the sport like Paul Campbell-James and Phil Robertson also found opportunities in the ACWS, and Peter Burling later took Outteridge's place at Team Korea before winning the Red Bull Youth America's Cup. 49er Gold Medalists and World Champions Iker Martinez and Xabi Fernandez, along with Nathan's own Olympic mate Iain Jensen, were yet more 49er talent flowing into the America's Cup realm.

"Chris was really the first one who got the chance and he really excelled," Outteridge said. "If it wasn't for Chris, then they wouldn't have come to the rest of us 49er and dinghy sailors, offering jobs."

In September 2012, Outteridge was picked up by Artemis Racing and thrust onto an even bigger stage as it became clear that the giant catamarans would be fully foiling downwind. Nearly overnight, Outteridge was in a lead-

ership role with people coming to him for answers. The young Aussie credited Iain Percy with quickly integrating him into the team.

"Percy did a great job of embracing the younger guys, guys who had experience in foiling boats and letting us have some input," said Outteridge. "In previous Cups, you'd never have that chance, you'd just sit there and listen and learn. That's what I thought was going to happen here. When I joined the team, I was the backup helmsman behind Terry [Hutchinson] and Loïck [Peyron]. When we shifted to foiling, everyone looked at me and asked what I thought, and that was really cool, to have that development and to be integral in so many aspects of the boat."

With a lot to learn about both wings and foils, the time spent on the AC45s was the stepping-stone from a small two-person dinghy to the AC72. Especially for Artemis, who didn't bet on foiling initially.

"First off, not many people had sailed with wings before, so having a pretty basic wing, with not much control except for twist and camber, you could learn how to deal with that first," Outteridge said. "The only thing that was really missing from the 45 was foiling, so we turned our AC45 into a foiling boat in March [2013], were out sailing by April, and did about 35 days foiling on the 45. If we hadn't done that, there's no way we would have sailed in the America's Cup.

"Everything that we learned from sailing a foiling 45 scaled up to a 72, in terms of how to trim, how to steer, how the daggerboard works, how the rudder lift works—all these complicated things that you see the 72s doing. From the outside, you just see a boat sailing around, but all the little details we learned from the 45 in the space of two months.

"We were designing boat two to foil while we were sailing the 45, so there would be critical moments when we would come in and say 'We need to have this system on the 72; otherwise, it's not going to work.' So that kept delaying boat two. Boat two was basically designed before I joined the team, but as we started to learn that boat one wasn't performing the way we needed it to in order to be competitive, they started changing the design of boat two.

"When we first started sailing Moths, we had big foils with really aggressive control systems, and as we got better, we made the foils smaller and smaller and we'd go faster and faster. But we didn't have time, so we decided that our first set of foils would be what we thought were small foils. A second set would be a refined set of small foils. So basically we got a foiling 72 that was going to be really hard to sail because if we designed a big set of foils to learn on, we were going to be too slow. And we didn't have any time."

It was heady stuff for a 27-year-old who, nine months after experiencing the high of winning an Olympic Gold medal, found himself dealing with the worst of lows—the accident that destroyed boat number one and took the life of teammate Andrew "Bart" Simpson. From sailing singlehanded Moths and the double-handed 49er, Outteridge was helping to keep a team of 130 people moving forward. With little sailing opportunity while the second Artemis boat was being altered, Outteridge headed to New Zealand on a spy mission.

"I went to New Zealand for two weeks to watch what they were doing and came back and said, 'We need this size rudder.' What we got was 90 percent of what they had—and we had eight days of training and they had 80. It was really impressive to see that our design team was able to shift from the direction they were going. It's really hard to swallow your pride and say, 'We're wrong, so let's go in this direction and let's listen to a young guy who's never been in the Cup before and get his ideas.' "

It wasn't possible to equal the prep time the other teams had, but the effort to get the second Artemis boat on the water and ready for racing was enormous.

"We were sailing every day we could, so what we learned on one day, we had to implement the next," Outteridge said. "You have to stop on the water, stop for half an hour and talk to the guys on the chase boat about everything—does the rudder look okay, do we need to change this or that—and give guys time to digest what happened. Half an hour later, you're doing 40 knots again, just trying to learn as fast as you could. We had a really good plan of how to learn, but it was the steepest learning curve I've ever been on. Everyone on the team would say that—it's just a shame it had to end so soon."

With Artemis out of the Louis Vuitton Cup, ACTV put the young Outteridge to work as a broadcast analyst providing television commentary alongside Tucker Thompson and Andy Green. All that time that Outteridge had spent closely watching the other teams' maneuvers and planning Artemis Racing's choreography suddenly came in very handy.

"I spent this whole year watching Team New Zealand, Prada, and OTUSA sail, watching video after video to see what they were doing. The one-boat races were better for us than the two-boat races, because we could see exactly what was going on. We could analyze specifics—at this time before a maneuver, the strategist crosses the boat and goes to the pit, then the trimmer runs across

and so on. You can see them stand on the buttons to switch gears on the winches. That kind of analysis helped us so much, because we could watch details of what they were doing.

"So now that I see them racing, I have a really good understanding. I can see a certain guy cross the boat and know there's a gybe coming in the next 30 seconds, which are tiny little details that no one picks up. So now, while I'm commentating, I'm trying to observe those little things as triggers to what's about to happen and I'm trying to pick up little details when they do something good or when something abnormal happens. The main thing to watch is the starts and where they position themselves, what they do around mark one and at the bottom marks."

Asked what advice he would have for the young 49er sailor that he was not that many months ago, setting out to take a chance on the America's Cup, he said, "Just be prepared to deal with whatever happens. Know that things aren't going to go as you planned and learn as much as you can, about things that aren't even relevant to sailing."

winds to win unopposed races, not to mention the absurdity of one-boat "races." As a result, some sanity prevailed with a change to the Racing Rules of Sailing for the America's Cup that allowed the umpires to disqualify an opponent who had not started after a reasonable amount of time, awarding the point to an opponent who had started.

Lessons were being learned in the tactics, especially at the start, and in the boat-handling department. Luna Rossa realized the importance of foiling smoothly through gybes that ETNZ had already mastered; the Italians, on the other hand, were falling off their foils whenever they gybed, losing 10 to 15 seconds or more.

Luna Rossa was learning and improving, but so was ETNZ, who was already way ahead in the game. ETNZ had led at every mark, trailing officially only in one start by less than one second.

After ETNZ developed an insurmountable lead in the Round Robins, they decided to bow out of the series to add new modifications to their boat. The Kiwis were pegging their development program to be ready for the start of the America's Cup. The task involved evolving the boat while at the same time not trying to show too many cards to the Defender before the start of the Match.

As winner of the Round Robins, ETNZ opted to bypass the Louis Vuitton semi-finals.

LOUIS VUITTON CUP SEMI-FINAL, AUGUST 6 TO 15

Artemis Racing versus Luna Rossa Challenge

The Louis Vuitton Cup resumed on August 6th with the semi-finals, an elimination round that would send Luna Rossa or Artemis Racing home. The first team to win four races would go on to face ETNZ in the Louis Vuitton Cup Final.

Experienced Cup watchers, having witnessed only four ETNZ–Luna Rossa races to date, were eager to have another match-up to gauge the competitiveness of the teams.

Despite the troubles that Artemis Racing had endured, there were high expectations for the newly launched second boat, Artemis Blue, that had been on the water only since July 22. The match-up with Luna Rossa would finally pair two boats with different design philosophies.

The real question was how Artemis Blue would stack up against Luna Rossa, and for that reason the semi-finals were closely watched by all sides. If the races between the Swedes and the Italians were too close, it would make ETNZ's superior performance look even more intimidating, and put some worry into the defender camp, too.

Beyond the boat speed questions, there were plenty of areas of concern for Artemis Racing, given their more limited experience with foiling. Furthermore, efficient crew techniques, optimized tuning for various conditions, and basic readiness to execute tactics and strategy were not aided by having zero AC72 race time to date.

Meanwhile, Luna Rossa had been working on finding the changes in gear and crew work to bring the boat closer to potential. A smoothly executed race by Italy would be a good sign to start the semi-final series.

Luna Rossa opted to step their first wingsail for the semi-finals. Their second wing remained in the shop due to damage it sustained during training. The decision suggested confidence on two levels: a willingness to start a race against Artemis with the older wing, and a focus on looking past the semi-finals entirely.

For Race 1, Artemis Racing had a dominant start, leading Luna Rossa at the first mark, but the Italians quickly outclassed them with smooth gybes and better downwind speed. The Swedes showed they had some potential upwind, making gains against Italy, but Luna Rossa was able to pull away, and won by nearly two minutes.

The exciting discovery during Race 1 was that the two boats were different enough to have asymmetric performance profiles. Artemis was capable of being faster upwind, while Luna Rossa usually was much faster

LUNA ROSSA CHALLENGE

Skipper/pit: Max Sirena

Helmsman: Chris Draper

Tactician: Francesco Bruni

Wing trimmer:
Xabi Fernández

Wing grinder:
Lele Marino

Trimmer:
Pierluigi de Felice

Pit/grinder: David Carr

Bow: Nick Hutton

Primary grinder:
Wade Morgan

Strategist/grinder:
Giles Scott

Freestyle: Marco Montis
Manuel Modena

Hydraulic grinder:
Simone de Mari

Artemis Racing found themselves off the pace in Race 1 of the Louis Vuitton Cup Semi-Finals. (© 2013 ACEA/Photo: Abner Kingman)

downwind. This gave either boat the prospect of catching or passing, and kept the racing much more interesting.

Luna Rossa's experience was telling, but the upside possibilities for Artemis held out hope.

The pressure was on Artemis to execute smoothly, especially downwind where the Italians had already measured themselves against ETNZ and were steadily raising their game. Italy was also showing the benefit of having had more time to refine rudder and lifting foil shapes. Upwind, where the boats sailed with their leeward hulls in the water, Artemis was seeing the benefits of a more hydrodynamic hull shape for the task, and likely also had an advantage with their more sophisticated wing.

New tactics were evolving, too.

Luna Rossa's Chris Draper and Artemis Racing's Nathan Outteridge, two of the youngest hotshots at the helm, were mixing it up with each other at the start.

But it wasn't clear given the speed differences on the course that it was really worth it for either team to take big risks at the start, potentially incurring penalties or, worse, sustaining major damage. But the young skippers still sailed aggressively at the starts as if the AC72s were dinghies.

Sailing better was the true order of the day, though. Luna Rossa was doing that, and Artemis, for all their potential, needed to catch fire, and soon. Luna Rossa was up 1-0, and needed only three more semi-final wins.

A 2:05 margin for Luna Rossa in Race 2 revealed the stark difference between being in the water or on foils. Because Artemis Racing's foils were not sorted out yet, the Swedes lost more distance on gybes. The race also demonstrated that the upwind leg was a good place to catch an opponent, but the downwind leg could be close to impossible, especially when a windshift skewed the course.

Artemis spent Thursday's off-day improving their gybing techniques, among other issues, hoping not to make gifts to Luna Rossa several times

ARTEMIS RACING

Skipper/tactician:
Iain Percy

Helmsman:
Nathan Outteridge

Pit: Curtis Blewett
Stu Bettany
Andy Fethers

Grinder: Chris Brittle

Grinder: Julien Cressant

Grinder: Craig Monk

Grinder: Sean Clarkson

Jib trim: Thierry Fouchier

Wing trim: Iain Jensen

Wing assist:
Rodney Ardern

per downwind leg. Artemis needed to press whatever advantages they might have upwind, and stay close downwind, hoping for opportunities.

The Swedish team won slight advantages over their opponent in the starts, but after the short reach of the first leg, their advantage was lost as the battle shifted to Luna Rossa's sweet spot, sailing off the wind. It was becoming quickly apparent that Luna Rossa was further up the learning curve, working on the refinement that's one of the core reasons the Challenger Series was created. And the Italians were getting the job done in the semis and began to look ahead to ETNZ in the Louis Vuitton Cup Final. Artemis Racing had enormous potential, in both sailors and technology, but time was running out.

Race 3 saw Luna Rossa start with a small lead, and slowly extend it, taking another win. Artemis was improving, either by staying even or by not losing as much ground.

The semi-finals had been much closer than the Round Robins. Artemis trimmed their losing margins from 1:57 in Race 1 and 2:05 in Race 2 down to 1:17 in the third race. The Swedes were getting faster, but not improving fast enough to win.

A race win for Artemis was not out of reach, but with Luna Rossa becoming increasingly solid, it would take excellent crew work by the Swedes and probably some mistakes from the Italians for that to happen.

With little to lose and their backs to the wall, Artemis came out swinging in the pre-start of Race 4. Artemis, to leeward, luffed Luna Rossa enough to make the Italians tack away, but Draper soon tacked back and Artemis was so close that even though the Swedes had the right of way, they weren't leaving Luna Rossa room to keep clear. Artemis started slightly ahead, but with a penalty.

Artemis carried a 130m lead as the boats began the first downwind leg, but between the penalty and better gybing from the Italians, Luna Rossa had little difficulty wiping that out and spent the rest of the race pulling away steadily.

A boundary penalty on Artemis Racing didn't help either, but changed little. Luna Rossa was just showing themselves to be faster, reassuring for the Italians, now going into the Louis Vuitton Cup Finals with more upgrades, such as a more advanced wingsail yet to be installed.

Artemis Racing spent over $100 million for what turned out to be four races, and lost all of them. Without the tragic accident on boat one, and several other development setbacks, the story could easily have been different, but none of that could be undone. It was a technical and logistical mountain to climb, aside from the expense. They responded to a succession of major setbacks, and a sad tragedy, with an enormous sporting effort just to be able to compete in the regatta at all. The story of Artemis was something bigger than just winning and losing races, even if they might have preferred otherwise.

EIGHT Sailing the AC72–Foiling

When Pete Melvin co-wrote the design rule for the AC72 catamaran, he knew there were two distinct areas of development that could determine the winner of the 34th America's Cup: the hard wing, an aspect of ORACLE TEAM USA's Cup-winning monster cat brought forward to this new era of Cup technology, and the foils. As it turns out, the 131' wingsail, initially regarded as the radical innovation of this America's Cup cycle, was overshadowed by the realization that these giant catamarans could foil not only downwind but upwind.

From the beginning of Melvin's role on the AC72 design team of Emirates Team New Zealand, the watchword was "stable flight." The team learned pretty early on that getting as much of the huge cat out of the water as possible was the key to speed. Consequently, the foils underwent a tremendous amount of development, from early models tested on the team's SL33s to the "V"-shaped version that led ETNZ to win the Louis Vuitton Cup.

"When we were working on the rule, we knew you wanted to get as much lift as possible when you were going fast downwind," Melvin said. "For instance, in the 2010 America's Cup, sailed on giant multihulls, the maximum amount of lift we thought we could get was about 50 percent of the weight of the boat. At that time, we were still relying on the hull to provide pitch control, so what's come out of this is the boats all now have elevators (the horizontal foils on the rudders).

"At Team New Zealand, we developed a new type of foil that allows you to keep your height above the water more or less steady. No one had been able to do that before, at least not on a course-racing boat that was not going downwind. We developed that mostly on our SL33 test boats—they came with the stock constant curvature "C" foils and with those kinds of foils, you can generate 50 percent boat weight lift before they get unstable. But we noticed that when we could get one boat up fully foiling for a few seconds, it would really accelerate away from the other boat—and that got the wheels turning. How, with such a huge potential benefit, can we achieve stable flight downwind? So our design team came up with the 'up-tip' type of boards. We refined those on the 33s, and our 72 is designed to do that and fortunately it worked right out of the box."

As with many new Cup revelations, ETNZ's first problem was how to test something as radical as foiling without showing their hand too soon. Opposing teams and sailors now freely admit the sheer number of hours spent on Waitemata Harbor, keeping a very close eye on the Kiwi's development plans. How did ETNZ keep the prying eyes at bay?

"When we first achieved stable flight, it was on the SL33s and we did a pretty decent job of keeping those sailing sessions out of the eyes of our competitors," says Melvin. "They would come out every few days and watch us—and when they did, we would go back into 'normal' mode. After a while, they would get bored and go away.

"But they could see what we were developing and they were probably wondering why we were sailing with these strange looking foils, though I'm sure they were figuring out what we were doing just by analyzing the shapes that we had. When we launched our 72, that was when pictures started appearing on the Internet. There were cries of it being Photoshop; people couldn't believe it."

Now that the foils have been proven to be a success, Melvin can admit that even he was somewhat caught by surprise.

"When we wrote the rule, we honestly weren't sure if we could fully foil," said Melvin. "All we knew was the higher the lift we could generate, the faster we could go. That was a central focus of our foil development program, to try to push that limit. Initially, we thought that if we could get 70 or 80 percent lift, that would be a giant gain over our competitors. The boat would accelerate like crazy, so incrementally we pushed it until we could fly 100 percent of the time.

"Our initial foils on the 72 were a little more conservative and even more stable than the foils we have now. Some of it is technique, though, to achieve stable flight—steering, trimming, and the setup of your wing and sails, the elevators. We're still on a very steep learning curve but we were able to design foils that have less drag, but are a little less stable than our original foils. There's a compromise between foiling stability and drag—you can have larger elevators, which give you more pitch stability, but it's more drag. Trialing these solutions and understanding exactly how hard and where you can push the envelope—that's where we had a good advantage initially, because we had more time on the water doing that."

All the teams had to compromise when it came to foil size and shape—for instance, a larger foil means the boat can lift at lower wind speeds, but the larger foil means more drag, especially at higher speeds. And the higher speeds bring their own problems, such as cavitation. As ORACLE TEAM USA and ETNZ navigate the trade-off between drag and speed, at least it's a decision that can wait until nearly the last possible moment—all foils are premeasured, so teams have until 8:00 pm the night before a race to declare their foils.

As a designer, Melvin enjoyed watching the other America's Cup teams launch their new boats, seeing how each design team put their personal stamp on the AC72 Rule that he and his staff put together. While no design truly surprised him, he doesn't mind borrowing a thing or two he's picked up along the way, especially from the team they face for the America's Cup.

"Clearly, we were in a little bit different design space than Oracle. They went for a much more aerodynamic solution but with a little bit of a compromised structure. Their boat was clearly more flexible than ours. We went for a stiffer structure and perhaps gave away some aerodynamics, though I'd say we've worked hard on aerodynamics since we've seen their boat and they worked pretty hard on stiffening their boat up. With foiling, you need to have fairly good stiffness control of your boat, because if the whole boat is moving it's hard to control your foils."

Gino Morrelli puts some numbers to the AC72: "It's a 72-foot, 45-foot wide, 12,000-odd-pound beast that can fly a hull in about 6 knots of wind, and can fully go airborne like this in about 10 or 12 knots of wind."

Top-end speeds over 50 mph have been flashed in racing, documented on LiveLine telemetry. "It can do that in about 20-something knots of wind, so it's about a 2-point-something windspeed boat," says Morrelli.

As fast as a wingsail multihull is, a foiling cat is faster. Getting the boat up on foils and keeping it up was key to winning the 2013 America's Cup.

With foils it takes about 10 to 12 knots of wind to fly barely, 16 to 18 knots to fly fully. The payoff for getting an AC72 up on foils is immediate; the boat speed jumps by about 5 knots at the low end when the leeward hull gets airborne, and the gain at the top end can be twice that or more, with top speeds going from the 30-plus-knot range into the 40s and edging toward 50 knots. Foiling has changed the game.

THE FOILS

"These are the really weird curved daggerboards we've been developing. They're what really . . . the whole game is about," said Morrelli. As for the hulls, "We call them a 'board-delivery device.' They barely even touch down even during tacks and gybes."

A few smaller boats have effectively used lifting foils in the past, such as the Moth dinghies, and in the last few years the A-Class catamarans, but fully flying a large multihull on foils was rarely done except for isolated situations.

"The French had been playing with foils for 15 years, foil stabilized," Morrelli said. "But they were still basically sailing on the main hull, leeward hull being lifted, but not trying to fly the whole boat, except for boats like *Hydroptère*, which are completely other animals. We've been following some of those trends and some of those trends have been dictated by carbon rigs and carbon sails, because we didn't really have the power to get the boats out of the water until engines got better."

Upgrading the engines took improving multihull designs in all areas, including the structural platform, the rigging, and the control systems.

"The problem has been in the past—even with Kevlar sails—they are too elastic and our boats are so stiff in righting moment, that to get the hull out of the water you've got to translate all that power through the rig, through the shrouds and the mainsheet, to get the boat out," says Morrelli. "And if the rig is twisting and flexing to get the boat out, then you are giving up that power and the boat doesn't come out of the water. So it's been the evolution of sail development, and lines, hydraulics, to translate the power back into the platform. Now we have plenty of power and now we can lift the boat out of the water."

Having the power to fly is one thing; having the ability to control a foiling cat was another feat completely new in the 34th America's Cup.

AC72s on foils are "dynamically supported," where the motion of the water over the foils creates the lifting forces that elevate the hull out of the water. That sounds straightforward, but it cuts both ways. Foils come with inherent issues, including that as speed increases, lift increases, which can make the foils themselves rise to the surface of the water and suddenly lose effectiveness, setting off a sequence of losing support, dropping back down, slowing, and then accelerating again to repeat the inefficient cycle. Or if the boat gets out of hand, for example, the angle of attack can increase too sharply, shooting the bows skyward while dropping the transom. Out of control is not a recipe for winning.

HOW THEY DO IT

It's obviously critical to control the angle of attack of the daggerboard foils, letting the crew adjust the board to suit speed, angles, and wind conditions. The goal is to sail the boat in a steady balance and let speed build, to say nothing of just keeping the boat upright and intact. There is just one problem, though: the rules don't allow the crew or an onboard system to actively adjust the angle of attack of the foils when the boat is racing. The rules also don't allow any adjustment at all of the foil angles on the rudders during the race. The daggerboards can be raised and lowered while sailing, but under the AC72 Class rule there are strict limits on managing the boards.

Pete Melvin explains the restrictions: "According to the rule, you are allowed to adjust rake and you're allowed to adjust cant. The rule also states that you can't move the lower bearing but you can perform any sort of rotation you want. So there's a possibility that if you had, say, a trim tab on your daggerboard, you could control lift that way and it would require far less power and force to actuate that than to move the entire board. But when we were working on the rule, our group thought that limiting moving parts on the foils would reduce cost and complexity, but possibly that was a mistake. If we'd known these boats would be fully foiling, there could have been a better solution."

In the tradition of unintended consequences, the AC72 Class rule was written this way to control costs and promote healthier designs, but it created a huge technical challenge for the design teams.

The Class rule actually started out differently in draft form. Morrelli says: "Oracle let us write a rule that said there was unlimited development of the foils: you could have flaps; you could tweak your rudder; you could have active controls; you could have a wand dragging in the water like a Moth, the sailing dinghy. It was basically an open game; there were no rules. Whatever you brought that could fit in the box, you could run."

But the Class rule is the product not just of designers. The Class was shaped by a meeting of the minds between the Defender and the Challenger of Record, who at that point in time was Club Nautico di Roma, represented by Mascalzone Latino. Compromise was involved.

"The Italians vetoed that extreme open example because they thought it was too expensive," Morrelli says. "It would be detrimental to the Cup developing boats that were reliable, and they squashed it."

The performance potential of lifting foils was too great to be left untapped, though. The question became how to control an AC72 catamaran on foils within the AC72 Class rule. Smaller boats can rely on crew movements fore-and-aft to achieve stable flight on foils, but the AC72s were too big for that approach, so more creative solutions were necessary. "That left designers with a problem of trying to find 'how do we fly it without flying the boat?' It's not like an airplane, you have a stick, and you can change the rudder and the ailerons," Morrelli says. "We basically had to build a boat that was self-flying, because there was very little opportunity to articulate the boat without sensors."

Emirates Team New Zealand's technique was to attach their foil to a curved daggerboard. When the board is lowered, the meeting of the extended foil and the rest of the board forms a V shape instead of an L. The ETNZ boat sits on the V so that when boat speed increases, and lift increases, the foil rises higher in the water with both legs of the V at an inclined angle instead of nearly horizontal.

"The advantages/disadvantages are this V is self-leveling," Morrelli said. "As it raises up to the surface at high speed, it loses lift, because it stalls a little bit, and it settles back down—where a true L will go completely out of the water, and you have to find another way of controlling the angle of attack and the amount of lift it creates."

Because the foils extend to their tips at an upward angle instead of flat, as the foil reaches the surface, the portion of the foil with water flowing over it, generating lift, is reduced incrementally, and the boat comes down gradually to an equilibrium point. The idea is to balance the forces as speed changes, avoiding the all-or-nothing conditions that a more horizontal lifting foil encounters.

It's not the only solution for an AC72, but for the pragmatic New Zealand team, it seemed to fit.

"There are these ways that people are trying to control their dag-

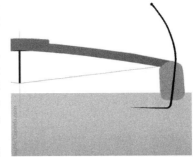

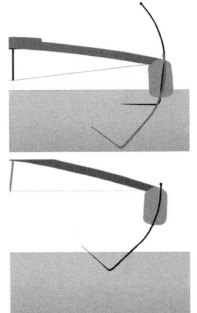

Top to bottom: Daggerboard in retracted position. Daggerboard in extended position. AC72 foiling on extended daggerboard. (© 2013 CupInfo.com)

Emirates Team New Zealand leading at Mark 1 in Race 7 of the America's Cup. Note the tip of their daggerboard foil showing just above the water. (© 2013 ACEA/ Photo: Ricardo Pinto)

gerboards with almost car-like suspension systems," said Morrelli, noting that those alternatives bring penalties in weight and complexity. "We've opted for this. . . . It's a rather simple, robust system of flying our boat.

"In the upwind position, by having articulating bearings at the deck and the bottom, we can put our foil basically vertical when we want lots of lateral resistance, lots of side force, and not so much lift. In light air we can actually rake the board back and take the angle of attack out of it, so it's not lifting very much. It's draggy, but it's not lifting."

DEVELOPMENT OF THE FOILING CONCEPT

Morrelli & Melvin's experience with foiling actually goes back to power boats, where as long as power is sufficient, the decision to foil is primarily a calculation about saving fuel costs. But adapting foils to multihull sail-boats has been a series of explorations, first in development classes like the A-Class cats and then in limited-production boats.

"We started with A's probably five to six years ago," Morrelli said. "Then we started playing with the Nacra 20, that's about five years ago, and that was the first production attempt at building a 20-foot boat—a carbon boat with curved foils and carbon rig—and it's been pretty successful. From that we moved to the SL33 and the F17 in the years after that."

As a platform for foil development, and to give their crews hands-on experience, Emirates Team New Zealand used a pair of Morrelli & Melvin–designed SL33s. "We actually designed [the SL33] a year before the Cup even went to catamarans, so it was only fortuitous that we had a boat already designed and already under construction. We were building them in New Zealand just by chance.

"We did most of our daggerboard experiments on these boats because they were easy to do and cheap to do, relatively," said Morrelli. "A daggerboard on one of these is about a five-grand, eight-grand problem. A daggerboard on our AC72s? A pair of boards is $400,000. So we didn't want to make many of those."

America's Cup teams are limited to building ten boards for the big boats, but as long as the test platform is a boat under 10 meters, there's no limit on the number of daggerboards that can be tried.

"So we made lots of these," Morrelli said, referring to the SL33 boards. "We can build these in the shop, and whack them off and change them. So that's where we've developed to. The boats are very fast, flying downwind now on foils very steadily."

TESTING AND DEVELOPMENT IN THE AC

Foil development was also a function of time factors and the nature of attacking the AC72 design problem within the context of the America's Cup. The teams were allowed to build two boats, six wingsails, and ten daggerboards/foils, but the lead times for design and building made it impractical to feed very much real-world data back into major changes to the hulls and wingsails. The first boat by rule couldn't even be launched until about a year before Louis Vuitton Cup competition started. ETNZ was the first team with an AC72 in the water and they still had to commit to the design of the second of two AC72s just weeks after boat one got wet. The schedule let them validate their first design in a general sense, but not spend a lot of effort to test and optimize on a large scale, let alone explore concepts that were more radical.

Even if the teams were not restricted by rule in the number of hulls and wingsails that they could build, and even regardless of budget, there simply wasn't the capacity to build and deploy enough iterations in a short enough time to take advantage of a methodical step-by-step development program for all the major components. The end result was that the AC72 hulls and wings had to be good enough, subject to minor modifications, but not perfect, and a lot of the performance deltas in Louis Vuitton and America's Cup racing would come from boat handling, maneuverability, and foiling performance.

That meant a lot of resources funneled into the boards. And even with all the design ingenuity at hand, the foils ran into limitations of physics.

"It becomes a material science problem," Morrelli said. "We're building those things as thin and as deep as humanly possible given our level of technology and understanding. They're pretty much solid carbon, but the way we build them, the way they are manufactured under high intense heat and pressure, the most aerospace part on the boat is really the daggerboards."

"They take about three months to build, once we have a set of tools. They are super labor-intensive."

There appeared to be differing schools of thought when it came to building daggerboards, though. "In fact, we were shocked when Oracle's broke," Morrelli said. "The first day sailing they broke one of their daggerboards and it popped up and it floated away." That's not what the ETNZ guys would have expected. "Ours would sink like a stone . . . and be down in 18 feet of mud."

With a lot left to learn, and the ability to keep drilling into the foil problem, teams were building and testing them even into the summer of 2013 as racing was under way.

Foil development was always expected to keep going, probably going on until the last second, Morrelli said. "How small can we make it and fly upwind? And compare it to a boat that's got an 80 percent lift fraction as opposed to 100 percent, work it back to an 80 percent boat, and test the delta between those two extremes."

TRICKLE DOWN—OTHER FOILING SAILBOATS

America's Cup racing has often been a test bed for design and technology that transfers to mainstream racing classes, cruising boats, and other civilian applications. But not always. Wingsails, for all their efficiencies, may require too much specialized handling to ever see widespread adoption, but foiling technology is another story.

"All of this board development is going to trickle into racing, big time," Morrelli said. "We're already stealing it and sticking it on our cruising cats. The sail-area-to-weight ratio that benefits from curved boards and angled boards and 'J'-boards is being approached by cruising boats like our Gunboat series or our custom MM65 series on a regular basis right now. We've already got clients looking for us to design basically semi-lifting—what we call lift fractions—to start putting lift fractions onto cruising cats, big custom carbon things. That trickle is happening as we speak. We recently just stuck a set of big asymmetric canted-end foils on one of our Gunboats, escalating that war down there in the Caribbean. That's a 62, it's a 40,000-pound boat. So they are benefiting from some of that experience, too. The next generation of custom cruising cats will definitely get some of this stuff. For doing Antigua Race week or Heineken or Caribbean 600, you're going to see some pretty wild 90- to 100-foot cruising cats flying a hull around the course in the near future."

Nacra 17

Want to fly your own small catamaran? Off-the-shelf lifting foils may be coming soon to a beach near you. Morrelli & Melvin's design for a 17-foot beach cat with curved foils was adopted as a new class for the 2016 Olympics. Intended for a crew of two, the Nacra 17 has retractable curved foils to go with a high-aspect sail and a carbon rig.

"It's really a fun boat. It's also a boat that misbehaves," Morrelli says.

"It will pull wheelies. This boat doesn't have 'T'-rudders, so you use your body weight and you move your body weight fore and aft to control the angle of attack, and by raising and lowering the board you get more or less surface area, so it's a combination of board position and body weight.

"You can get these things to nearly fly with just barely the transom touching and the leeward bow . . . completely out of the water. So they are quite fast, quite active fiberglass hulls, carbon rigs, carbon boards. They weigh about 313 pounds, and retail at about 26 grand, and you can't get one." At least not yet. The first hundred boats were pre-sold to the Olympic sailing teams, in sets of ten boats, for use in their national trials.

The small boats are instructive as to the advantages of the foils. How much faster is the Nacra 17 than a similar cat, or even the larger ex-Olympic-cat, the Tornado? "[The Nacra 17] doesn't have an advantage over anybody in light air," Morrelli says. "In fact with the curved boards we actually give away a little bit of performance, because in light air you really want the straight super-deep boards, but at about 6 knots of wind it crosses right over to [where] the curved-board boats are faster. As soon as you can fly a hull, the curved-board boats are faster these days. Anything above 8 to 10 knots, they're faster downwind all the time. It's still a close race upwind with some conventional—what we call conventional—cats."

What did foils do for the SL33? "On our little test boats, the SL33s, the fastest we could make those go before we started putting the foil package on was about 24 knots, because we just ran out of stability, we

Cup-Speak

AC34. The 34th America's Cup Match, sailed in San Francisco, California, in 2013.

ACWS. America's Cup World Series, a series of fleet racing and match racing regattas that preceded the 2013 America's Cup, raced with AC45 yachts.

Bearaway (verb). To turn the boat from a higher course, nearer the wind, to a lower course, further from the wind, on the same tack. Also as a noun, the maneuver of bearing away.

Boundary Penalty. Punishment applied to Cup yachts for sailing past the edges of the race area by the America's Cup umpires. The course perimeter is set electronically by the race officials and an amber light flashes a warning onboard a race yacht as it approaches a boundary.

Box Rule. A set of rules that defines a class of yacht primarily in terms of maximum and minimum parameters, with minimal details on the shape of the yacht provided that it fits inside the "box." A box rule is a relatively open approach to a Class Rule in contrast to a formula-based rule that tries to control specific aspects of the shape of the yacht in more detail.

Class Rule. A set of design specifications which the race yachts must satisfy. The yachts that sailed in the 2013 America's Cup were catamarans of the AC72 Class Rule.

Clysar/Cryovac. Trade names for high-performance shrink wrap film used, among other applications, as the "sail cloth" for the rigid-wings of the AC45s and AC72s.

Code Zero. An asymmetric tight, reaching soft-sail, often used for sailing upwind.

Daggerboard, daggerfoil. The retractable appendages used by the AC72 yachts to resist leeway and to lift the hulls off the water.

Development Class. A type of Class Rule that permits significant modification to the yachts of the Class.

Fleet Race. A race among three or more yachts at the same time, in contrast to a match race.

Foil (noun). In AC34, the hydro-foiling element of a daggerboard or a rudder that provides a lifting force for the boat. Or, more broadly, used to refer to the entire daggerboard. In general, any airfoil or hydrofoil might be referred to as simply a foil.

Foil (verb). To sail a boat borne primarily on the lifting foils of the daggerboard and rudder, with the hulls clear of the water.

Flaps. Movable element or elements of the wingsail that trail behind the spar that help shape the camber of the wingsail. AC72 rules permitted any number of elements in trail, and in practice the flaps were divided into multiple panels to allow trimming the wing in different configurations varying with height.

Gennaker. An asymmetric tight, reaching soft sail, often used for sailing downwind or reaching.

Gybe, gybing. A maneuver whereby a yacht that is sailing downwind or reaching turns its stern through the wind.

Hook. To gain leeward position on the same tack and use right-of-way rules to gain control over the windward boat, forcing them to luff into the wind or tack. Primarily a tactic for AC72s during the pre-start.

Knot. Shorthand for one nautical mile per hour: 1 nautical mile equals about 1.15 statute miles.

Layline. The direct line of travel which allows a boat to reach (lay) the mark or gate on the most effective point of sail, without having to make additional tacks or gybes. A boat that hasn't reached the layline upwind can't reach the mark yet. A boat sailing past the layline has unnecessarily sailed extra distance.

Match Race. A race between two yachts.

Nautical Mile. 6,076.12 feet, which is longer than the statute mile of 5,280 feet by about 15%.

Platform. The hulls, cross beams, and bracing structure of an AC72, but not the wingsail or rigging.

Soft Sail. Traditional flexible sails. On an AC72, only the jib, gennaker, and code zero were soft sails.

Spar. On a wingsail, the forward element which provides the structural support of the wing in addition to playing an aerodynamic role.

Starboard Tack. On a point of sail where the sails are on the port side of the boat and the wind is coming over the starboard side.

Port Tack. On a point of sail where the sails are on the starboard side of the boat and the wind is coming over the port side.

To Tack, or Tacking. When sailing upwind, to change direction from port to starboard tack or vice-versa by turning the bow through the eye of the wind.

Wingmast. Usually meant broadly to refer to the wingsail, or just to the wing spar, though more precisely a wingmast is any mast that is large enough in profile to generate lift. Wing masts were developed on beach cats in the 1960s, with soft sails trailing behind them, and were forerunners of the complete wingsail.

Wingsail. AC72 mainsail, with a rigid articulating structure consisting of the spar and flaps, covered with heat-shrink film.

ran out of righting moment," says Morrelli. "By the time we got the full package on, those boats can go over 40. So we added 16 knots of top end to the little boat."

HELMING AN AC72: "IT'S HYPER"

Once an America's Cup team made their design bets and put their boat on the water, the size, speed, and power of the large foiling cats changed the game for helmsmen, too.

"You have to be super-careful because it's super-controllable," Morrelli said. "You can throw the boys off the back of the boat by flicking them. When you are rotating the boat about the daggerboard . . . there's no resistance."

Getting the right sort of person on the helm was a priority, made more difficult because there was no proven pool of AC72 foiling skippers. Teams had to figure out which sailors had the skill set to excel. While ORACLE TEAM USA's James Spithill and ETNZ's Dean Barker transitioned to multihulls from experience in America's Cup Class monohulls, most of the new talent came from small high-tech dinghies, either foilers or trapeze boats that are high velocity and physically intense.

"That's why I think we've seen this really healthy transition to the 49er sailors," Morrelli said. "Because they were born at the end of a flicking tiller, you get an innate sense of that pressure point. . . .

"That's obviously where the 49er sailors came from. We're almost transitioning, where a lot of the guys in my generation may be surpassed as we go to foiling, and this 49er crowd, the Moth crowd, is going to be the drivers of the next go-around."

Beyond the sensitivity needed just to get the boats cranked up to speed, AC72 helmsmen must also bring the anticipation and tactical awareness to manage all that energy around the course. Match racing at 40 to 50 knots is a recalibration of the normal scale of yachting experience. Ten seconds down the racecourse is 600 to 700 feet away.

"It's more like aiming a rocket," Morrelli said. "You're not really sailing a boat. You are looking at targets and you are aiming. There's no trimming going on anymore. You basically set the thing and go. You grind the jibs down; they're self-tacking. You grind them down, and they are staying. And you are aiming the boat to hit the target. The only one trimmer is the wing trimmer. He's basically trimming for twist. The things are so fast it's only when they are whacked up, way overpowered, that they are dumping the mainsheet."

"It's probably like F1 [Formula 1, racecar driving]," Morrelli said. "A real good F1 driver has feeling that a normal human being doesn't have."

There was no precedent for racing boats like these around the buoys, and barely any for sailing boats like this at all. Nobody's ever really done it before and everybody's learning.

NINE ORACLE TEAM USA's Penalty

On July 26, 2013, America's Cup Regatta Management (ACRM) personnel preparing the AC45 class yachts for the Red Bull Youth America's Cup regatta discovered something strange on the Team BAR AC45. The forward kingpost, a compression strut on the underside of the boat, was unusually heavy—about five pounds heavier than a standard one. When the Measurement Committee examined the inside of the kingpost, they found a mix of resin and lead tailings. This was a startling discovery because the AC45 Class rules forbade adding weights to the kingposts. Any additional weights could be added only in a specified area below the chainplates in either hull (see illustration on page 128).

The Measurement Committee immediately notified ORACLE TEAM USA (OTUSA), the owner of the Team BAR (Ben Ainslie Racing) AC45. ORACLE TEAM USA launched its internal investigation and on August 4 they reported the issue to the International Jury, which began their own investigation. Further examination showed that the BAR AC45 wasn't the only boat that appeared to have modified kingposts.

And with that began a falling of dominoes that rocked the America's Cup.

On August 7, Ben Ainslie, skipper of Team BAR, who was "surprised, disappointed, disgusted, and angry at what had happened," notified the jury that his team wished to retire after finishing the America's Cup World Series regattas. Ainslie elaborated that "BAR was loaned the AC45 for competition by OTUSA and the boat was prepared/maintained by OTUSA. As skipper of the boat, I had no knowledge whatsoever that the boat was being raced out of measurement."

The next day, ORACLE TEAM USA also voluntarily asked to be retired retroactively from the ACWS series, and they publicly admitted "that prior to racing in the regattas the yachts were modified without the permission of the Measurement Committee." The changes to the boats reportedly extended back to include the last four of the ACWS regattas, affecting the results of two ACWS seasons. But at the same time, OTUSA claimed "the modifications had no impact on the performance of the boats."

Russell Coutts explained: "After the discovery, we had our designers run the VPP to determine the impact of the weight. I think the finding was the weight would induce something like a 1/100th of a degree angle change to the boat. The performance impact was hardly measurable. It induced a near insignificant improvement upwind and a similarly small detriment to downwind speed."

The jury requested a detailed report from the measurement committee and began interviews and hearings to investigate what had taken place.

First it was up to the jury to weigh the facts. The International Jury consisted of five members: David Tillett (Australia), Bryan Willis (Great Britain), Josje Hofland (The Netherlands), John Doerr (Great Britain), and Graham McKenzie (New Zealand). While the members shared the experience as an ISAF (International Sailing Federation) judge or ISAF committee member, they had diverse backgrounds and experience that included engineering, law, and liberal arts. David Tillett, the chairman, a lawyer, had been an international yachting judge for over 20 years; this was his fourth America's Cup as juror.

In mid-August, the jury investigated the issue in the context of OTUSA having allegedly violated Rule 69 of the ISAF Racing Rules of Sailing, America's Cup Edition.

69 ALLEGATIONS OF GROSS MISCONDUCT

69.1 Action by the Jury

(a) When the Jury, from its own observation or a report received from any source, believes that a person associated with a Competitor may have committed a gross breach of a *rule*, good manners or sportsmanship, or may have brought the sport into disrepute, it may call a hearing. The Jury shall promptly inform the individual in writing of the alleged misconduct and of the time and place of the hearing. If the individual provides good reason for being unable to attend the hearing, the Jury shall reschedule it.

(b) If the Jury decides that the person committed the alleged misconduct it shall either:

(i) warn the person or

(ii) impose a penalty by excluding the person and, when appropriate, disqualifying a *yacht*, from a race or the remaining races or all races of the series, or by taking other action within its jurisdiction. A disqualification under this *rule* shall not be excluded from the *yacht's* series score.

The jury interviewed sixteen members of OTUSA and five members of ACRM, and examined the evidence. On August 19, they decided to also consider if OTUSA violated Article 60 of the Protocol as well. Article 60 is aimed at protecting the reputation of the America's Cup by prohibiting conduct that is prejudicial and detrimental to the regatta and the sport of sailing.

Protocol Article 60.1
PROTECTING THE REPUTATION OF THE AMERICA'S CUP
The favorable reputation of the America's Cup, its regattas, events, selected venues, Officials, sponsors, commercial partners and its Competitors is a valuable asset and creates financial and other tangible and intangible benefits for all. Accordingly, each Competitor shall not (and shall use its best efforts to ensure that any team member, owner, officer, employee, contractor, affiliate, agent or representative of the Competitor shall not) and each Official shall not make or cause to be made, or authorize or endorse, any public statement, or engage in any other act or conduct or any activity, in each case, on or off the water, that is prejudicial or detrimental to or against the welfare or the best interests of the America's Cup, or the sport of sailing, or that may impair public confidence in the honest and orderly conduct of the America's Cup, any Event, or in the integrity and good character of any Competitor, Official, selected venue, sponsor or other commercial partner of the America's Cup. Conduct contrary to the welfare or the best interests of the America's Cup includes, but is not limited to, public statements that unreasonably attack or disparage a regatta related to the America's Cup, an Event, a selected venue, a funder, a sponsor, a commercial partner of the Event or a Competitor, another Competitor, an Official, or the commercial viability or integrity of the America's Cup or any of its regattas or events, but responsible expressions of legitimate disagreement are not prohibited.

The result of the jury's investigation led to the jury identifying six OTUSA members who allegedly committed gross misconduct:

Bryce Ruthenberg (OTUSA yacht rigger)
Andrew Walker (OTUSA yacht rigger)
Kyle Langford (OTUSA sailor and yacht rigger)
Matt Mitchell (OTUSA sailor and yacht rigger)
Dirk de Ridder (OTUSA sailor)
Sailor X (OTUSA sailor, name redacted, see Notes, page 208)

On August 26 to 29, the jury held hearings to determine if OTUSA as a team had breached RRSAC 69 and Protocol Article 60, and, if so, to prescribe penalties.

The jury took testimony from the six OTUSA members who had allegedly committed misconduct, plus Nick Nicholson (chairman of the measurement committee), Russell Coutts, Jimmy Spithill, and four other members of the team.

On September 3, the jury published their findings. They revealed five incidents of breaching the AC45 Class rule.

1. A bag containing lead tailings was placed inside the forward kingpost on OTUSA Boat 4 (a.k.a. Boat Spithill) at the Newport regatta. The placement of the bag was established at the Jury hearing but the Jury was unable to discover when it was removed, who removed it or why it was no longer in the forward kingpost.
2. A bag of heavy ferrous tailings was found inside the main kingpost in Boat 4. The Jury was unable to discover when it was placed there or who put it there.
3. Lead tailings and resin were added to the forward kingpost on boat BAR.
4. The lengths of each of the main kingposts used on Boats 4 and 5 were found to have been extended by the addition of a 8mm carbon composite plate ("C-plate") without receiving authorization from the Measurement Committee.
5. The top ends of the main kingposts of Boats 4 and 5 were fitted with 80mm spigots without permission from the Measurement Committee. All other boats that raced in the ACWS regattas were found to have fittings with the standard 15mm spigots.

The jury concluded the following: One, adding weights to the kingpost enhanced performance to a small degree; Two, the extended kingposts (with the "C-plate") on Boats 4 and 5 would assist in straightening the spine if the kingposts were dipped down toward the middle; Three, the addition of the 80mm spigots on Boats 4 and 5 improved reliability, as the standard short-length spigots had been identified as having problems.

The jury cleared the team's upper management, including chief executive Russell Coutts, skipper Jimmy Spithill, and general manager Grant Simmer of any wrongdoing.

But they found five OTUSA members in breach of Racing Rule 69 by altering the placement of weights and changing the measurements of the boats.

The jury dismissed wing trimmer Dirk de Ridder and yacht riggers Bryce Ruthenberg and Andrew Walker from the event. They suspended grinder Matthew Mitchell for the first four races and delivered a warning to wing trimmer Kyle Langford.

The jury's report stated that de Ridder gave instruction to Ruthenberg and Walker to add weight to the forward kingpost of Boat 4 at the Newport regatta. The jury also felt that de Ridder had not cooperated fully with the investigation. Despite the fact that de Ridder signed an interview

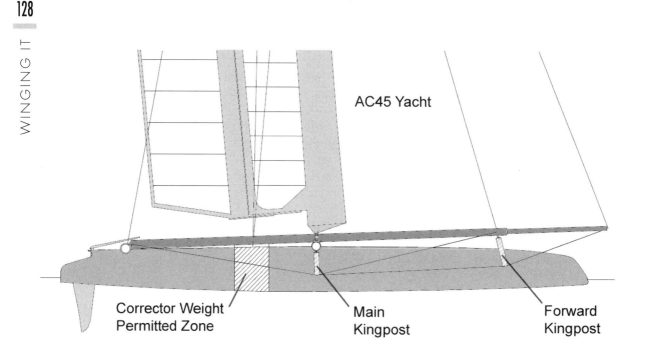

AC45 Yacht

Corrector Weight
Permitted Zone

Main
Kingpost

Forward
Kingpost

AC45 showing the permitted area for corrector weights, and the location of the kingposts. (Illustration: © 2013 CupInfo.com)

statement from mid-August, the jury believed he had given conflicting testimony during the hearing.

The jury deemed that both Mitchell and Langford should have been aware that it was a violation of the AC45 class rules to add weight. But given Langford's inexperience (he was 24 at the time of the hearing and it was his first America's Cup), and his cooperation with the investigation, Langford was only given a warning. Mitchell was an experienced Cup sailor, with OTUSA being his fifth Cup campaign.

In addition to the penalties against the five members, the jury also levied two other penalties against the team itself for violating Article 60.1 of the Protocol.

The first was a two-point penalty (two-race penalty) against OTUSA to be applied in the America's Cup match: OTUSA would now have to win eleven races to win the Cup, as opposed to nine. David Tillett, the chairman, said that the jury arrived at the "two-points" because it was "a question of balance: one would be tokenism, four potentially crushing. Two was considered significant . . . and appropriate for the conduct involved." Deduction of races was not unprecedented. In the 2000 Louis Vuitton Series, American Challenger Team Dennis Conner was penalized one point, representing one race, for using an improperly sourced rudder (the rudder was made in Australia, a breach of the rules since the boat had to be built in the country of the challenge). In 2003, the American Challenger One World was penalized one point, again representing one race, in the Louis Vuitton Cup semi-finals for conduct by staff who illegally obtained yacht design information from the New Zealand team.

Second, OTUSA was fined $250,000 ($125,000 to go to the Andrew Simpson Sailing Foundation and the other $125,000 to a section 501(c)(3) charitable organization selected by the mayor of San Francisco to provide support to at-risk youth in the San Francisco Bay area).

Russell Coutts called the penalties "outrageous, ridiculous" and "grossly unfair." "We've got penalized two points in the match for something that a few of our sailors did on an AC45 more than a year ago without the knowledge or approval of management or the skippers," Coutts said. "I think it's an outrageous decision."

Public speculation on penalties had ranged from a mere monetary fine all the way up to forfeiting the America's Cup to Emirates Team New Zealand. There was no easy answer for the jury when it came to deciding the sanctions against the team. No amount of cheating was acceptable, but what should be the balance between the misconduct and the punishment?

Was it fair to punish a team in the America's Cup for something that had taken place in the ACWS? With the ACWS series concluded, and OTUSA's entries retroactively withdrawn, the jury had no punishments of consequence that could be confined to the ACWS alone, had that been an acceptable course of action in their view. It is important to note that, while it was a series of exhibition races in a one-design warm-up class, the ACWS was part of the America's Cup event defined by the Protocol of the America's Cup. Furthermore, the penalties that the jury applied were within the guidelines established in Article 15.4 of the Protocol. Therefore, the jury's penalties, and the fact that they impacted the Cup match, were in compliance with the Protocol.

The fallout and penalties that resulted from the cheating scandal were significant because they nearly prevented ORACLE TEAM USA from successfully defending the Cup. The expulsion of wing trimmer Dirk de Ridder was likely to have a negative impact on performance, at least initially, because his replacement, Kyle Langford, had not sailed extensively with Jimmy Spithill prior to the match. Glenn Ashby, the wing trimmer on Emirates Team New Zealand, said: "I know Dirk personally and I worked with a lot of the guys over there in the last America's Cup with the coaching and sailing. He's a big loss for those guys."

Perhaps just as significantly, the disruption at the highest levels of the OTUSA leadership caused by the investigation and hearings in August also hobbled the Defender's two-boat training program in the weeks leading up to the race, distracting key personnel from exclusively focusing on preparing the boat and crew for the Match.

TEN Louis Vuitton Cup Finals

AUGUST 17 TO 30: A BEST OF 13 SERIES

It was once again a match between Emirates Team New Zealand and Luna Rossa. But this time the winner would go on to meet ORACLE TEAM USA in the America's Cup match.

The Louis Vuitton Finals was viewed, in part, as a test to determine how far the Italians had progressed since July. Luna Rossa's match against Artemis yielded increasingly aggressive pre-starts and improved boat-handling skills, including reliably foiling through gybes. The Italians had also installed a new wingsail and made other modifications for the finals.

Meanwhile ETNZ wasn't sitting still, exiting the Round Robins early to gain more time to put the boat into the shed for their own tune-ups; they also found time to conduct some additional on-the-water testing.

Expectations were for Luna Rossa to be sailing at a much higher percentage of their potential, but most observers expected ETNZ to beat them again. ETNZ was even regarded as the favorite to win the America's Cup.

But if Luna Rossa could press the New Zealanders hard enough, it would be evidence that the Kiwis were not going to be an unassailable Challenger.

The seven-leg racecourse was history now. The Louis Vuitton Cup Finals and the America's Cup would both be using only the five-leg Course 1. The five-leg courses were projected to last 25 to 30 minutes, depending on conditions, and allowing for the logistics of resetting for a second race would allow two races per day to fit within the scheduled broadcasting slot.

This change to the two-per-day race format, which required an increased level of crew fitness, opened the possibility of tactical opportunities created by their opponents making errors due to fatigue—not to mention an increased risk of gear failures. Likewise the effects of gear damage could cascade from the first race of the day into the second.

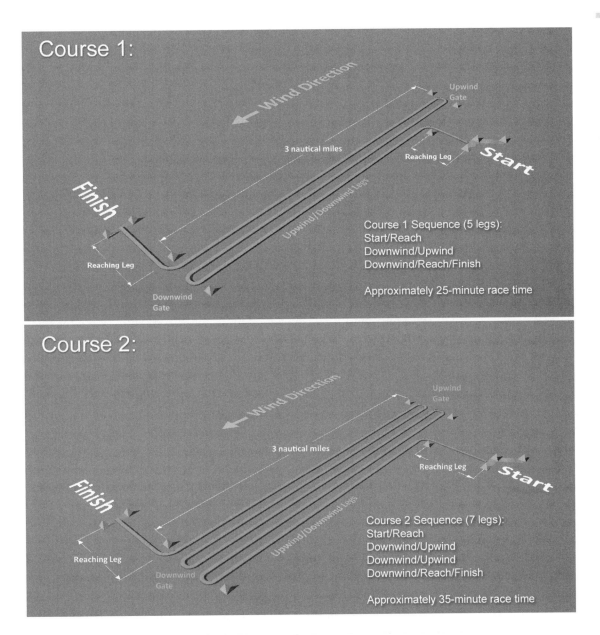

Course 1:

Wind Direction

Upwind Gate

3 nautical miles

Reaching Leg

Start

Finish

Upwind/Downwind Legs

Reaching Leg

Course 1 Sequence (5 legs):
Start/Reach
Downwind/Upwind
Downwind/Reach/Finish

Approximately 25-minute race time

Downwind Gate

Course 2:

Wind Direction

Upwind Gate

3 nautical miles

Reaching Leg

Start

Finish

Upwind/Downwind Legs

Reaching Leg

Course 2 Sequence (7 legs):
Start/Reach
Downwind/Upwind
Downwind/Upwind
Downwind/Reach/Finish

Approximately 35-minute race time

Downwind Gate

(© 2013 CupInfo.com)

Since ETNZ and Luna Rossa had spent July skirmishing, with only four official races between them and all won handily by ETNZ, the Louis Vuitton Cup Final would be the big test of how much both teams had improved.

Though they almost always looked a step behind the Kiwis in the Round Robin, Luna Rossa showed good crew work and a better speed in the semi-finals, much improved from the opening rounds.

It would have been shocking if Luna Rossa eliminated ETNZ, for no other reason than that they were sailing different generations of boats, and from the same group of designers.

There was no reason to expect a change in tactics. Starts had been limited in engagement between the two teams, generally some luffing away from the line with the leeward boat trying to hook the windward boat at the right time, making a run for the starting line while the other was recovering. The wrong kind of damage in the pre-start could put an end to a team's participation, and was a huge risk to be taken, especially considering the small advantages to be gained. Anything more than a small repair, especially if it involved structural issues, might not be repairable in time. But even the chance of being eliminated via collision or accident might not stop fighting instincts from coming into play. Luna Rossa's Chris Draper, fresh from putting some moves on Artemis, would probably want to try to put ETNZ at a disadvantage. If the Kiwis were confident they had the faster boat, they might avoid getting caught up.

Race 1, Saturday, August 17

Beginning in Race 1, the Bay's current ebbed, a departure from the flood tide that occurred more often during the semi-finals. This changed the tactical picture, especially on the upwind legs.

Wind limits were raised from the semi-final to the final, to 21 knots, plus or minus the speed of the current (subtracting from the limit for a flood tide, adding to the limit for an ebb tide). On Saturday, August 17, as the finals were about to begin, the wind was averaging just a bit too high, 19.4 knots over an adjusted 19-knot limit, prompting a 20-minute delay from the Race Committee. Nobody was happier than Luna Rossa. The lifting fittings on their starboard daggerboard had broken loose, with the board delaminating at the attachment point. Starting the race at 1:30 instead of 1:10 gave them just enough time to rig a quick repair with glue.

There was no serious pre-start engagement, and ETNZ got away at the start slightly ahead of Luna Rossa. ETNZ rounded Mark 1 first, but as the boats bore off the wind and headed downwind Luna Rossa throttled back. Their daggerboard had failed again.

"When we bore away, the board went down and we saw the pin coming out again," said Francesco Bruni, tactician on Luna Rossa. "When you have no control of the board's up and down, it's basically race over."

ETNZ expanded their lead as Luna Rossa limped along far behind. As they did so, speculation quickly turned to whether ITA would be able to start in Race 2. Each team was allowed the option to postpone the second race of the day, but just one time per match. No reason was required. ITA was hoping for the wind to pick up again before the start of Race 2, and stay over the limit long enough for the second race to be cancelled.

ETNZ only had to complete the course to go up 1-0. But the race was not over yet. Just after rounding the top gate, ETNZ fell off her foils at speed, stuffing the bows underwater for over half their length, slam-

ming the boat to a halt. The wave of water threw two grinders overboard and caused some damage to the boat. ETNZ crew Chris Ward and Rob Waddell were rescued from the water. Parts of fairings, the end plate, and trampoline were ripped loose. However, ETNZ was able to finish with just nine crew members still on board and take the first win.

Luna Rossa Challenge in Race 1 of the Louis Vuitton Cup Final. (© 2013 ACEA/Photo: Gilles Martin-Raget)

Skipper Dean Barker had seen that the Italians were in trouble on Leg 2, but the New Zealander carried on.

"There are things we want to try when we get the opportunity so we were mucking around with different things," Barker said. "The top mark was supposedly going to be a routine maneuver."

"As we started turning down, there was quite a distinct puff on the water," said Barker. "There was a good increase as we bore off and we really stuck it in. You're hanging on, that's for sure, but it didn't feel as bad as it may have looked. First, we made sure the guys were safe, especially the two who went over the side. Then we set about securing all our loose bits. The guys did a very good job of getting rid of the damaged fairing and putting some trampoline on to cover the hole that was left. We were ready to go again."

Chris McAsey, grinder on ETNZ, recounted the incident: "I'm on the forward pedestal, behind Jeremy Lomas and we were the first guys to go under. The first thing I was thinking about was just holding on, then the next thing I know there's a wall of water coming at me. I felt an arm link behind me—that was Derek Saward, who was also trying to hold onto Rob Waddell, who was on his way over. Behind him was Chris Ward, who unfortunately no one was holding onto! But it's hard to know exactly what happened because now, it's just a blur."

It was a reminder of how quick fortunes could turn. Observers speculated whether ORACLE TEAM USA, with narrow hulls upfront, would have survived such a plunge.

Having survived a potential capsize, ETNZ only had to strip off some damaged elements of the boat, looking a bit ungainly, but *Aotearoa*, ETNZ's AC72, was ready for the second race.

"The damage isn't bad—it will be a late night but it's just fairings, nothing structural," said ETNZ's McAsey. "We've always had a lot of faith in the boat. I've said that with the tragedy that happened here in May that you really had to look inside yourself, to see if you really wanted to get back on the boat after that. We all felt the same, that it was good to go with our boat and this just strengthens that."

Luna Rossa, unable to make the needed repair on the water, won a reprieve as the wind continued to rise over the limit and racing was done for the day.

Race 2, Sunday, August 18

The issue lurking on Day 2 was whether all the damage from Race 1 was repaired on both boats. Luna Rossa had fixed their daggerboard attachment. ETNZ said that careful inspection took place overnight to be sure nothing structural was overstressed. A strong ebb tide kept the wind limit down near 18.8 knots.

At the gun, ETNZ started close and to windward of Luna Rossa, drag racing them across the line, spoiling the Italian wing's air flow enough for the Kiwis to pull ahead. The Kiwis then broke the overlap, and sailed down directly in front of Luna Rossa before reaching the first mark. It was a powerful move: Dean Barker was able to avoid being luffed by Chris Draper because his boat accelerated so fast, thus rolling over the opponent to lead 10 seconds at the mark. A few feet too far back and Luna Rossa could have held them out at the mark.

ETNZ gained downwind, out to a 23-second delta at the downwind gate. Luna Rossa wasn't losing much, but they hadn't shown they could gain yet, either.

Then it became apparent that ETNZ wasn't tacking. They didn't appear to be racing, instead just nursing the boat upwind. Their hydraulic system wasn't responding, leaving the crew unable to trim the wing or control the angle of the foils. It wasn't even an option to ease the wing and let it swing free in the wind: the mechanics of ETNZ's wingsail needed hydraulic pressure to move in either direction. Their tender was quickly at *Aotearoa*'s side, technicians coming aboard as the AC72 sailed past the top of the course. Outside help is forbidden during racing, of course, but ETNZ had no way to safely maneuver the boat when they could not control the wing, and certainly not with winds in the high teens. Help was needed first to get control of the boat, even though it disqualified them in the race, and then to be ready for the second race of the day if possible.

Luna Rossa, meanwhile, now took their turn to sail to the finish, completed the course uneventfully and tying the match at one point apiece.

The problem on *Aotearoa* was traced to a small battery in the electronics of the hydraulic system—a part worth just a few dollars had sidelined the boat. The wall of water from the boat's plunge the day before was not thought to be at fault, but somehow the shore crew's detailed maintenance review the night before had missed the failing power cell. With a fresh battery swapped in, ETNZ was ready for the second race of the day, but the wind was now over the limit again, climbing as it followed the normal daily San Francisco Bay cycle.

Max Sirena, skipper, Luna Rossa, remarked about the starting tactics: "To win the start to leeward in a big breeze, you have to be quite ahead of them, otherwise it's really easy for the windward boat to roll—unless you're really tight to leeward and then you can luff."

Cracks in ETNZ's armor had finally appeared—nearly capsizing in one race and dropping out of a second race with mechanical failure. They looked faster than Luna Rossa, though by a smaller margin than during the Round Robins. Luna Rossa's crew work was catching up to ETNZ level.

Race 3, Monday, August 19

Fatigue of preparation, racing, and recovering from multiple days of damage was threatening to catch up with the sailors, and the shore crews, too. Two days with breakdowns, meaning a lot of time on the water followed by more time in the shop, and the Day 3 question was whether the boats were fully repaired and reliable enough to finish two races in the same day. There were even complaints from some observers, questioning the complexity of the boats, which overlooked the goals of a development class. A boat that never broke was probably overdesigned and slow.

This was the dual purpose of the Louis Vuitton Cup, putting the challengers to the test, making the final Challenger stronger, not just eliminating the slowest candidates. The America's Cup match was also a two-race-per day schedule, and the boats and crews would be pushed at least as hard. For now, there was still time to make the boats fast, find out what broke, and fix it.

Race 3 offered another of those opportunities before long. Luna Rossa was again keeping pace with ETNZ, just 20 seconds behind at the downwind gate, but tacking coming out of the mark they damaged the bottom of the wing and had to withdraw.

"There are a few sheaves on the bottom of the wing, in the control panel," Luna Rossa skipper Max Sirena said, explaining the problem that caused them to drop out of the race. "The control cable is attached to the flaps that are coming down to the base, and this sheave broke."

Observers who had previously been critical of the AC72s became even more vocal now, questioning the design of the boats, and why the cats were breaking this far into the regatta. Others felt that the sailors were going at it perhaps too hard and that they needed to back off to preserve the boats.

"It is so frustrating because we want to do a full race," he said. "The conditions are pretty tough for this boat—they're pretty fragile. It's the first generation, so maybe if we continue with this boat, in the next Cup we will have fewer problems. When it's a new class, you always have breakdowns. But I really am not surprised because we really are pushing the boat hard for the first time.

"It's hard for people to understand, but when you are sailing around the course alone, even in 20 knots, you are a little bit scared. Anything can happen, like putting the bow down, which happened to Team New Zealand. Then, when you have another boat next to you, the scared goes away because you want to beat the other guy. So you push way harder than normally and unfortunately, because we are sailing a new class of boat, there is a lot unknown and we discover that even in the race. But there is no other choice, we go out and race, and if the boat breaks, it breaks. If you are scared to break the boat, you should change jobs."

ETNZ was handed another point, now up 2-1, with five more points to go.

After three straight days of sailing and a breakdown in every race, the next day, Tuesday, was a lay day, sorely needed for sailing crews to refresh and shore crews to go over the yachts yet again.

Observers were holding their breath to see if the two boats could complete the same race, which had not been an issue in the Round Robin provided they both started.

Lost in the disappointment from Monday's fizzled Race 3 was the hint from Luna Rossa that they thought they had been faster downwind at times than ETNZ. A good puff of wind or less adverse current might be the dismissive explanation from some quarters, pointing to the 300m lead the Kiwis carried by the bottom of the downwind leg, but the Italian crew was genuinely excited at what they saw, and Cup fans would be too if Luna Rossa were to roll past ETNZ in the same water.

Races 4 and 5, Wednesday, August 21

Winds for Wednesday were the lightest seen in the series, 13 to 14 knots at race time. Slacking current promised to give the teams plenty of room to work with for the start, without maximum flood or ebb tides pushing the boats around in the pre-start. The previous race had shown that a leeward position might be fine if you could hook underneath the opponent and luff them head-to-wind or further, but if the windward boat came back down and matched tacks before the gun, the advantage was largely gone.

Advantages at the start weren't going very far in any case, to date, on these courses. Barring breakage, the AC72 fundamentals of executing smooth crew work, sustaining foiling through gybes, minimizing tacks, and constant attention to managing the boat, especially in maneuvers, were still going to be the foundation of a win. That questions about boat-speed were in play was a credit to Luna Rossa, though the Kiwis didn't quite look worried yet.

In the Race 4 pre-start, ETNZ initially stayed below Luna Rossa trying to get a hook, but later disengaged and went above the Italians. On the first reach, ETNZ rolled over the top of Luna Rossa, leading by 12 seconds at Mark 1. New Zealand looked stronger in the light wind, and built a 33-second lead at the leeward gate. On the upwind leg, with ETNZ leading by over 400 meters, Luna Rossa committed a boundary penalty. The Kiwis stretched the lead and rounded the windward gate well ahead. New Zealand was much faster in lighter air and won by over a mile. New Zealand now led the series 3-1.

Race 5

Winds remained light in the second race, the sea breeze not building. The boats started tight together, Luna Rossa to windward, but not in position to blanket ETNZ, leaving the Kiwis the inside position at the first mark and another early lead. Heading downwind the boats were right on top of each other to the first gybe, but Luna Rossa's wing hung up and they lost ground, unable to sail the better angles with ETNZ. Still, good crew work kept it from getting worse.

At the downwind gate the delta was 18 seconds, the Kiwis turning left and the Italians turning right, heading inshore, but soon coming back together. Upwind the lead was down to 60 meters, with both boats nearly on top of each other out to the left boundary. Both were edging up onto their foils, screaming along. This was a boat race! Luna Rossa tacked, ETNZ followed. Midway across, ITA came back again, trying to stay in the better conditions, ETNZ trying to stay in phase and cover them. Luna Rossa tacked again, not wanting to mess with the boundary. ETNZ covered but could not maintain position, Luna Rossa was working them out of phase. It was an AC72 tacking duel, close tactical racing, the boats nearly foiling upwind.

ETNZ opened up the lead a little bit, but the race stayed close enough that if someone saved a tack getting to the gate, things could change. NZL turned right at the top gate, heading offshore for the favorable current downwind. ITA had to turn left at the gate, 1:06 behind, sailing inshore and fighting the current, looking for wind but not finding it. ETNZ's lead was soon about 1000 meters, just too far away, and they never looked back.

Despite the outcome, Luna Rossa's performance was earning respect.

"They've really stepped up their game and it's good, because we really need to be pushed," said ETNZ's tactician Ray Davies. "They did a nice job down the run and made some good decisions to make it really hard for us."

"We didn't sail that well in the first race, but in the second race we pushed the boat pretty hard and put some pressure on them," Max Sirena said. "The big difference today is they were able to hold us in a difficult position in the pre-start. They are doing a good job and there is something in the boat that is giving them the possibility to hold that position. We are hoping that if we can get to the reaching mark first, we can be in front at the bottom gate. We need to analyze the video and see if we can improve our speed on the first reaching leg."

Despite a final margin of 1 minute, 28 seconds, and the Italians now in a 1-4 hole for the Louis Vuitton Cup, the takeaway for the day was exciting. This was the first flash of AC72s really going at it head to head out on the racecourse, the upwind tacking duel of classic monohull match racing transferred to giant twenty-first-century multihulls, an achievement even some professional sailors and designers had said was impossible. The action didn't span the entire race, but it was electric while it lasted. "You can't match race multihulls," went the refrain, but now it was happening. Plus, both AC72s had completed back-to-back races. After so much criticism, frustration, and complaint, the 2013 America's Cup was starting to turn a corner.

Race 6, Friday, August 23

Racing resumed Friday with only one race—Race 6—on the agenda. The teams were thankful for the chance to concentrate on one race, and the luxury of having one lay day to prepare for it. Luna Rossa at least might have welcomed two lay days for the practice opportunities, which was briefly the subject of discussion between ACRM and the competitors, but only one rest day was agreed upon.

What Luna Rossa wanted even more were conditions in what they felt was their sweet spot: 16 to18 knots of wind. To win they also needed the combination of delivering great crew work, not breaking anything, and not being unlucky. That's been the standard checklist for America's Cup competitors going back over 100 years, and foils and wings didn't change it. A few mistakes by the opponent wouldn't hurt either.

But ETNZ was trying hard not to give them that mistake. Their submarine excursion showed how quickly even a little lapse could lead to trouble. But when Luna Rossa made things close in the last race, the Kiwis also showed that they still held a few cards in the tactics and speed departments, and they likely had plenty more left to reveal.

Flood current for Race 6 would make the pre-start wrestling more difficult, but the skippers and crews usually still felt pressure to do something aggressive. The psychological benefits of winning the start are probably overstated by broadcast commentators, and even over-weighted by the teams, if evaluated on a risk-reward basis. So far it was hard to win these races in the pre-start. That could more or less happen back in monohull days, where getting the favored side of a lopsided course and clocking a 30-second margin via putting a penalty on the other boat were advantages rarely overcome. In the Louis Vuitton Cup, speed, crew work, and tactics on the racecourse were telling the tale.

The closer the racing, though, the more the starts mattered, even in AC72s. ETNZ may have felt more driven now to engage either because Luna Rossa was getting faster, or because they wanted to prepare for the next opponent. ORACLE TEAM USA had been training and becoming increasingly enthusiastic in their practice starts. With the luxury of two boats to train with, OTUSA also had the benefit of a second boat already in service to fall back on if they damaged one.

At race time the winds were lighter than forecast, 14 to 17 knots. ETNZ, to windward, sailed over the top of Luna Rossa again at the start, passing them and getting into the early lead at Mark 1. Getting to leeward of ETNZ in the pre-start was becoming risky unless the leeward boat managed to hook them and luff them away from the line with perfect timing. Dean Barker and crew were too adept at accelerating the boat and putting the turbulent exhaust from their wing where it would most disturb the other boat.

ETNZ soon had a 300 meter lead and then stretched it to 500 meters before reaching the leeward gate. With the flood tide, tactical options for the upwind leg were few. The only partial relief from the strong currents coming into the bay was to tack early on Leg 3 and sail near Alcatraz Island where there was some relief from the current. The alternative path would have been to sail immediately for the shoreline after rounding the gate, but the flood current made that rounding unattractive, though it didn't stop some race observers from criticizing Bruni, the Italian tactician, for not trying something else. A trailing boat had two bad options: follow the leader with little opportunity to gain, or an even worse option —fight a strong current, and lose.

Going to the windward mark, ETNZ was working on foiling their boat upwind again, a trick still not perfected while maintaining a high enough angle to the wind to make the technique pay off consistently, but still signs were there that ETNZ had another level of performance on tap. ETNZ didn't get much farther away, but by the time the Italians rounded the upwind mark, there was little that Luna Rossa could do. The boats could sail so deep to the leeward mark, gybing just a couple times on the way, that a sizable lead was all but impregnable under normal conditions. The racecourse, in a flood tide, gave few tactical possibilities for a trailing boat. ETNZ won by 1:56.

The writing on the wall was becoming clear, though, New Zealand was plain faster.

"It would've been nice to have had a better start," said Chris Draper, Luna Rossa's skipper. "We can talk about the start as much as we want, but the cold reality is they're going to sail past us whether they're to windward or leeward."

Now down 5-1, Luna Rossa's mission was coming down to just trying to win another race.

"We're going to give it everything we have in the last two races," said Draper. "We're very aware that we're a bit more competitive when the breeze is up. It would be good to have two races tomorrow and it certainly would be good if there were a bit more breeze."

Meanwhile, ETNZ was trying to make the most of the Louis Vuitton Cup Final, honing their tools for the America's Cup match.

"The boat's going well. We have our modes figured out reasonably well across the range," said Barker. "We're always learning. We were mucking around at one stage on the upwind leg. It's quite interesting the way the boat responds in different conditions."

Race 7, Saturday, August 24

With the finals standing at 5-1, ETNZ needed just two more wins to reach the necessary seven points, and could close out the Louis Vuitton Cup on Saturday.

Luna Rossa was hanging their hopes on lots of wind to extend the series. And wind they did get on Saturday. A number of predictions had conditions ranging "from *fresh* to *frightening*," in the words of Regatta Director Iain Murray. The racecourse area on San Francisco Bay alternates from weather conditions that run like clockwork to a micro-climate roulette defying reliable predictions. Race Day arrived, and the upper wind range settled into the low 20s, just enough to race.

For the Louis Vuitton Final, average winds had to stay under a 21-knot limit for 15 minutes before the principal race officer (PRO) could start an LVC Final Race, plus or minus adjustments for the current. Once the race had started, though, the winds still had to stay under the limit for a five-minute average or the race would be abandoned. The exception was that a race could not be stopped for high wind once at least one of the boats had begun the second-to-last leg, which was the final downwind leg, Leg 4 on this course. An abandoned race would not count and would be re-sailed.

Saturday's flood current added about 2 knots of breathing room to the wind limit for the first race, and if they raced in the permitted 23 knots it would be the windiest AC72 race to date. The current would be diminishing in the second race, bringing the wind limits down slightly. If winds were right near the threshold, however, it would be a tense time for sailors and fans as to whether the finish line, or Leg 4 actually, could be reached before the race was scratched.

Higher winds also emphasized boat handling and keeping gear intact. Mistakes in these strong conditions led to breakage. The mitigating factor was that both teams had trained in Auckland in much higher winds than they'd been permitted to race in San Francisco, so they were not without experience in stronger air. The boats had originally been designed for winds into the 30s, and the trade-offs in hulls and wings especially had been engineered to balance performance across that spectrum. Did Luna

Rossa's preferred racing conditions extend beyond the high teens into the low 20s, though? It might become spectacular racing for a while if NZL and ITA could complete a race in that sort of wind. And more so if Luna Rossa's performance in a "fresh" breeze was what they thought it was.

Race 7 started with a drag race to the first mark, and a 4-second delta with ETNZ in the lead; then the boats did their bearaways and headed downwind on the inshore side, with a slim lead of 130 meters for ETNZ. The Italians followed ETNZ briefly, then tacked away, and the Kiwis matched them. Luna Rossa gained on a better gybe. The lead narrowed to 100 meters. Luna Rossa soon gybed back, possibly looking to take another piece out of the lead, but gybed poorly and lost ground instead, the lead growing from 100m to 300m. Then Luna Rossa started taking it back, sailing higher speeds than ETNZ even though the Kiwis appeared to be sailing with a more favorable flood current. Luna Rossa's gaining downwind gave hope that they could eventually roll up to ETNZ and maybe pass. The higher winds might be their sweet spot.

ETNZ managed a 27-second delta at the downwind gate, but Luna Rossa was still looking fast. Upwind ETNZ turned right, and Luna Rossa turned right. ITA saved a tack. The lead was down to 200m. Then ETNZ began to stretch the lead again, aided by a Luna Rossa tack, the gap now in the 300 to 400m range. Toward the top of the leg, ETNZ pulled out to 700m. With downwind speeds so much higher, the downwind lead would be a multiple of that.

Upwind, ETNZ had built a lead that was going to be insurmountable; the delta at the upwind gate was 1:56 for NZL by the time Luna Rossa got there. Even with the Italians' extra speed downwind, it wouldn't be remotely enough to close up the distance they had already given away. The finish delta was 1:58. ETNZ won Race 7, one win away from going to the America's Cup.

Saturday wasn't going to be the day for that win, however, as the wind average continued rising, following the normal daily San Francisco Bay cycle.

The higher wind had shown that Luna Rossa had good speed in the right situations. There were just limited places to make use of it.

"The boat was going pretty well downwind, the problem is there's a one-way track upwind," said Franceso Bruni, Luna Rossa's tactician. "There is so much to do and the leading boat is just going to extend. I thought about going to the shore after tack one, but I thought it was too risky a solution. After that, there was not much we could have done differently."

"I still say there is a little bit of a difference in performance upwind. Downwind I think we can be quite competitive, definitely better today than yesterday."

It was the starts that were beginning to figure big finally, and Barker was giving ETNZ the early advantage by winning the starts. The first boat to the reaching mark would turn downwind with a slight lead, and likely be in a position to defend from ahead on the single upwind leg. Barring mistakes, now that yachts were closer in performance, a trailing boat had to work very hard to get out of a hole.

Bruni remarked, "I would have loved to start to windward but that is not easy with Dean Barker when he enters on the port side, which is kind of the controlling position. He had a perfect direction going back to the line so there was not much we could have done differently. But definitely the start made a difference; I think the windward position was key today, as yesterday. Apart from that, I think we made a couple of mistakes with the boards up and down downwind, but I think we did sail pretty close to 100 percent."

The AC72s were putting on a decent show now, and the ability the crews were demonstrating in managing the boats was a phenomenal achievement. Some of the mainstream press in San Francisco was writing outright dismissive coverage of the racing, suggesting in one bitter article that since Luna Rossa wasn't winning enough that they should quit. That level of analysis, if that's the proper term, encapsulated everything that the uninitiated didn't understand about sailing at the level of the America's Cup, especially in 2013.

Chris Draper, helmsman of Luna Rossa, commented, "It was full on, probably the windiest race we've seen. Pushing the boats in that breeze and sailing the boats hard in that wind is impossible to get over, even to people who have sailed all their lives, what these boats are like to sail. It's just incredible. Even though we weren't winning and the Kiwis were sailing away from us, it was still an amazing race to do. Ten years ago, we'd have set the world speed record! And we're racing these boats around marks."

Dean Barker on ETNZ shared Draper's excitement for sailing AC72s in such conditions. "It's been a little while since we raced in this much breeze, but it was awesome sailing in these boats," Barker said. "You don't focus too much at the speed, but you know you're going fast. There are different types of vibrations as you go through different speeds, but you definitely know when it's really ripping, the thing feels like it's going to shake itself to pieces."

He also pointed out that, for them, it wasn't just about winning, it was a development game all the way. "There're always improvements and gains to be had so I think it's a matter of using what you've got, and developing," said Barker. "That's the big challenge. The more racing, the more time you go around this course, there's always areas you know you can improve."

"But you get to a certain breeze strength and it's very hard to get around the mark, accelerate up on the foils and get stable, it just takes a lot of work. The loading changes so quickly. We're still playing around with different things upwind and trying to learn at the same time as race. Getting consistent will be the key."

Chris Draper wanted to win as much as anyone, but he was also honest about what the team could and couldn't achieve.

"It's frustrating for us as a team," lamented Draper. "We'd love to buy some time back, but we just can't do that. We've gotten a lot better and our performance numbers show that, but so have the Kiwis and it's impressive to see. I think if we were able to go back and do everything again, we would do a way better job."

Race 8, Sunday, August 25

The Italians pointed out that they weren't losing so much because of decisions they had been making on the racecourse, but because of decisions they made months earlier when designing, modeling, and tuning the boat. Whether a derivative of ETNZ's first-generation boat was ever consistently going to beat ETNZ's second-generation boat is another fair question.

Reductive focus on win-loss records shouldn't cloud the fact of what had been accomplished with these boats. A year before, a spy shot of ETNZ's AC72 up on foils was derided by Internet sailing mavens as a hoax, not possible, and certainly not feasible for racing in the Louis Vuitton or America's Cup. Now, as the 2013 Louis Vuitton Cup revealed, the crews had learned to fly them around San Francisco Bay close to 50 miles per hour, water turning to smoke behind them, different terraced levels of

Luna Rossa chasing Emirates Team New Zealand downwind in the final race of the Louis Vuitton Cup. (© 2013 ACEA/Photo: Gilles Martin-Raget)

harmonics in their vibrations and other noises singing to the helmsman, crews springing from hull to hull for the next tack. Racing these boats so well was a tremendous achievement for both Emirates Team New Zealand and Luna Rossa, no matter who won the Louis Vuitton Cup. Race 8 started with light winds, around 10 knots. ETNZ again won the start from windward and cut in front of Luna Rossa, leading by 16 seconds. The New Zealanders saved two gybes on the downwind and opened a 1:31 margin at the downwind gate. Upwind, the distance was huge, getting to 800m. The wind picked up slightly, but Luna Rossa trailed by 2:58 at the windward gate. Across the finish line the margin was 3:20 as Emirates Team New Zealand won the Louis Vuitton Cup!

ETNZ had come through in very good shape. They had stumbled, falling off their foils in Race 1, and had other problems with gear, though losing only one race to breakdowns. With Luna Rossa sailing better, the tactical match was less one-sided. Tactician Ray Davies looked darn good, but with boat speeds becoming less lopsided, Luna Rossa's Francesco Bruni sometimes got the better of the exchanges. But if ETNZ no longer looked incapable of making a mistake, the last few races also showed they had speed potential that had only been hinted at so far. They just flat out sailed away from Luna Rossa upwind, were beginning to make foiling work for them when going to windward, and probably had a lot more tricks where that came from. ORACLE TEAM USA was going flat out, but their work was in practice, training in-house. Would that be enough when it came time to face Emirates Team New Zealand for the America's Cup on September 7?

ELEVEN

A Team of Rivals—OTUSA Trains with Two Boats

Would the Defender be ready? That's been a question in every America's Cup match since the first match in 1870. However, that question has become even more relevant after the 1995 defense. Since then, only a single defense candidate represented the yacht club holding the trophy, breaking with 124 years of precedence by not holding trials between Defender candidate teams. While there has only been one Defender team, per Cup cycle, after the 1995 series, these Defender teams have fielded a two-boat team: an "A" boat and a "B" boat, a trial-horse. For 2013, ORACLE TEAM USA had America's Cup winner James Spithill on the "A" boat, dueling against four-time Olympic gold medalist Ben Ainslie on the "B" boat. The Australian-born Spithill was a scrappy, often brilliant skipper who took to the boxing ring to stay fit, and might have pursued the sport professionally had he not found a career racing sailboats. Ainslie, already knighted for the unprecedented honors he brought to Britain's national sailing team, had never done the America's Cup. He had jumped from the aborted TeamOrigin campaign back into the 2012 Olympics, then joined ORACLE TEAM USA just for this purpose. (For more on Ainslie, see sidebar on page 85.)

Spithill and his team had to be ready for Emirates Team New Zealand when the America's Cup match started on September 7, 2013. The team claimed they were racing as hard as anyone did in the Louis Vuitton Cup. The challenger selection series had seen several breakdowns, crew overboard in a near-pitchpole, and some boat-to-boat contact in the pre-starts, not to mention sometimes clocking 50-mph-plus top speeds. But was the Defender really going to the limit in testing as hard as they would in a race?

"We are pushing as hard as we can," Spithill said. "It's hard not to be at full throttle on these boats, there really is no in-between. If you look at our racing versus the Challengers' racing, it's quite a lot different. We're getting pushed, we're getting under a lot of pressure—and that's exactly what we need."

ORACLE TEAM USA took advantage of opportunities during the Louis Vuitton Cup Final to duplicate race conditions as much as they could, not just racing on the actual course with the official boats present, but even, when possible, with the television broadcast environment up and running.

"It was great to test our program with the cameras and under the pressure," Spithill said. "The whole tone was different in the team, we've learned a lot. That's why we designed our campaign on a two-boat program, having two very competitive teams and two competitive boats."

Training with two boats at once was an option that all the teams were permitted. But in the combination of circumstances and finances only OTUSA, believing it necessary to their chances of winning, managed to do so with their own boats. ETNZ did not sail both of their boats at the same time, concentrating resources on boat two once it was ready. Luna Rossa built only one boat, though training with it at times against ETNZ. Artemis Racing had the issue decided for them when their first boat was wrecked in May before their second boat was launched.

The Challengers relied on finding their competition in the challenger selection series, the Louis Vuitton Cup. OTUSA was committed from the outset to the principle that in a challenge cup the Defender should not interfere in the challenger selection process, potentially altering the outcome and diminishing expectations for the America's Cup match itself. Fielding two boats with two crews and sailing together was their only route to gaining race experience. OTUSA hoped that the arrangement would turn out to their advantage.

"We're going to play our two-boat card as much as we can," Spithill said during the summer of 2013. "That's one of our trump cards—you've seen the challenger racing and you've seen our racing and I think it's pretty obvious who has the better racing. So we're going to keep pushing hard— that's why we hired a lot of good sailors. We've got two great boats and we're going to capitalize on that, push the race team as hard as we can. At this point in the game, I think everyone's got their gear and it's time to just get out there. It's a pretty good problem that we've got right now, to have two very competitive boats." Even in late August, Spithill hedged on which boat would sail in the match, saying they didn't know yet.

Ben Ainslie, new to both OTUSA and America's Cup multihulls, had been skippering boat one, sparring with Spithill, trying not to hold much back. "You can't sail these boats at less than 100 percent downwind just because of the nature of the boat—they are really close to the edge," Ainslie said. "One small mistake and you're in a lot of trouble. It's zero-tolerance sailing. But in testing, we can do more upwind, like change modes and the setup a little bit."

Though Ainslie has designs on taking the wheel of his own America's Cup Challenger in the future, members of the OTUSA camp noted that, as intended, Ainslie's role here was to push Spithill, off the water as well as on.

And nobody admitted that Ainslie had accomplished that more readily than Spithill. "Ben Ainslie is the best sailor in the world," Spithill said in August. "So for me, it's great to be pushed. You can only get better if you're training against someone who's very good. What he's done with that group of guys, it's a fantastic program. But also we're pretty good mates, so we're able to develop the boats at the same time. Without him, there's no way we'd be able to progress as we are. And it means we have options—if we have two sailing teams, we have the ability to have everyone backed up. You never know what can come up during the Cup, sickness or injury—you saw what happened to the Kiwis—so we're prepared if something happens. That's the only thing we can do now—be as prepared as we can."

The preparation would be continuing all the way to the Cup's starting gun on September 7, 2013. Ainslie said it had to.

"You're learning all the time," said Ainslie. "It's a massive learning curve, maybe a little bit steeper for me than anyone else. As a sailor, it's rewarding, almost like being back at sailing school, the first time you were sailing an Opti or something. You're learning how to fly, learning the nuances of the boat, the racecourse. When the game changed to multihulls,

ORACLE TEAM USA boats practicing starts and match-racing. (© 2013 ACEA/Photo: Abner Kingman)

suddenly we had to try to catch up with all the multihull experts. But we have a great team here and hopefully we can push Jimmy and the guys. They're doing really well and I'm very confident in their abilities. I think we can keep pushing them, keep them honest, put them under a bit of pressure and that's really what they need to be properly prepared for the race."

Emirates Team New Zealand Skipper Dean Barker has played Ainslie's role himself. Barker got his start leading the in-house "B-Boat" in aggressive style, tuning up Russell Coutts thoroughly in the 2000 Defense of the America's Cup, and ultimately sailing at Russell's insistence in the final race of the 5-0 "Blackwash" in Auckland.

ORACLE TEAM USA had a brief opportunity to gauge their performance against Challenger ETNZ during the Louis Vuitton Cup Final when the Kiwi boat dropped in, sailing near the OTUSA boats as they were training on the racecourse. Ainslie watched as Barker lined up against Spithill. While Ainslie joked about being a little bit annoyed with Dean and the boys for joining in, it was a tantalizing moment even for the sailors themselves to have the chance to gauge their performance against their upcoming America's Cup competitor. In advance of the Match, the question had to be asked: Who was faster?

"I think the speeds are pretty even," said Ainslie at the time. "I think our boats are a little bit higher, a little bit faster, but I think you'll find the overall speeds are pretty even. If you asked me right now who I'd put my money on, I honestly couldn't tell you."

TWELVE

America's Cup Match: The 34th Defense of the America's Cup

September 7 had arrived. The 2013 America's Cup, the vision of giant wingsail catamarans, now transformed into foiling flying 50-mph beasts that awed their creators, stunned the spectators and commanded the sailors' complete respect. Some said the day would never come; some in the city of San Francisco or in the Cup world tried to keep it from coming amid a mini-industry of honest skeptics, heartfelt traditionalists, and the just plain mean and myopic trying hard not to enjoy a boat race they had never seen.

Two of the most advanced racing craft on the water were going to meet for the most historic, most famous, and most difficult-to-win trophy in sailing.

ORACLE TEAM USA had won the Cup 43 months earlier, brought it home to the City by the Bay, and now the New Zealanders were set to take it back, if they could. ETNZ had launched the first AC72, foiled the first AC72, built another for the Italians, were the first to launch a second AC72, foiled that one too, and swept the Louis Vuitton Cup except for one DSQ. In the process, the tough, practical, and hardened ETNZ had taken on the aura of an irresistible force. When Luna Rossa began breathing down New Zealand's neck upwind in the Louis Vuitton Cup Final, the Kiwi boat *Aotearoa* did everything except utter the Road Runner's "Meep-Meep" as it took off to parts unknown. Dean Barker and Grant Dalton and their boys likely had a whole deck of cards still up their sleeves, and they had been upgrading their performance at every chance. They were in the tenth year of their quest with one goal: get the trophy back.

They faced a vast yacht-racing industrial complex. ORACLE TEAM USA was the only team to field two boats simultaneously; throughout the summer Olympian Ben Ainslie sparred with Cup-winner James Spithill. OTUSA's boats sprouted uncountable trick bits, backed by an incredible array of real-time computer analysis and real-time brain power. The basic shapes were honed in all the countless virtual regattas that their designers could run, and both actual OTUSA boats had been pounding the water together since June. They had the resources of a local expert like John Kostecki as tactician, and the oversight of legend Russell Coutts, both an engineer and sailor, who had been behind every winning America's Cup program since 1995 except one. ORACLE TEAM USA had at its disposal every resource except for the one thing that no America's Cup campaign ever has too much of—namely, time.

The defense looked to come down to three factors. The first was boat speed. If one team had it and the other didn't, almost nothing else would matter. A little boat speed will make you famous, a certain Kiwi once said, and it certainly had.

The great anticipation of the America's Cup is that nobody knows the answer to that question about speed until the first race. The limited comparisons available so far just weren't enough to know. OTUSA may have had some sense how they compared to what ETNZ showed in the Louis Vuitton Cup, but nobody except ETNZ knew the Challenger's potential and nobody but OTUSA knew the Defender's.

Publicly, OTUSA had been offering the idea that the differences showed USA faster upwind, but both sides had been playing smoke and mirrors since before the boats were launched. With only one upwind leg, and two downwind legs, there wasn't room to concede a large margin anywhere, no matter how fast you can make it up in the other direction.

If the boats were close in speed, or at least had asymmetrical advantages and disadvantages, then it might be a heck of a boat race. There had been a few memorable minutes during the Louis Vuitton Cup where the boats were right on top of each other, threatening to pass, and the outcome was not certain. It was true edge-of-your-seat stuff, but those moments had been few and far between.

The second factor after speed was crew work. A poorly executed gybe that caused the boat to drop off her foils could cost 100 meters to 200 meters. Bigger mistakes, such as burying the bows, could be even more costly.

The third factor was reliability, given the issues witnessed during the Louis Vuitton Cup. Could either boat make it through nine to eleven races without failures? That factor might not decide the regatta, but it has put teams on the ropes when they should have had a fighting chance. In 2003, TNZ's frequent breakages (including both a dismasting and a broken boom) made it easy for Alinghi to triumph. In 1983, it took the vastly superior *Australia II* seven races to beat *Liberty* because the Australians had gear failures early in the series.

After the first three issues, tactics then entered into the picture in two main categories: the start, and the rest of the race. Sailors are hardwired to be aggressive at the start of a race, and the adrenaline of an

America's Cup match plus testosterone would be hard to resist. Still, it's an enormously risky roll of the dice, the reward of a 5- to 15-second jump at the first mark, versus the risk that damage or a penalty could bring something much worse. Nobody had yet really managed to win an AC72 race at the start.

Tactics really come into play only if the boats are close in speed and the crews are similar in boat-handling skills, but the narrow racecourse of the 2013 match took away many of the macro options on the upwind leg, and more so in a flood tide. The biggest opportunities for tactics had usually been found in the approaches to the marks and coming out of the roundings, where being able to minimize tacks and gybes could add up quickly.

As to which boat had the edge in the three factors and tactics, some of the answers would be known as early as Mark 1, where the boats bear off from the reach to downwind, and a lot more would be clear by the end of that second leg. The biggest reveal might be on the upwind leg, when the differential in advantages could show itself. The 25 minutes or so that Race 1 would last would not necessarily tell the whole story of the Cup, but it would say a lot about what everybody had been up to for the last three years, and what they accomplished.

And none of that should get lost in the noise. These boats were incredible, and did what many experts thought wasn't even possible. Sailing them stretched the sailors, the shore crews, the designers, and everyone else involved. It would be an historic America's Cup in one form or another.

THE MATCH

The America's Cup match would be run as was the Louis Vuitton Cup Final: two races per day on the five-leg course. The main difference for race management from the previous round was that the nominal wind limit rose to 23 knots instead of 21.

Each race would be worth one point. The first team to score nine points would win the America's Cup.

The complication was that as a result of the OTUSA penalty, their first two points would be taken away. They were effectively starting out at negative two points. Though the docking of the first two points wasn't that complicated of a concept, it defied easy explanations of the standings throughout the match.

For Race 1, the America's Cup Park on Piers 27 to 29 and the Village at Marina Green attracted a combined 46,000 spectators. So many people were drawn to the America's Cup Park during the race that the San Francisco police had to close off admission before the pier exceeded its structural capacity.

CREWS FOR THE 34TH AMERICA'S CUP

ORACLE TEAM USA

Skipper/helmsman:
Jimmy Spithill

Tactician:
John Kostecki (Races 1-5)
Ben Ainslie (Races 6-19)

Strategist: Tom Slingsby

Wing trimmer:
Kyle Langford

Jib trimmer:
Joe Newton

Off-side trimmer:
Rome Kirby

Grinders:
Shannon Falcone
Joe Spooner
Jonathan MacBeth
Gilberto Nobili
Simeon Tienpont

Emirates Team New Zealand

Skipper/helmsman:
Dean Barker

Tactician: Ray Davies

Wing trimmer:
Glenn Ashby

Trimmer: James Dagg

Bow: Adam Beashel

Pit: Jeremy Lomas

Grinders:
Chris Ward
Rob Waddell
Grant Dalton
Chris McAsey

Float/grinder:
Derek Saward

RACING

Races 1 and 2, Saturday, September 7

Winds as light as 12 knots had been expected, but by race time it was blowing 17 knots. High tide and slack water would occur between race starts, so the current would be a minor factor compared to most races.

ETNZ entered from port, OTUSA from starboard. Pre-start engagement between the two was limited, the teams looking a bit wary the first time in the starting box, keeping some distance apart. They sailed away from the line, ETNZ tacking, OTUSA gybing to leeward of them with 1 minute and 10 seconds to go, and the two yachts sailed back, OTUSA centered on the start line, ETNZ several lengths to windward. They were slightly early, slowing to avoid being over the line. ETNZ was setting up to try the drag race tactic that had worked so well against Luna Rossa. With 10 seconds left, Challenger and Defender were idling along at 15 knots. Could ETNZ spoil OTUSA's air and get ahead in time, just like the Kiwis had rolled the Italians? If not, OTUSA would have the early lead.

The gun went off, and the 72-foot cats were off in a frenzy of acceleration, already doing 30 knots as they crossed the starting line, trying to leap up onto their foils and kick ahead. At first, ETNZ wasn't blanketing OTUSA's wind so much as they were coming down at a hotter, faster angle toward the mark, showing huge bursts of leeway as the boat tried to stabilize on her foils, skidding sideways toward the Defender. The boats converged, now edging past 40 knots, ETNZ straining ahead. Dean Barker dropped *Aotearoa* right in front of OTUSA, throwing the irreplaceable

The Challengers. (Photo: Chris Cameron/© 2013 Emirates Team New Zealand)

boat into his competitor's path like it was a beach cat, his transom missing OTUSA's bowsprit by what looked like just feet. There were audible gasps from people watching onshore.

This was already a wildly aggressive battle, with a few moments that seemed at the edge of control.

Spithill had turned OTUSA's bows up as ETNZ had passed, either to avoid ETNZ's bad air or in an attempt at a luff, but it was too late, and OTUSA fell off her foils with the move. The Defender signaled a protest to the umpires, but no penalty was given. ETNZ led OTUSA around Mark 1 by 3.5 seconds as they headed downwind. The New Zealand boat had topped 42 knots, over 48 miles per hour, on the first leg.

Downwind, ETNZ was the first to gybe away, off onto port and maybe better current, but setting up starboard tack right-of-way for NZL when the yachts met again. Boat speeds were in the mid-30s as they worked their way down the first leeward leg. When they came back together, ETNZ was clearly ahead at the first cross, but the lead was bounding between just 30 and 50 meters and sometimes less. Another cross and ORACLE TEAM USA came in with starboard rights this time, though ETNZ held their course, getting past OTUSA with just a second or two to spare. Another protest came from the Defender, but no penalty from the umpires.

It wasn't clear who was faster yet, and that was an answer in itself. ETNZ looked to be going slightly better, maneuvering slightly better, but there was no advantage building yet.

With the downwind gate coming, OTUSA made it first to the lay line, setting up to turn left at the gate. ETNZ came in and gybed ahead of them,

Race 1, just after the start, Dean Barker on Emirates Team New Zealand maneuvers his boat ahead of Jimmy Spithill on ORACLE TEAM USA with just feet to spare. (© 2013 ACEA/Photo: Abner Kingman)

Emirates Team New Zealand, leading ORACLE TEAM USA on Leg 1 of the first race. (© 2013 ACEA/Photo: Ricardo Pinto)

with the same intention. OTUSA, up to speed earlier, gained rapidly on ETNZ and had to bear off just short of the point of contact, unfortunately falling off her foils briefly as she did so, just enough to let ETNZ to round clear ahead by 4.5 seconds. The difference over the leg was measured in tenths of a second.

OTUSA built her speed back, though, and carried it around the mark, while ETNZ was slow coming out of the gate and pointing too high. Both yachts were on port tack right after rounding when a much faster OTUSA got her bows just overlapped to leeward of ETNZ, and was about to luff ETNZ, probably passing her, and maybe giving NZL a penalty, too. New Zealand saw it coming and had to tack away. OTUSA kept going and looked to be ahead. The upwind battle was on.

Soon it was ETNZ on the left, OTUSA on the right, both on starboard tack. ETNZ hit the boundary and had to tack and try to cross OTUSA. OTUSA conceded nothing and passed them. ORACLE TEAM USA was now leading on Leg 3.

Trading leads, ducking each other on crosses, differences in boat speed were minimal and they could catch each other. The Match was on, it was seriously on.

Both set out on a longer port tack up the course, promising to be the setup for the mark rounding. ETNZ was a few lengths to windward and behind, but not by much.

On OTUSA it looked possible they could tack and cross ETNZ, which would consolidate their gains with the upwind gate getting closer and let them lead around the mark. When OTUSA did tack, though, ETNZ was ready and immediately tacked to cover, matching the Defender on starboard tack a few lengths directly ahead of OTUSA, right in her path. Trying to sail in the bad air coming off the Kiwi boat wasn't going to work and OTUSA had to tack away, downspeed, in what was the final critical exchange of the match.

The wind was picking up, a few knots greater at the top of the course, and ETNZ's usual magic began to return. They were tacking a little faster than the Defender, saving tacks now, and the combination quickly added to a real lead, 300m as the Kiwis reached the top gate. ETNZ rounded 25 seconds ahead. It had taken most of the first three legs to do it, but they had broken away again.

Downwind, ETNZ opened the lead slowly but steadily. OTUSA couldn't really close up and the downwind leg didn't really offer them any more opportunities from behind than Luna Rossa or Artemis had found. ETNZ carried around the bottom gate uneventfully, and took Race 1 by 36 seconds.

AC72s crossing on the first day of the 2013 America's Cup. (© 2013 ACEA/Photo: Gilles Martin-Raget)

Race 4: ORACLE TEAM USA worked to protect the favored left side of the course against Emirates Team New Zealand on the upwind leg, and was able to lead by 16 seconds at the windward mark. (© 2013 ACEA/Photo: Gilles Martin-Raget)

OTUSA looked close enough, though, that with a few better breaks and improved tactics, the win could have just as well been theirs.

Race 2 went off in a similar fashion, but the boats started to engage this time in the pre-start. A bit too early for the starting line, Spithill to leeward tried to hook under Barker, hoping for the luff or a penalty. He got neither. His starboard bow made glancing contact with ETNZ, apparent in certain angles of the television relay, but not detected by the umpires. When there is contact, a penalty is expected, but it would have been a matter of judgment who received it, depending on whether Barker had been trying hard enough to keep clear and whether Spithill had given him room to do so. Crossing the starting line, Barker to windward managed to get close enough this time to spoil Spithill's air, and ETNZ was ahead again at Mark 1.

The pattern was the same after that, though. OTUSA was close, seven seconds, at the downwind gate, and hung in close, not gaining upwind. ETNZ threw a close cover on them from ahead, and the more OTUSA tried to break free, the more distance they lost on the tacks. OTUSA lost 39 seconds upwind; there was no catching on the final downwind leg, and ETNZ won Race 2 by 52 seconds.

ETNZ now led the Match 2-0, and had shown how tough they were as a crew.

The starts had not worked out for Spithill; Barker had taken control both times.

"We just didn't get as tight as we would have liked to on the first start and they were able to get over us at the reach mark," Jimmy Spithill said. "On the second one, we luffed tighter, waiting for the hook. We thought we were going to get a penalty, but it didn't go our way. In the second race, there really weren't any passing lanes; they did a great job and didn't make any mistakes."

The skippers had taken enormous risks with their boats in the starts, especially in Race 1.

"These are two guys at the top of their game and they're at the wheel of a $10 million carbon fiber missile," Ashby said. "These guys are definitely in control, but it's like a riding a motorbike or in a car—you don't know you've crashed it 'til you've crashed!"

It was an even deeper hole than it looked for ORACLE TEAM USA, since their first two wins would be wiped out because of penalties imposed by the jury. But the takeaway on all sides was that the boats were much more evenly matched than any previous AC72 racing. A breathtaking Race 1 was a thorough rebuke to skeptics of multihull match racing.

"Close," however, for OTUSA didn't mean they were winning.

Races 3 and 4, Sunday, September 8

Saturday's opening races showed that this was a real battle. ETNZ now needed seven more wins to OTUSA's eleven. And where was OTUSA going to get those wins?

Opinions varied wildly on who had the speed edge and where. Some saw ETNZ's big gain upwind in the second race as proof their boat was plain faster; others pointed out that OTUSA did in fact pass ETNZ, and instead tactics shaped Race 1's outcome where the Defender might just as well have won. OTUSA had been sailing with damage to their wing covering in Race 2, but then that was part of the competition, too.

For the less partisan, consensus was that the boats were very tightly matched downwind. The more passionate ETNZ fans saw the win totals, and the final delta in Race 2, and liked their chances. Excited ORACLE TEAM USA fans saw their boat catch the Kiwis and make them work awfully hard for the points.

The main issues turned to what else the teams could find in their tanks, with the wild card being what much lighter or stronger conditions might bring to bear on the match-up. The boats were close enough that crew work and tactics could mean the race, and small mistakes at these speeds were all that was needed to lose.

Race 3, Minimal Flood Current

OTUSA got a slight jump in the pre-start, and Dean Barker couldn't use his signature move to close them out by Mark 1, giving OTUSA a lead on the first leeward leg, the first time the Defender had led downwind.

The job for Spithill then was to keep the Kiwis behind him. The teams matched gybe for gybe. Into the bottom gate Emirates Team New Zealand took an extra gybe, but splitting away just 10 seconds behind.

In the tacking duel that ensued upwind, Emirates Team New Zealand began chipping away at the Defender's lead, drawing closer.

At the boundary on the city side of the course, ETNZ tacked onto port, which put them in a special situation under the America's Cup Racing Rules that gave them the right of way over OTUSA on starboard. Normally OTUSA would have had rights, but instead had to tack short of ETNZ, and below them, to leeward, leaving the Kiwis in control and continuing to cover, more or less shutting the Defender down.

OTUSA lost the race on the upwind leg, forced to take an extra tack and sail hundreds of meters farther. A tacking duel played to ETNZ's strengths and put them close enough to make the tactics work.

Three races done and ETNZ was getting the upper hand, time and again. They had done it from in front when OTUSA seemed to be catching up, and now they had done it from behind.

The New Zealanders were already a third of the way to taking the Cup. They looked like they had the speed to do it. Not a lot more, but just enough. Having the speed made good tactics look easy, too. They were tacking faster, having fewer issues in gybes, and doing a better job in the starts. The speed alone threatened to grind the Defender down over time; there was only so much you could do against a faster boat. Being slower against a better-sailed boat wasn't going to work at all. And, close or not in some ways, ORACLE TEAM USA was already effectively 5 points behind in a 9-point match.

The legions of New Zealanders flocking to the America's Cup Park on Piers 27 to 29 were elated. There may be no nation so attuned to sailing, and a basic point of honor was on its way to being restored. Media, whether sailing, sporting, or otherwise, was impressed by what OTUSA was capable of, but they could also see that ETNZ was beating OTUSA following the same pattern that had beaten Luna Rossa. OTUSA was a much faster opponent than Luna Rossa, but sailing from ahead, ETNZ was identifying OTUSA's weaknesses and dismantling the team on the racecourse.

ETNZ could tack faster, so they made OTUSA tack as much as possible. ETNZ was accelerating their boat better, so they set up starting scenarios that would pay off. If OTUSA made a bad tactical call, ETNZ seemed to be waiting in anticipation and pouncing. The opinion was forming quickly that for all the capability OTUSA was showing, it wouldn't be enough to win.

Race 4

The second race of the day.

Again the start shaped up with OTUSA to leeward, TNZ to windward, in Dean Barker's usual drag race position. After the gun, both boats got an even jump off the line, but Jimmy Spithill found an extra gear in clear air and the boat was screaming along. ETNZ couldn't gain and couldn't sail down to beat OTUSA to the first mark. As they went across the reaching leg, Spithill sailed up, away from Mark 1 and not rounding it, to hold Barker out to windward well past the mark before gybing away on his own terms with the lead. It was a bit of a manhandling, a show of aggression on Spithill's part now that he had found an opening for it.

Downwind, OTUSA held a narrow 130m lead. ETNZ flopped off their foils in a gybe, giving up a bit more. Nearing the bottom gate, OTUSA dropped off, too, retracting the wrong foil by mistake. ETNZ was following by just a five-second margin at the bottom gate. Upwind would be the test.

It looked to be another Kiwi overtaking maneuver on the beat, using their upwind speed advantage to roll over the top of the Americans on the race toward shore. But ORACLE TEAM USA shifted deftly into point mode, as close to the wind as the boat would allow, and forced ETNZ away and back into the adverse current. For the first time, ORACLE TEAM USA appeared to be sailing their own game, matching the Kiwis in upwind boat speed and not being dictated to on tactics.

OTUSA led by 16 seconds at the windward gate. On the final leeward, ETNZ was close, but not gaining. There was no room for another error with the foils on OTUSA, not with the margin holding at just 110m down the leg and the boats tearing along at 40 knots and more, but ETNZ couldn't gain either.

The finish delta was a scant 7 seconds, with the boats ripping across the water at the finish as ORACLE TEAM USA took their first win of the regatta.

The moment was electric for the event. USA's victory energized fans, teams, organizers, and (nearly all) the media.

The sense at the America's Cup Park was that everything had been taken up a notch in the last two days. Seeing on an electronic screen someplace that, yes, the boats were fast was well and good, but that captured nothing of the wow factor of the two of them screaming into the finish line, crowd cheering, the Challenger seven seconds back, the series re-set from a sweep to a battle, and no idea what would come next.

Nobody had beaten ETNZ until now except for the single dead battery race when the hydraulic system failed in the challenger series. In Race 4, OTUSA had aggressively won the start, dictated the terms of the reaching leg, given up nothing downwind despite a miscue with the foils, and bested the Kiwis on tactics and mode changes on the upwind leg.

Doing things right, OTUSA could beat ETNZ. It wouldn't be by much, but they could do it.

And not only that, the America's Cup had just brought two days of racing to live national TV in the U.S., broadcast on a major network. And delivered close racing, actual match racing, epic match racing. The pre-starts had action to them, there were lead changes, close deltas at the marks, close crosses—it was edge-of-the seat stuff nearly all the way, or, in Race 4, all the way through to the end.

The event had endured years of criticism, not just skepticism but outright dismissal of the new boats, the format, nearly every feature that had been put in place. Experts had been certain that racing multihulls would never be interesting to the public; they were too fast, too fragile, too dangerous, too complicated, and at heart just wouldn't work. You couldn't match race multihulls, and in any case the contest would never be close.

The public wouldn't watch sailing on TV, and people weren't going to come out in San Francisco for a boat race. Race 4 put an end to that talk. The vision of the 2013 America's Cup running on all 72 cylinders was powerful stuff.

On the piers and in Marina Green, a whole other set of fans was now cheering, too, partially for the American victory, and partially because the gauntlet had been picked up. It seemed like anything could happen.

Monday, Lay Day

OTUSA was out on the Bay on Monday, training hard in wind conditions that trended into the upper 20s, utterly flying, a hawk among the Golden geese of the Superyacht Cup fleet. What they were learning is anybody's guess. ETNZ had braved winds 10 to 15 knots higher with their boat one, so that was not unknown territory for them either, but ETNZ instead spent the day in their boat shed, surely working something up.

Race 5, Tuesday, September 10

With the battle joined, Tuesday looked exciting. ETNZ was up 3-1 on the scoreboard. OTUSA had erased half of their penalty, and still needed another win before scoring points, but now that either team had shown they could win, a different energy level surrounded the event.

By some counts OTUSA could have been up three races and tied on points with better tactics, a few better breaks, and one or two of the non-penalty calls. The New Zealanders were looking tough, but not invulnerable. And regardless of what OTUSA could have done, New Zealand was the one winning.

Barker was matter of fact about the Race 4 loss. "The second one we could have done better, but what we take out of that race is the fact that we sailed—by our standards—a pretty average race and we were still pretty close at the end," he said.

Spithill had talked enthusiastically in Sunday's press conference about the momentum having shifted to his team, which might have been more an attempt to get into his competitors' heads than a deep insight. Each race was its own race, as events would soon reinforce.

Race 5 was expected to be in strong winds, 18 to 22 knots.

Detailed analysis of the data so far showed OTUSA closing the gap in average speeds upwind, downwind, and tacking. The numbers showed the boats becoming much closer in performance on all points of sail. Both teams had made mistakes on Sunday; OTUSA's just cost them less than they did ETNZ.

Spithill went head-to-wind at the line, getting Barker underneath him to leeward, the Kiwis trying for the hook but undermined by the flood current moving both boats to the pin end. Barker sitting further downwind at the gun had little leeway to give on the reaching leg, and it was Spithill this time who could put the bow down, hit the throttle, and ruin his opponent's air. It was an excellent execution by Spithill of the technique that Barker had been taking to the bank all summer. Spithill was in command, leaving Barker behind by a half dozen boat lengths heading downwind.

Coming into the bottom mark with ETNZ close but not gaining on starboard, with ORACLE TEAM USA ahead, tactician John Kostecki called for a foiling tack so they could quickly head back into the "cone" behind Alcatraz, where the flood current, near its maximum strength for the afternoon, would have less impact. But the tack was slow, with the Americans seeming to completely stall out. Tacking onto starboard when they reached the right-hand boundary, ORACLE TEAM USA crossed ahead of Emirates Team New Zealand, but the Defender inexplicably chose to continue across the flood current toward shore. ETNZ continued offshore, staying out of the flood current, and when the boats tacked and came back together Emirates Team New Zealand had the lead, continued to build on it, and never looked back. They won Race 5 by 1:04.

After a brilliant start for ORACLE TEAM USA, one bad foiling tack, and a decision to let ETNZ head out of the current alone, had spelled disaster.

Criticism mounted for OTUSA tactician John Kostecki. Others blamed him less than the fact that the setup on OTUSA's boat had Kostecki grinding a winch, head down, so often that he couldn't focus on the other boat enough to stay on top of the situation and guide Spithill. ETNZ's arrangement gave Ray Davies, their tactician, better awareness and easier communication to Barker.

Whatever the reason, the pattern of losses was continuing: boat-handling mistakes, tactical missteps, and not enough speed.

OTUSA was now down 4-0 in points, needing ten wins to the Challenger's five. Another loss and ETNZ would be able to win the trophy back in only two more days of racing.

Jimmy Spithill, ORACLE TEAM USA skipper (left) and Dean Barker, Emirates Team New Zealand skipper, at the post-race press conference on September 10, after the Defender postponed the second race of the day to regroup. (© 2013 ACEA/Photo: Abner Kingman)

Race 5: Emirates Team New Zealand was still sailing away from ORACLE TEAM USA. (© 2013 ACEA/Photo: Ricardo Pinto)

Race 6–Postponed

An intense group conversation could be seen on board the Defender's boat between races. Ten minutes before the start of Race 6, as permitted by the rules, ORACLE TEAM USA requested postponement of the second race of the day. Each team was permitted to do so one time only for the entire span of the match, and only for the second race of the day.

Since it was a card that could be played only once, it was often regarded as an option only if damage to the yacht guaranteed a loss. OTU-SA's boat wasn't damaged, and under the rules it didn't have to be in order to make the request. Spithill, on board, had polled his crew, and they had agreed with the decision.

Whether it was wise to play the postponement card and not have it in hand in case the boat suffered damage in the first race of a future day was one question—but the fact that Spithill had played it at all suggested how deep their trouble was. It was a very public no confidence vote.

Onshore, the move was not very well regarded by some. To critics, OTUSA's refusal to race made them look afraid of ETNZ.

A thorough defeat of OTUSA in Race 5 despite a masterful start, and then the disarray culminating with the decision not to race, drained all the energy from the proceedings. ETNZ was looking like they couldn't be stopped. OTUSA looked desperate.

The post-race press conference was marked by a somber mood among the participants and audience alike. Criticism of the foiling tack and ensuing tactics abounded. John Kostecki had been up on stage next to Spithill the first two days, but he was not present at Tuesday's press conference, his absence interpreted as a question concerning his future in this edition of the Cup. Inquiry was made as to whether ORACLE TEAM USA's other AC72 could be brought into service. The substitution of wing trimmer Kyle Langford for the excluded Dirk de Ridder was a topic for the third race day in a row. There was concern about what message the decision not to race sent to fans. With the Kiwis still needing to win five more races, ETNZ's skipper and tactician were asked if the Protocol for the next defense in Auckland was ready to be signed with Patrizio Bertelli, Luna Rossa's CEO, who happened to be standing in the media room.

The tone was that the regatta was slipping away from OTUSA, and maybe it was gone already.

To Spithill fell the task of bringing balance back to the dire tone of the proceedings, and to overcome the inference from the media that what he described as a re-grouping was instead a collapse. There was a lot to handle. Langford was doing a great job and absolutely not a factor in the losses, Spithill said as he had repeated since Race 1. No decision had been made on what changes would be made for Thursday, he said, and when asked to guarantee that Kostecki would be on the boat, Spithill was quick to point out he couldn't guarantee that he himself would be on the boat.

ETNZ's Ray Davies rightly ducked a question about the next defense as being above his pay grade, not to mention outright premature.

The closest anyone came to giving the Kiwis a tough question was America's Cup–winning tactician Gary Jobson, here again as a TV broadcaster, who probed Dean Barker to see how concerned he was about losing the last two starts to Spithill and what the NZL crew might do to get better. Barker registered no worry on the subject and said that they would carry on as before.

The crowd in the room wasn't hostile, but the assumptions about the outcome of the Match, and OTUSA's ability to compete against ETNZ, were unmistakable. The American team was nearly written off.

There were theories that the re-grouping explanation offered publicly for the ORACLE TEAM USA postponement was a smokescreen for more serious problems with the boat—the wing, the foil system, a mismatch in their preparation, or something else that gave the team reason to expect a loss in the second race of the day.

On the television broadcast, Nathan Outteridge offered a perceptive take, saying that OTUSA had won one race, New Zealand had won one race, and OTUSA had lost three races. Though definitely not giving full credit to everything ETNZ had done right in their wins, Outteridge's calculation dovetailed with the point of view that James Spithill expressed Tuesday that, much more so than in America's Cup monohulls, teams pay huge penalties very quickly for small mistakes in AC72s.

New Zealand was now up 4-0 in points, with OTUSA yet to get on the board. The Kiwis needed five wins, the Americans ten.

Wednesday, September 11

ETNZ kept their boat in the shed on Wednesday, giving the AC72 and the crew a certain amount of respite, although they all worked on improving aspects of their operation, according to Dean Barker. For his part, Spithill said ORACLE TEAM USA would be doing all that, plus sailing on the water.

Race 6, Thursday, September 12

ORACLE TEAM USA put Ben Ainslie on the boat, replacing John Kostecki. Ainslie would work with Tom Slingsby on tactics while Spithill concentrated on helming. There were changes in the jib configuration, which had made ORACLE TEAM USA slow in tacking, and many as yet unseen adjustments.

The winds for Race 6 were 12 to 13 knots. ORACLE TEAM USA blocked ETNZ away from the line, started directly ahead of them at the gun, and led by 8 seconds at Mark 1.

Emirates Team New Zealand swept both races on September 12. (© 2013 ACEA/Photo: Gilles Martin-Raget)

Upwind, a split at the bottom of the leg allowed ETNZ to pull even, the boats taking turns ducking each other at crosses, New Zealand chipping away until finally the Kiwis had enough edge to try hunting their opponent when they came together, the confrontation known in match racing as the "dial-down." The America's Cup Racing Rules allow the right-of-way boat on starboard tack to "hunt" the give-way boat on port, something the normal rules prohibit. Hunting is when the starboard tack boat keeps pointing right at their opponent, even as the opponent is trying to keep clear, until the give-way boat ultimately has to turn away, sailing the wrong direction, downwind on an upwind leg. The meeting of the boats is essentially a game of chicken, threatening a head-on collision that the starboard tack boat gets to win. This was a first for the AC72s.

It's a bit of a swat on the nose, and here the dial-down cemented a small lead for NZL that they used to keep OTUSA on the boundary. NZL left OTUSA two bad choices, either too many tacks (each adding slightly to ETNZ's lead) or else OTUSA not tacking with ETNZ sitting on them from ahead. Again ETNZ converted a small lead at the top mark into an unrecoverable gap on the final downwind leg. OTUSA made gains downwind, about 100m out of the 590m lead, but using half the leg to do so.

ETNZ won Race 6 with a finish delta of 47 seconds. New Zealand was up 5-0 on points, not even counting the penalty, and four wins from taking the Match.

Race 7

Winds were up slightly, 16 to 17 knots. ETNZ to weather again won the drag race on Leg 1. Downwind trailing by barely 60m, a slow gybe cost USA another 40m.

Upwind, ETNZ covered. OTUSA tried to get out of phase, but in the tacking NZL's lead grew halfway up the leg to 300m, insurmountable unless something went wrong for ETNZ. At the windward gate, the lead hit 400m. They would be well on their way home by the time USA got there 55 seconds later, with a 1000m lead downwind for ETNZ.

ETNZ won Race 7 by 1:06. They were now three victories from the Cup while USA still needed ten races.

A trailing ORACLE TEAM USA couldn't match ETNZ upwind. Changing the crew had not changed the outcome.

The press was all over Spithill. How could OTUSA keep going? Why couldn't they win?

"Well, we're going to fight the whole way," Spithill said. "We're going to go out every single race thinking we can win. We have to, and we believe that. We still have a couple of options with the boat that we are going to make changes in this day off. A little bit of it depends on the weather, but we are going to have to be pretty aggressive now and obviously push as hard as we can, but look—we know if we sail well out there we can win races."

ORACLE TEAM USA leading
Emirates Team New Zealand on
September 15. (© 2013 ACEA/
Photo: Abner Kingman)

Spithill's strong conviction didn't quiet the press. In the context of the events of the last few days, and the score, and the negative penalties, and winning the starts only to lose the races, this looked easily like bravado on Spithill's part. Prodded again on the topic, he showed his boxing skills, slipped away and did a little counter-punching.

"I think the question is, imagine if these guys lost from here, what an upset that would be," Spithill said, referring to Dean Barker and crew sitting next to him. "I mean they've almost got it in the bag. So, that's my motivation. That'd be one hell of a story, that'd be one hell of a comeback, and that's the kind of thing that I'd like to be a part of. I've been involved in some big fight-backs, you know, with some big challenges, and facing a lot of adversity, and that'd be the kind of thing I'd love to be involved in. I know I speak on behalf of all of the team, so that's our motivation going in to the rest of this series. We feel we've got just as much chance to win this, and we're going to do everything we can."

He was the team leader and wasn't going to admit defeat until the Match had actually been lost. After being on the defensive for so many days in the post-race briefings, Spithill was also trying to put the spotlight on Dean Barker, who up until then had mostly enjoyed the luxury of trying not to look too confident in the face of good results. Spithill was talking tough, but time to back it up was running out.

Race 8, Saturday, September 14

ORACLE TEAM USA did not sail in practice on Friday, a sign that in addition to giving the sailors a chance to refresh, though by no means rest, OTUSA also was making modifications to their boat. On Saturday, one visible change to 17 was a much shorter bowsprit.

OTUSA was getting out-tacked, out-pointed, and eventually out-raced on the upwind leg. Downwind they were somewhere between even and ahead of Emirates, but that wasn't going to cut it. Emirates Team New

Emirates Team New Zealand leading near the top of the upwind leg. (© 2013 ACEA/Photo: Gilles Martin-Raget)

(© 2013 ACEA/Photo: Ricardo Pinto)

Zealand needed just three more races to take the America's Cup. OTUSA needed ten.

Better tactics to windward would help. In Thursday's racing ETNZ did everything they could to make the contest about their greatest advantages over the Defender. OTUSA got trapped near the boundary, with no good way out, having to tack repeatedly and lose ground each time. ETNZ had done better playing the flood current protection near Alcatraz Island, but Saturday would be an ebb current race, changing up the tactical landscape.

At the start of Race 8, Spithill couldn't get any advantage on Barker coming to the line, and ETNZ won the start. Downwind, USA traded gybes, ETNZ getting the better of the Defender by one maneuver. Delta at the leeward gate was just 8 seconds.

Upwind the boats started a tacking duel, working up the shore near the city, looking for small advantages in the wind. ETNZ tried to cover, but OTUSA started making gains, a 70m lead down to 50m. Nearing the top of the course, ETNZ was to the left of OTUSA, both on port tack. OTUSA had been inching up, the lead down to 5m, but the boats were several lengths apart across the course. OTUSA tacked to starboard, hoping to get to the left side and set up for the mark rounding. ETNZ was ready for their move, and tacked right on their track, dead ahead, a repeat of the way ETNZ had put an end to OTUSA's threat in Race 1.

NZL tacked in front of OTUSA, cranking hard in her turn with OTUSA close, and the boat coming out of the tack suddenly heeled up at nearly 45 degrees, the classic small-boat capsize about to happen with a 13-story wing at 20 knots. *Aotearoa* looked like it was going over. The boat hung there nearly ten seconds, somewhere close to the knife's edge, possibly the whole challenge campaign hanging in the balance. The crew called out "Hydro! Hydro!" apparently not having the pressure in their system to control the wing. The ETNZ wing was not self-tacking, and they needed the hydraulic system to ease the wing.

Spithill, sailing at 26 knots, had planned to duck below, saw his opponent's AC72 head up in his path, dead ahead. OTUSA had to crash-tack away to avoid a collision. There was no telling how quickly ETNZ was going to come down, in what direction, or where the boat would be headed after she landed.

ETNZ was penalized for tacking in front of OTUSA and not keeping clear, but by the time the Kiwis gathered their wits, they were far enough behind that the penalty was done. OTUSA was 300m ahead, about to take a big lead onto the final leeward leg. Downwind that quickly became 700m, and ORACLE TEAM USA won Race 8 by 52 seconds.

With their second victory, OTUSA had erased their penalty, and any wins after this would score points. ETNZ might have lost everything had they flipped over. Nothing appeared to be damaged, but OTUSA had finally broken TNZ's aura of invincibility. Sailing better, OTUSA had drawn close, and a simple mistake with big consequences had given them the opportunity to win.

The Match stood at 6-0 on points, with the penalties cleared, ETNZ still needing three races, OTUSA now needing nine.

Race 9, Try 1, Second Race of the Day

Winds were coming in at 19 to 20 knots, delaying the start by 15 minutes.

At the start, Spithill was slightly back and to windward of ETNZ, not close enough to roll over them in the drag race, and Barker to leeward held OTUSA past the reaching mark before bearing off with a small 60m lead downwind to ETNZ. Both boats were right on top of each other. Delta at the downwind gate was 7 seconds, with ETNZ barely ahead, when the winds built over the limit again and the Race Committee abandoned the race.

Barker was pleased by the starts, but still recovering from the near-capsize.

"We had two leads round Mark 1, which is something that we've been working hard on, so that's encouraging," Barker reported. "And then sailed the runs well. The second we were shaken up, it was still tight, but we felt we're in a pretty nice spot, the boat felt better, we made some changes from the first race, and I think it would have been an interesting race. But tomorrow is another day and we'll come out absolutely full on to make sure we win some races."

Jimmy Spithill was happy to have something good to talk about, getting ahead of the New Zealanders, even if it had been while they were looking at the world from 30 to 40 feet in the air. "I think we've gained a lot in that we've improved our boat," he said. "We've seen we've come from behind on the upwind leg and passed. So that is a huge step for our

A turning point: On the upwind leg of Race 8, Emirates Team New Zealand nearly capsized, heeling to 44.8 degrees. ORACLE TEAM USA had to crash tack to avoid a collision, and thus, a shaken-up ETNZ was penalized by the umpires. (© 2013 ACEA/Photo: Abner Kingman)

team and a huge confidence booster. It's exactly what we need. The guys have already got more ideas, and they are going to work all night again. And we'll come out tomorrow ready to try and step it up once more."

Races 9 and 10, Sunday, September 15

Barker was aggressive in the start of Race 9 (second attempt), but Spithill held ETNZ to windward, away from the line, letting USA break away first, and taking a 4-second lead at Mark 1.

USA extended on the first downwind leg to nearly 200m at the downwind gate. Delta was 18 seconds.

With NZL working the shore side of the course and OTUSA on the other, a right shift helped USA edge out to a 300m lead. The Kiwis were not gaining. USA was also battling to round the upwind gate before wind limits might cause the race to be abandoned. They were well ahead, a delta of 33 seconds.

ETNZ split from the Defender on the leeward leg, hoping there was something that could be done other than follow, but Leg 4 was no kinder to ETNZ when they were losing than it had been to anyone else. A 500m lead grew to 740m.

OTUSA won Race 9 by 47 seconds. The score stood 6-1 for ETNZ. The first to nine points now would win.

There was something more than just the victory if you looked closer. ORACLE TEAM USA had gained on every leg of Race 9.

At the start of Race 10, winds were near the limits of 21.5 knots.

NZL wanted the pin end. Barker sailed down past the lay line a bit, trying to get Spithill on his right, and block him from the line. Spithill tried to chase him closer to the line, tried to push him too far to lay the pin. After the starting gun, NZL maintained the overlap, preventing USA from getting in front. It was a 3.5-second delta for NZL at Mark 1.

Onto the downwind, USA cut a 200m lead to 120m, but a slow rounding for USA gave up distance to NZL. It was a 10-second delta at the downwind gate.

Upwind, OTUSA closed up the lead, down to 150m. Wind on the left looked better, but NZL tried the right looking for better current. NZL soon tacked back, with the lead under 100m.

A long port tack paid off for USA. The boats converging, OTUSA pulled in front and crossed ahead by 20m, taking the lead as NZL, on port, had to duck.

With the upwind gate coming, there was a big cross near the port lay line. USA had to dip. NZL was back in front!

On the next tack, they might make the gate. NZL couldn't get in front, crossing each other just below the gate. OTUSA didn't hunt them, and instead went to the left mark. NZL went to the right. Less than a one-second delta was between them at the upwind gate. Two legs remained.

ETNZ gained on the offshore side of the course and was ahead again

by just meters as they came together on the final downwind leg. Spithill went behind them and stayed on port gybe, but he lost distance. NZL pulled out to 100m. There was no place to make more gains for OTUSA. NZL had a line to the mark and the finish, and won Race 10 by 16 seconds. The score was now 7-1.

Race 10 would stand as the height of the battle, one wild race where the lead changed hands four times, and the deltas at the marks were never larger than 11 seconds.

The AC72 yachts had been amazing to watch, especially in person, where the size and visceral speed of the boats was almost hard to comprehend. A 131-foot-tall boat, with a footprint the size of a tennis court, screaming across the finish line 8 feet in the air, seconds ahead of their opponent, was an adrenaline rush even for spectators. It was a technological achievement that even the authors of the Class rule didn't know was possible when they started.

"I can honestly say this is the most fun and exciting sailing I've been involved with," said Ben Ainslie after the race.

"If you didn't enjoy today's racing, you should probably watch another sport," said Barker.

OTUSA leading ETNZ on September 15. (© 2013 ACEA/Photo: Abner Kingman)

Though USA and NZL had been clocked nearly equal if you looked at average speeds, USA had gained on only one leg, the upwind. Even then they had lost the lead. But the Defender and Challenger had never looked so equal since the Match started.

Spithill wouldn't confess as to exactly what they had changed on-board 17 to improve their performance, but he was willing to say they weren't done.

"This is a development boat. Like any racing sport, whether it's F1 or Moto GP, you're constantly learning how to race them," said Spithill. "Even today we have a heap of stuff we'd like to do to the boat."

The question was whether ETNZ would give them time to manage it.

Race 11, Wednesday, September 18

Two races away from winning the Cup, ETNZ could now win the regatta if they swept the day. OTUSA was getting better. They seemed to have fixed their weaknesses, and the teams looked even. With ETNZ needing two races to OTUSA's eight, splitting the daily outcomes as on Day 7 would do the trick before too long.

At the start of Race 11, the boats were late rather than early to the line for a change, Barker with position ahead. Mark 1 showed a 3-second lead for NZL.

On the downwind leg, NZL loosely covered, keeping a 6-second lead at Mark 2. NZL turned left, USA turned right, giving separation to USA as they started Leg 3 upwind.

The right turn paid off for USA, and they took the lead, but a tacking duel erupted, sustained until finally NZL succeeded with a lee bow tack onto USA, right ahead, and USA had to short tack to get away, giving back the lead to NZL.

The tacking duel continued, but OTUSA trailed by about 120m at the crosses, both teams working the left side of the course to minimize current.

NZL was hanging on to a 100m lead, but USA was making gains now in the middle of the course, with both boats on port tack. The lead went down to 50m, then down to 30m. USA tacked to starboard, but NZL just made it past them without having to duck. NZL tacked on them and USA tacked back. NZL got the better of the exchange.

USA came into the gate on starboard, NZL on port. USA was downspeed and gave NZL about a 100m lead around the mark. It was a 16-second delta at the windward gate.

A 300m lead for NZL downwind. USA was gaining slowly, but it was too big of a deficit to overcome with not much time left. OTUSA got close, very close, but ETNZ rounded Mark 4 at much better speed and held them off.

ETNZ won Race 11 by 14 seconds. Match total now stood at 8-1—match point for NZL.

USA was close, and starting with a lead rather than behind might have made the difference. A slow tack at the top of Leg 3 put them in a hole they couldn't get out of, despite cutting NZL's lead from 300m down to under 100m on the second-to-last leg. Race 11 had been close, and USA might have had enough boat speed, but ETNZ prevailed on tactics in the start, upwind, and at the downwind mark.

In Race 12, Try 1, the wind limit was called 15 seconds before the start, abandoning the race, and rising winds prevented another start before time ran out for the day.

Race 12, Thursday, September 19

America's Cup match point now. ORACLE TEAM USA's back was to the wall, every race now a must-win for them

In the pre-start, USA and skipper Jimmy Spithill caught NZL on their back foot and got a nice jump at the line while ETNZ was headed up, though still it was just a 5-second delta at the line.

Downwind, both gybed, 110m lead for USA, but NZL gained slightly on the gybes. Coming into the gate, OTUSA ahead rounded first, turned left, taking the offshore side. NZL turned right, 11 seconds behind.

USA went up to the right-hand boundary, then tacked. Both boats now on starboard, NZL made gains, the lead going to NZL. They tacked to port. Cross coming, lead going back to USA, who had right-of-way and crossed ahead. USA tacked at the left-hand boundary and when they came back were well ahead of NZL—a 115m lead. USA consolidated their lead, tacking ahead of NZL, and bounced them back to the left.

It was a struggle all the way up the leg, though. USA crossed the tide line, NZL got a boost from the ebb current. Both settled in on port for a long tack. USA gained slightly and tacked to protect the favored left side now. NZL stuck it out on the right. The USA lead was 145m.

NZL had an extra tack before rounding the gate. USA clear ahead rounded first, turned right, and went for the offshore and some favorable current. NZL turned left, behind by just 10 seconds.

On the final downwind leg, the gap started out at 200m, but was quickly up to 400m. USA had a much better angle. Quickly it was an-over-500m lead for USA.

ORACLE TEAM USA won Race 12. Match score was 8-2 for NZL—still match point.

Race 13, Try 1: Winds over the limit scratched the second race of the day just as the boats were entering the starting box, pushing Race 13 to Friday.

Race 13, Friday, September 20

The Heartbreaker

ORACLE TEAM USA had a new measurement certificate, now with a longer bowsprit in order to fly a code zero in the very light conditions expected.

Race 13, Attempt 2: Very light winds reported at 7 to 11 knots. Low fog was heavy on the windward end of the course, near the Golden Gate Bridge.

With the unusually light breeze, USA set up immediately for the line on a time-and-distance start. NZL came back and got to windward of them. Slight lead for USA at the start, just 20 knots boat speed on the reach to Mark 1, where usually the yachts were going 40 knots plus. USA luffed NZL, keeping them away from Mark 1. All was in slow motion compared to earlier races.

It was a 10-second delta for USA at Mark 1. USA ahead, NZL slightly behind and to weather. Downwind boat speeds were only in the teens. NZL got advantageous current first and pulled nearly even. Then NZL found some wind, enough to fly a hull, and soon built a lead. They were 400m ahead while USA was still trying to find better wind, and 600m ahead by the bottom gate.

USA rounded 1:41 behind, but not the biggest factor. ETNZ was racing against the clock. There was a time limit of 40 minutes this course, per the Sailing Instructions, and it took 14 minutes just for Legs 1 and 2

Race 12: ORACLE TEAM USA was able to cover Emirates Team New Zealand and protect the favored left side of the course on the way to winning their fourth race of the match. (© 2013 ACEA/Photo: Ricardo Pinto)

to be completed. If New Zealand could finish in time, they would win the America's Cup.

NZL headed off to the right, USA went to the left, got better wind, and started chewing NZL's lead down to 350m. But filling in from the ocean into the Bay, the wind up the course was better, and NZL got it first. They extended their lead to 700m.

NZL needed to finish in the next 14 minutes, and they had not even rounded Mark 3 yet. There were 12 minutes left under the time limit. NZL rounded Mark 4 and started Leg 4, the final downwind leg. The first downwind leg had taken 11 minutes. Slightly better wind and they could make it.

USA dropped to 1000m behind, and in this wind that didn't matter anymore. The only race was against the clock.

Downwind, time ran down, 7 minutes, 6 minutes, with NZL barely halfway down the course. At 5 minutes to go, NZL still had to reach Mark 4 and sail the finish leg. They were finally getting to 20 knots on the downwind leg in between gybes.

With a minute to go, they weren't quite to Mark 4. It was just not in these conditions to sail a complete race. 40:00 passed on the timers. The Regatta director called on the radio for the race to be abandoned, per the rules. ETNZ kept going toward the finish, but they had been watching the clock, too. Just a few hundred feet away in the gray, listless San Francisco overcast lay the finish line, as close as Emirates Team New Zealand got to winning the America's Cup.

Race 13 would be sailed again.

There was enormous frustration, some for fans who didn't expect that the time limit would play a factor. The ETNZ crew was sorry to see a chance, however improbable, slip away, but knew that it wasn't something to dwell on at the time.

Said Dean Barker, "I looked at the clock and it was counting back up from the start and it became clear that we weren't going to make the time limit. It's there for a reason and in the light conditions we had, it was difficult to get around the course in time. It's tough on the guys; they put a lot into the race. It's about being able to put it behind you—you can cry or you can laugh and get on with it.

"This is the third race that we've been in the lead and haven't won, either hitting the wind limits or running into the time limit. Any one of those three points would have been nice right about now. But there's no loss of confidence. We know we can easily get this done; it's just a case of going out there again tomorrow and racing hard."

Race 13, Try 3

Collision Course

NZL needed one win, from anywhere.

The Race 13 start was scheduled for 2:33 pm, with more wind this try. NZL went deep into the starting box, USA staying closer to the line and to

Race 13 (abandoned)-Emirates Team New Zealand couldn't get the point they needed to win the America's Cup. (© 2013 ACEA/ Photo: Abner Kingman)

windward. Spithill came down and tried to get under NZL for the hook. Barker came down, too, prevented the hook, and had a start clear ahead—USA 3 seconds behind.

Foiling downwind on starboard, USA was within 20m, then gybed away. NZL followed after about 10 seconds, but USA gained by being farther offshore. The boats looked even. USA gybed back, bringing starboard right-of-way with her as the boats converged. NZL crossed narrowly on port, very boldly, ahead by fractions of a second, and with a collision looking imminent USA headed up to avoid. USA protested. USA took the lead and NZL gybed to follow them.

The umpires penalized NZL for a port-starboard violation. USA was now out to 120m. Coming into the leeward gate, USA could lay the left-hand mark. NZL was diving to round to the right. USA, sailing between NZL and the mark, changed at the last second to a right-hand turn around the other mark, holding NZL away and forcing the Kiwis to gybe twice, way downspeed, and continue slowly now to the left-hand gate. It was a solid OTUSA gain for a split-second decision, and they led by 20 seconds at Mark 2.

Upwind, USA was on the right side, out to a 375m lead. NZL tacked to get to the left. USA kept going right, then finally tacked to cover and on port got a big shift and pulled out ahead. USA didn't want to get too far away, though, and came back again to tack ahead of NZL. The lead shrank to under 150m. NZL was too far to the right side of the course, though, and USA got the better of the shift and the current. NZL had to tack underneath them—being on the wrong side of the shift killed their chances. USA got out to 350m by the windward gate, which would open up into a huge lead downwind.

Race 13, on September 20: Emirates Team New Zealand (on right in photo) started clear ahead, but cutting it too close on a downwind cross brought trouble for the Kiwis. (© 2013 ACEA/Photo: Ricardo Pinto)

USA won Race 13 by 1:23.

Review would later show that NZL would have been safely across OTUSA's path by a matter of meters, but the umpires had established that a safe cross would be regarded as missing the other boat by 10m at a minimum. The consequences were just too great to force a helmsman to come closer than that to an opponent before trying to avoid a collision. The gains OTUSA made from the penalty and ETNZ's gybe soon after were leveraged into the position they used to switch gates at the last possible instant, pushing ETNZ even farther back.

After being within minutes of losing the America's Cup before time was called earlier in the day, USA brought the score up to 3-8, with NZL still one point away from winning the Match.

"We believe we can win, it's as simple as that," said Spithill. "We've worked so hard this whole campaign. From the start of this regatta, we were off the pace and we were honest about it and critical about it inside our own team. But now, we believe we've got the boat to do it, we've got the tools to do it and the guys are doing a fantastic job on board. If you look at the people involved in this campaign, the fact that we are at match point— we get the best out of our people when they're at that sort of pressure. We take it one at a time, get back out there tomorrow and try to do it again.

"If you look at the start of the regatta, it seemed as though everything was going against us. Four days out from the start of the regatta, we didn't know who we were going to race with. We'd lost our wing trimmer and had lost two points before we'd even started to race. But it feels to me as though it's starting to turn. There is so much support in San Francisco— the message, the energy, it's starting to affect the entire team. We feel as though the tide is turning and it's starting to go our way."

Races 14 and 15, Sunday, September 22

Race 14

The wind was light and spotty, especially at the leeward end of the course. Barker went to windward and even though Spithill couldn't pass him, USA used the overlap to push him out above the reaching mark, keeping him there nearly to the shoreside boundary, wringing all they could from the position.

USA was sailing slightly faster, but NZL was matching USA's gybes, just slightly behind and to weather, with USA out to a 175m lead. They went into the leeward gate 24 seconds apart.

On the upwind leg the lead was bouncing between 100m and 300m as they sailed through different patches, the wind getting softer as they went up the leg. Sailing in better current, and finding better wind, NZL cut the lead and, trading a few tacks, gained more, as close as 50m. ETNZ was only 15 seconds behind at the windward gate.

USA tried to cover, but in the spotty wind it wasn't easy. USA actually sailed into a dead zone, and ETNZ started to catch up. The lead was down to less than 50m before ETNZ's wind died, too. Another split, but NZL didn't find the wind this time. USA did and started foiling, sending OTUSA out to a 700m lead.

The two tacks were highly unequal, and NZL closed up quickly yet another time, under 250m. USA gybed for the mark with NZL coming fast, but OTUSA was just far enough ahead to round and stay out of trouble.

ORACLE TEAM USA won Race 14 by 23 seconds. The match stood at 8-4.

Second Race of the Day, Race 15

They started even at the gun, in a drag race. NZL, to weather again, couldn't pull ahead. USA led into Mark 1 by 3 seconds.

Downwind, trailing by about 100m, NZL gybed. USA, in the middle of the course, quickly multiplied their lead on a windshift. NZL, headed to the shoreside boundary, got lighter air, sailing 4 to 5 knots slower than USA. USA rounded the downwind gate 700m ahead, leading by 1:00. If the wind was this patchy, it might still be treacherous before the finish.

Upwind USA was 450m ahead. NZL gained, being out of phase with OTUSA until USA started covering. Only near the top was NZL finally in better conditions, closing to 275m. NZL gained 28 seconds on the upwind, trailing by 32 seconds.

Downwind, a big wind hole near Alcatraz played havoc, letting NZL get within 100m of OTUSA, but USA got out of it first, back up to speed, and won Race 15 by 37 seconds.

The America's Cup Match score went to 8-5 NZL-USA. Another match point had slipped away from ETNZ.

The light breeze had been a wild card in both races.

"It's really, really quite tricky," ETNZ's Glenn Ashby said. "We certainly saw less than 10 knots on our part of the racecourse a couple of times. It's tricky. Forecasting conditions is difficult, and certainly moding the boat is more difficult in actual fact. The boats go through such a big range of conditions. You get your configuration a little bit wrong, it doesn't affect one little thing, it sort of has a chain reaction and it affects the whole rest of the boat. Both teams were probably a little caught out by the conditions today, but that's yachting."

ETNZ was put away by aggressive moves at the start, an overlap that OTUSA used to maximum advantage. Much of the race was in difficult spotty winds, and typically in those conditions the leading boat often gets to the better wind first. What if NZL had started to leeward instead?

NZL had actually tightened up the race despite the light conditions, but there was a question of whether last-minute choices on sail selection had significant effect. Dean Barker didn't think that was a controlling factor. "We chose right on the cutoff in terms of having enough time to change sails," Barker said. "We made a call. We just looked at the conditions and the forecast we were sort of expecting. It was a tough call, we were expecting the breeze to sort of build more than it did, and it was probably the wrong decision, but it certainly didn't cost us the race. It wasn't the reason we didn't win the race."

Jimmy Spithill:

"The team is getting stronger each day. We made a couple more changes to the boat last night and I thought it made a significant difference in the boat in terms of performance. It felt really quick—and we're not done. There are a couple of other things we were speaking about today that we want to get to.

"When we were down 6-1, I said that we had a hell of a challenge on our hands, but stranger things have happened in sport. I thought we had the boat and the team to make a comeback and I wanted to be a part of that.

"We've faced all kinds of adversity—we capsized our first boat, we lost our wing trimmer, we lost two points, we've had all kinds of things happen. But the team hasn't made any excuses, they just stuck in and worked hard and it's made the team stronger. With the energy we have now and the changes we've made to the boat—the boat is just so much quicker than when we started this competition."

Dean Barker:

"We think we are fast enough (to get that last point). We have to sail well. We let ourselves down today, on both of the first downwind legs. We started behind at Mark 1 both times but we gave up too much distance on the downwinds. While the guys worked hard and made some gains upwind, it was never quite enough to put enough pressure on them.

"It was always going to be a battle, we knew that. They have improved since the first week but we feel as though we've improved as well."

Race 16, Monday, September 23

Start was postponed to 1:45, waiting for the wind to be consistent across the course, and even when it settled in, the breeze was light.

In the pre-start they came back to the line with USA to windward, NZL to leeward. USA accelerated better after the gun, got in front of NZL, and sailed down in front of them, the tables turned on Dean Barker again. USA led at Mark 1 by five seconds.

Onto the first downwind, light winds about 10 knots. Both gybed, with USA foiling first, and about a 175m lead for USA as both went to the offshore boundary. Gybing back, USA gained slightly, again up on foils first, a 210m lead. NZL started gaining slightly, gybing away past the middle of the course. USA let them go. NZL gained a lot on the offshore side. The lead was 50m as they came back on starboard, but NZL lost just enough in the gybe so as to not cross USA. Delta at Mark 2 was 13 seconds.

Upwind, the lead for USA was about 120m as they traded a couple tacks. Then they started across the course on a starboard tack, USA gaining in slightly better wind. The lead was up to 160m. NZL was still trading tacks, staying out of phase, but both were close as the left was the favored part of the course.

USA was looking for the long tack on port to set up their upwind gate rounding. NZL was following, but had lost slightly, lead out 200m, then down to 180m. USA had one more tack to the port lay line, then tacked to approach for a right-hand turn. NZL out to the right, saved a tack, rounded the mark, turning left. Delta at the upwind gate was 19 seconds.

Downwind, NZL came back from the shore side, gaining on USA, lead down to 140m, gybing away. USA gybed to starboard to cover. One slip here and NZL would get the lead. Past Marina Green they were at 30 to 32 knots. USA gained slightly, NZL gybed. USA gybed to cover. With a slightly better gybe by USA, the lead opened up to 180m. And USA kept doing better; they were soon out to 250m as the racecourse got shorter and shorter.

ORACLE TEAM USA won Race 16 by 33 seconds. The match stood at 8-6 now, getting close on points. This was the fifth match point race ETNZ had lost—five losses in a row after winning eight of the first eleven.

OTUSA, who had tied ETNZ on the number of wins at eight for each team, appeared to be confounding ETNZ a bit.

"The plan was to start to leeward of OTUSA and they did a pretty nice job of getting us compressed right down to the leeward end there, and they jumped us pretty quickly," ETNZ tactician Ray Davies said. "It was pretty evident about fifteen seconds after the start that they're very strong."

There was not enough time in the day to re-set for a second race, which was probably just as well for ETNZ. Upwind and downwind they were losing distance to ORACLE TEAM USA, who was getting their boat up on foils faster, and just able to sail faster than ETNZ downwind. Upwind, it was easy to say OTUSA was sailing smarter, but underneath it was beginning to look like a speed advantage, too.

Still, this loss was in unusually light air for San Francisco Bay, not normal conditions, and ETNZ had three races remaining to win one for the regatta.

"We still wouldn't trade positions, still would rather be on match point than having to win three more, but it's definitely a battle," Barker said. "There's no question the OTUSA guys have stepped it up a lot, and we need to be able to respond."

Did ETNZ want to race in higher wind?

"We're happy to race in anything; we feel comfortable with our boat across a range of conditions," Barker said. "We're not worried about sailing in any conditions. Both boats have their strengths and weaknesses but we feel that in any condition, if we sail well, we can win the race. There isn't any one particular thing—you increase your chances by leading around Mark 1 and that's something we haven't done as well as we could have over the last several races. There are lots of little things and you've got to be able to win races from in front as well as from behind. We've got to keep working hard on those options."

Was ORACLE TEAM USA frustrated because the 8-6 score at the end of Monday would actually have been 8-8 without the penalty?

"It's not frustrating, it's motivating, to be honest," Spithill said. "When it's very difficult and challenging, that's when it's the most rewarding. You have to play the cards you're dealt. We're not going to make excuses; we're going to work hard. We feel as though we've made great progress with the performance of the boat and that was evident today in the lighter air. As per usual, we'll go back tonight, work hard, and come out swinging tomorrow."

Spithill tried not to get into discussions about whether the penalty had been appropriate for the circumstances.

"We're sailors, we're athletes. We're not about the politics. Life's not fair sometimes but the beauty of sport is that you can win if you go win the race. We can win this Cup if we win the next few races. We control our own destiny."

Races 17 and 18, Tuesday, September 24

How much tension could one boat race stand? With the score at 8-6, this was the last day where Emirates Team New Zealand could win the America's Cup, but ORACLE TEAM USA could not. If there were two more wins by the Defender, though, it would force a monumental final Race 19, a single race for all the stakes.

Larry Ellison, who on one side of the street in San Francisco had the America's Cup, and on the other side had his company's annual meeting known as Oracle Open World, with 60,000 attendees, was scheduled to give the keynote speech to the convention Tuesday afternoon. The America's Cup had been expected to wrap up by September 21 even if it had gone the distance, but now the two events had overlapped. Ellison did the only reasonable thing possible given the circumstances. He skipped his own keynote speech to watch the America's Cup match on the water. Riding in one of the tenders from his 88m/288-ft. Feadship *Musashi*, he was in for something epic.

On Day 14, the flood tide made the pin end of the line a risky place to be, with the danger of getting pushed too low and trapped below the mark when the gun went off. More importantly, the flood tide meant that the upwind Leg 3, which held most of the passing potential for a trailing boat, would again be locked into the sheltering cone in the waters behind Alcatraz. The trailing boat could lose only by splitting, and instead would follow the leader with few opportunities to gain or pass until they got well up the leg. With passing on the downwind legs being rare, being ahead when starting the upwind leg was vital, and so the start loomed more enormously over these races than ever. Win the start, defend Leg 2, lock your opponent behind you on the early part of Leg 3, and there would be only a short window for him to pass.

Everyone knew it, and Dean Barker and crew were out to quash OTUSA's hopes before the series got any closer. The inverse logic of a series leader applied, in that ETNZ could afford to gamble and lose, while ORACLE TEAM USA didn't have that luxury.

Race 17

Winds calmed slightly to 18 to 19 knots with less than 10 minutes to the start.

USA entered on port, going deep into the box, 90 seconds to the start. NZL followed, USA turned back. 1:15 to start. Working back, moving slowly upwind, USA to leeward, NZL ahead and to windward, trying to block the line. At 15 seconds to the start, the two were slightly early. USA hooked NZL at the starting line, both went into a dial-up, stopping dead upwind on the line. A penalty was called on NZL for a windward-leeward violation. Still sitting nearly head to wind, NZL drifted downward toward USA and there was contact between the boats, though USA was bearing away, and a second penalty was given to NZL for not keeping clear after the start. Things were already going poorly for ETNZ, and they had not even crossed the starting line.

Onto the downwind leg, it was a 16-second delta for USA at Mark 1. They headed down the shoreside boundary, a 300m lead in place for USA. Near Marina Green USA gybed away. USA's lead was soon 400m. NZL followed. USA went out to the offshore boundary, then gybed. NZL followed. USA gybed in the middle of the course, able to lay the gate. NZL did the same, but the lead was now 530m. USA rounded, turning right, as did NZL 29 seconds later.

On the upwind, USA got up to speed and tacked to port, going for Alcatraz. NZL copied. The lead at the start of Leg 3 was 330m. The boats were doing some foiling upwind. NZL closed the lead as USA lost the protection of Alcatraz. USA went nearly to the left-hand boundary and then tacked back, the lead 210m as they crossed.

Both teams worked the left side of the course, tacking short of the middle and going up the shore. Getting to the top third of the course, they settled in for the longer port tack, anticipating the gate setup before long. NZL gained again, the lead down to 200m.

USA couldn't lay the upwind mark and had to short tack; NZL gained within 120m, and were within 19 seconds when they rounded the top mark.

Downwind the lead was 300m. USA came from the shoreside boundary to the center, NZL gybed over from the offshore side. USA gybed in front of their track, and consolidated their lead, covering from ahead at over 40 knots downwind passing Fort Mason. NZL gybed to port, USA matched. It was classic covering. There was not a lot ETNZ could do from behind on the downwind leg.

The margin from the start, with the two penalties, was never overcome. Had ETNZ been a little closer, could they have been near enough to turn an even start into a lead on Leg 3?

This was where OTUSA had been in the early races. Catching from behind was becoming hard to manage for NZL now. With a small gap, there might be a way to claw ahead in a tacking duel.

ETNZ had shown some gains upwind, and Ray Davies was a wizard at minimizing tacks. If they had been closer, that might have been enough to edge OTUSA at the upwind gate. It was the wrong race to have a disaster in the starting box.

OTUSA had simply sailed good covering tactics after that, and ETNZ still had chipped away, and beating OTUSA seemed like it could still be within their reach.

USA won Race 17 by 27 seconds. The match score was 8-7 NZL-USA on points, 9-8 USA on wins (see page 215). Had it not been for the penalties in the match, OTUSA would have already won the America's Cup.

"That start was an absolute shocker," said Barker. "We tried to mix it up a bit but really put ourselves in a bad, bad spot. We tried to bring them down the line, but we were just way too early; 40 seconds before the start we knew we had a bit on."

"We saw an opportunity there at the start and it was great to be able to put it together," said Spithill. "It was a really physical race and the boys really dug in."

ETNZ could recognize that their advantages were disappearing on the course.

"It's clear to see they were going pretty damn well," said Barker. "It was the first time that we recognized there was a condition where maybe we aren't as strong as we need to be. It's tough. We're doing all we can, the guys never gave up, but clearly the OTUSA guys were going well in that stuff."

Dean Barker continued, "The first race today, I made a really bad job of the start that put us completely on the back foot and took us out of the race at the start. It was nice to bounce back—the guys never give up, the belief is there. We executed everything well and did everything we needed to do and we were beaten. In the end, that's all you can ask of the guys. We know we can still win this; we'll go out and give it everything we can tomorrow. It's one thing to talk about it, another thing to do it. We have to go out there and do everything right—we know if we put the pieces together, we'll be successful."

Race 18

Winds 20 to 21 knots at last report. Either Emirates Team New Zealand would win the America's Cup in the next hour, or Wednesday would be the showdown Race 19 for the America's Cup.

Pre-start with USA to windward, NZL going for the hook. Protest by USA was green-flagged, no penalty. On a drag race to Mark 1, USA pulled ahead slightly, but was not able to drop in front. NZL leads onto Leg 2. Lead at Mark 1 was 5 seconds.

Early lead was 50m for NZL. OTUSA gybed slowly, losing some distance. Sailing 40 knots nearing the bottom gate, NZL reached the port lay line and headed for the left gate. USA turned right, 6 seconds apart.

With a 60m lead upwind NZL tacked early on USA, hoping to lee bow, but made a slow tack, letting USA pull very close. The boundary was coming fast, a dangerous spot for USA to be in. They tacked in unison, USA doing it a little better, getting a small lead out of it. NZL waited 30 seconds and tacked back to port, hoping to benefit more near Alcatraz while avoiding USA's bad air. By the time NZL got over to the shore boundary, they were 180m behind.

Both settled onto port tack. And USA gained. ETNZ tried getting out of phase with OTUSA, and every time they crossed, USA was 25m farther ahead. At the top of the course, the Kiwis couldn't lay the mark and needed an extra tack. USA was already away onto the downwind, and the lead was huge. The delta was over 56 seconds.

The lead was 940m as ETNZ rounded, out of range to catch OTUSA on the downwind leg, and USA won Race 18 with a finish delta of 54 seconds.

After being down 8-1, and facing match point seven times, OTUSA had evened the score.

The Match was now tied at 8-8 on points. OTUSA had won ten races to New Zealand's eight. Final Race 19 would decide the 2013 America's Cup.

ETNZ was only a hair slow on the Leg 3 cross, but USA leveraged it into an even position, then a pass, and then pulled away. OTUSA's tactics were good, and ETNZ may have given away some position they didn't need to, but it was also the sort of tactical victory that comes from having an edge in speed. And the upper portion of Leg 3 proved it. ORACLE TEAM USA was just sailing away from the New Zealand boat.

New Zealand just couldn't get that one race, not one in seven tries. OTUSA couldn't catch a break when the Match had started, 17 days earlier. Now every slip ETNZ made seemed to cost them a race, and with it another chance at the Cup was gone.

Dean Barker:

"Tomorrow is winner take all and it's going to be a tough race. Both teams are equally hungry to win this thing. We'll fight all the way til the end. You never focus on the ultimate outcome; you focus on the races that you've got. We've got one more race tomorrow. I think you have to give credit where credit is due—these guys have sailed themselves back into this regatta. They've been impressive. We're certainly very upbeat and we know we can win. There's an absolute belief in this team that we can win and we're going to go out there and give it our best shot."

Spithill:

"I think we've got it in us. We've come back from a very deep hole and we want this."

Glenn Ashby:

"I don't know what we've been doing these past two weeks—it's all just been training and the actual regatta starts tomorrow."

Race 19 (Deciding Race), Wednesday, September 25

Things had become very simple. The America's Cup would go to the first boat that could get around the five-leg course on San Francisco Bay and cross the finish line at the end of Piers 27 to 29. That would take less than 25 minutes from the 1:15 pm start, meaning a little after 2:30 the silver trophy won by the yacht *America* that August day in 1851 would be hoisted in the California sun, dripping with champagne.

The pure sporting occasion was off the charts. A seven-win streak for a comeback versus ten years of dedication just to get the opportunity. Somewhere between the joy and relief and a bit of something else, a lot of history would be taking place in that City by the Bay on September 25.

Race 19

After all the fireworks in the previous 18 races, the final race of the America's Cup saw a nearly simple time and distance starting strategy, with very little engagement, just a few testing moves. OTUSA was to weather, ETNZ to leeward in a drag race to Mark 1. They were neck and neck. Just short of the mark OTUSA fell off her foils, letting ETNZ round first. The delta at Mark 1 was 6 seconds.

Onto Leg 2, ETNZ just leading. OTUSA 35m behind, trying to roll up on the Kiwis. All the way down to the offshore boundary they sailed, gybing together. The lead was about 1 length with OTUSA directly astern of ETNZ at 40 knots on starboard tack. Into the gate, ETNZ turned left, ORACLE TEAM USA turned right, delta was 3 seconds. Utterly flying.

Upwind, a slight lead for USA as ETNZ tacked also to starboard. Lead went out to 70m, then ORACLE TEAM USA tacked. The cross came with ETNZ on starboard with right of way. OTUSA had to duck, and the lead went back to NZL—66m. ETNZ sailed out to the shoreside boundary. They tacked. Both on port, lead nearly even. OTUSA tacked, another cross coming now with OTUSA on starboard. ETNZ went behind them, no need to dip. OTUSA ahead.

Did New Zealand gain on the right? ETNZ tacked to starboard, cross coming again. Very close. OTUSA was still just ahead and could make it past. NZL went to the shore and tacked. OTUSA came back again, covering, still ahead, 120m now. ETNZ had to hang in with them. Winds were 17 to 20 knots. The point of no return was coming at the next mark, when exceeding the wind limits would no longer abandon the race.

ETNZ came back to the middle, but was still trailing. ORACLE TEAM USA was opening up a small lead, similar to the pattern of Race 18. Lead out to 300m. ORACLE TEAM USA was now foiling upwind. Saving tacks in the rounding would be the key. There was a lot of wind for the mark rounding, too.

ORACLE TEAM USA tacked on the port lay line, able to lay the mark, intending to turn right. ETNZ managed to point and lay the mark without an extra tack. USA was off and running for home, ETNZ rounding to the left. Delta at Mark 3 was 26 seconds.

On the final downwind the lead was 500m to ORACLE TEAM USA. Slow gybe very close to the boundary for ETNZ, and the lead was now 600m. The race was now on Leg 4—it would go into the books, no abandonment, the Cup would be decided. Halfway down the leg, the lead wasn't shrinking, 700m plus for ORACLE TEAM USA. OTUSA's wind dropped a bit, ETNZ closed slightly, but it was not enough. The racetrack was getting very short. OTUSA now on port gybe would need one gybe to starboard for rounding the final mark of the regatta; 44 seconds separated the teams at the finish line.

Golden Gate Yacht Club and ORACLE TEAM USA had defended the America's Cup!

The crew onboard 17 began to celebrate, and soon after crossing the finish line, a chase boat deposited Larry Ellison on board to congratulate his team, telling them that they had just won the America's Cup. Ellison soon took the wheel of the boat, too, slicing across the wakes of the spectator fleet as the historic fireboat *Guardian* filled the sky with arcs of water in celebration. One of the most incredible comebacks in the history of sports was complete, from down 8-1 at match point all the way back to a 9-8 victory.

On the other boat, though, the weight of high expectations, of a triumph almost in reach and now gone, had fallen on a crew that was still trying to comprehend the defeat. They knew what it meant to their fans back home, what it represented to their nation, and how fully committed they had been to a goal. For the last seven races, success and the vindication, the release that it would have carried had seemed nearly in hand. Grant Dalton had said that if they lost, there might not be any more Team New Zealand, that they might not be able to find the funding to compete again. And they had lost.

Onshore, Barker was solemn, saying little. Interviewed for TV, he relaxed slightly, but the look on his face was devastation. He could admit, though, that they had been studying their opponents, and had a pretty good idea what was coming. ETNZ had done everything they could do. It wasn't enough.

Dean Barker:

"Yesterday was really the first time we felt we had a bit on. We led around the bottom mark and watched OTUSA pretty much sail around us and sail away into the distance in the upwind, which had been our strength. We went into the race today with the attitude that we would do the very best we could—we led around the top mark but we saw today how dominant they've become upwind. It's very difficult to accept but I'm incredibly proud of Team New Zealand and everything the guys have achieved. We put everything into the race today, the guys' attitude was just phenomenal. We achieved everything we wanted to achieve—we got around the bottom mark in front and tried to hold them off, but we couldn't."

Grant Dalton:

"I probably slept better the last couple of nights than I did a week

Top: Race 19: ORACLE TEAM USA fell off her foils nearing Mark 1, giving an early lead to Emirates Team New Zealand. (© 2013 ACEA/Photo: Ricardo Pinto)

Bottom: The Cup Defended: ORACLE TEAM USA crew celebrates onboard after crossing the finish line, with the addition of a twelfth man, Larry Ellison, just right of center. (© 2013 ACEA/Photo: Gilles Martin-Raget)

ago, when I sensed that something was going on. I think the upwind deltas changed by a minute and a half in a week and a half. That's a huge improvement that they've made. We've improved a huge amount as well—we had a top speed at the bottom of one of our tacks of 14 knots— a week ago, it was 10 knots. But we just weren't quick enough, in the end.

"In Valencia in 2007, we were up 2-0 but we weren't nearly as strong a team as we are here. This was a completely different team in terms of its strength. My job now is just to support the guys, because they're just smashed—they're feeling this pretty bad. Everyone—the sponsors, the team, our friends, and families and a whole country, really—they're just devastated.

"We didn't feel as though we peaked properly in Valencia, we peaked more for the Louis Vuitton Cup finals. So here we made sure we hit it at the start of the America's Cup and we won the first two races. So we'd hit our peak and OTUSA was still trying to figure out how to sail at the start of the regatta. We've improved quite a bit but we didn't have as far to go. We are massively faster than we were at the end of the Louis Vuitton Cup but their rate of improvement was greater.

"[In terms of expectations] We were expecting 9-8, that's for sure. We always said the fastest boat would ultimately win, especially with the technology race that's been in play here, and that's what happened. We knew San Francisco would be a great sailing venue, it's amazing. We're biased toward Auckland, of course, but other than that, I can't think of anywhere better to sail."

Jimmy Spithill:

"I'd like to congratulate Emirates Team New Zealand. They are a tough team, a champion team. We had a lot of great battles against Dean Barker and his guys. He's a champion and he will be back. It's tough when you get to a winner-takes-all battle; it almost seems like a crime that there has to be a winner and a loser. I can't wait to race them again.

"We never gave up. I know everyone has questioned me relentlessly about this, but it really is about never giving up. I feel as though every-thing we went through really brought the team together and that's what got us through this. For me personally, I look back to the capsize. We didn't get back until two or three in the morning and the next day, the first guy to call me was Larry. I didn't know how it would go, but I told him I was fully responsible. He didn't want to hear that. 'You're a champion, you've got a champion team and this isn't the first bit of adversity you've faced and you'll come back from this.' It was one of the key moments of my life and I'll never forget that. It's what drove me this entire time. I felt I owed it to him, because he believed in me and believed in the team. I feel privileged to be part of this group."

Larry Ellison, when asked what he told the team when they were down 8-1:

"I just told them to listen to Jimmy Spithill! He said 'you know what 8-1 is? 8-1 is motivating.' I said, okay. I'll get behind that."

Emirates Team New Zealand skipper Dean Barker acknowledges cheers from the crowd and his competitors at the trophy ceremony.(© 2013 ACEA/Photo: Ricardo Pinto)

Asked about the role of Russell Coutts, Ellison continued: "Russell Coutts is our leader. When we were down 8-1 he told me it doesn't make any sense that they're faster upwind. We kept focusing on things we could do to the boat. We thought our boat would be okay, we just had to configure the boat properly. A combination of the engineering team and the guys out on the water finally broke the code, finally figured out what we had to do. It was Russell's perseverance. He talked a lot about driving the boat lower and faster instead of higher and faster, a matter of moding the boat, getting more horsepower. Russell wasn't out on the water, but a lot of his ideas, a lot of his strategies, a lot of techniques used to speed up the boat came from Russell Coutts. He has never lost an America's Cup—not a bad record."

Asked about Team New Zealand and the possibility that this had been their last America's Cup, Ellison concluded: "Team New Zealand—what a great team, what a great sailing nation. So many great sailors. No one should have the weight of a nation on his shoulders like Dean Barker has these past several teams. It's a fantastic sailing team. Dean is a champion and it's impossible to conceive of an America's Cup without Team New Zealand. I think they will be back."

HOW THEY DID IT

Even with the spray from fireboats and champagne bottles still hanging in the air, the question was how had ORACLE TEAM USA done it? Like the rest of the AC72 fleet, OTUSA had seemed slower than ETNZ when they first met on the racecourse. Not too much slower in the Defender's case, at least compared to the gaps Artemis and Luna Rossa showed, but at the start of the match ETNZ had looked stronger in nearly every respect, getting off the line faster in the starts, gybing more smoothly downwind, better in the tacks upwind, and when it counted most, faster to the windward mark.

By the end of the regatta, the starts were a toss-up, OTUSA was tacking better than ETNZ, and was at least even in other boat handling. Most devastating, upwind OTUSA was sailing away, and foiling to windward at times.

And OTUSA had continued to improve as the match progressed. "Yesterday was the first time that we felt we had a bit on," said ETNZ's Barker on the final day. "Yesterday in Race 2 we led around the bottom gate and watched Oracle pretty much sail around us and into the distance on the upwind, which had been our strength. Today we went in with the attitude to win the start, lead at the first mark and leeward gate and see what we can do. Today, again, we saw how dominant they'd become upwind."

"They just got better and better," said Grant Dalton. "They got about a minute and a half faster on the beat than they were nine days ago. We were sort of 50 seconds a beat quicker, and now they're 50 seconds quicker than us. So they've done a really amazing job to turn that around."

During the regatta, only a few changes to the OTUSA boat had been obvious, such as removing the bowsprit on days when the wind was up. Questioned about the modifications daily in the post-race press conferences, Spithill continued to refer to changes being made every day to the boat. The race schedule, becoming nearly constant in the later stages of the match, allowed little or no time for on-the-water testing to confirm that any reconfigurations of the yacht were actually faster, and some wondered how much change the Defender could be taking on. Unverified modifications to the boat in the middle of a regatta would be a huge risk if you didn't have a race left to lose.

Throughout the match, the teams could make changes to their yachts, have them remeasured and recertified by the measurers. ETNZ received 11 new certificates while OTUSA received 17. The margin primarily came during the first five days of the regatta, when OTUSA was recertified four times while ETNZ stayed unchanged. After that, both boats were being modified for nearly every race during the match. Since such small changes as modifying the angles of the rudders to suit the predicted conditions would result in a new certificate being issued, new certificates alone don't confirm that drastic steps were being taken.

Evidence since the match suggests now that most of OTUSA's technical modifications were made early, but that a lot of the gains resulted from continual improvements in crew work and techniques through to the end of the regatta.

The obvious question, though, was that if OTUSA could improve so much, what happened to ETNZ?

The Kiwis had been ahead of the game, it looked like. ETNZ had laid out their development program with the intention of being in peak form by the first race of the America's Cup match. They left the Round

Robin stage early, giving them two-and-a-half weeks to conduct tests and optimize the boat further before the Louis Vuitton Cup Finals began. And then they had what turned out to be another 12 days after the LVC Finals to keep working.

And ETNZ found results. By some measures they were 20% faster around the course by the time they began the America's Cup match compared to their earlier performance.

Everything had been stacked on being ready at the start of the AC match. Freezing development too early had limited their potential in Valencia in 2007. That lesson had been learned, and for 2013 ETNZ was still making adjustments to their boat right up to the days before the match began.

OTUSA, for their part, had enjoyed the entire summer to prepare, racing their two boats against each other, and should have been on the same trajectory for the first race. But the two development programs had a different underlying approach, and it nearly undid OTUSA.

ETNZ had gone ahead early with a solid dependable boat, a good all-around platform that had a high likelihood of performing well in a range of expected conditions. The team was confident that as foils, sails, and other features were optimized over time they would sail well when it came time to race. Being ready earlier than the other teams with boat one and boat two gave them experience nobody else had. The Louis Vuitton Cup bore them out, the NZ team looking smooth nearly throughout.

OTUSA on the other hand had designed boats that appeared to have greater potential. They were more refined designs in some aspects, but much harder to master. OTUSA's hulls were narrower, probably creating lower drag in the water, and certainly lower in aerodynamic drag. Among the visible clues, for example, OTUSA's foils were a bit smaller, likely having been optimized for lower drag, too. But being smaller and having less surface area at the same time made the design more sensitive to being in the proper configuration to generate sufficient lift. OTUSA more readily fell off her foils, especially in the reaching legs, throughout the match. The Defender's boat was harder to sail well, and at the start of the racing they had not really figured everything out. The potential was there, but they weren't achieving it.

ORACLE TEAM USA also admitted that they were hampered to some degree and lost focus while coping with the cheating scandal. Grant Simmer told *Sailing World* magazine that "the last month prior to the Cup was very hard because a lot of people were distracted by the Jury process, myself included. It meant we couldn't get on with our two-boat program. It was seriously disrupted and one of the reasons we went into the Cup certainly less prepared to race."

The Defender also lacked for a true opponent. Despite the aggressive intramural sailing between Spithill and Ainslie, they were still competing with two boats produced by the same designers, and more similar in philosophy to each other than to the rest of the AC72 fleet. Being ready

San Francisco fireboat *Guardian* salutes the America's Cup winners. (© 2013 ACEA/Photo: Gilles Martin-Raget)

for match racing usually involves fine-tuning the boat, trading possibly lesser performance in some areas for better performance in other, more important, aspects. Until the experience of actual racing, OTUSA couldn't be sure where their greatest weaknesses were.

In essence OTUSA had chosen a design that would take a lot of time to master when there just wasn't a lot of time available. And they had lost more time—months—than expected, with their capsize, and launched boat number two nearly at the end of April. They had built a lot of potential into their AC72, but would they be able to harness enough of it in time to win?

Surprises on Day 1

The biggest surprise for both sides came in the area of upwind speed. OTUSA had been confident by mid-summer that they were faster to windward than ETNZ, based on the configurations of the hulls and foils and observations of the performance of the boats. They were also willing to concede that ETNZ was probably a touch faster downwind.

Upwind mattered most. With the introduction of foiling, even in the AC72s, more time was spent on the single upwind leg compared to the two downwind legs combined. Factoring in tactics and racecourse factors, the upwind leg was the pivotal section of each race, making it the most critical aspect of the matchup between the boats.

The Challenger must have been worried a bit, too. By the time the match started, with all of their August downtime, ETNZ had improved their windward performance to the point where they were now faster than the Defender, while OTUSA now held maybe a small speed advantage heading to leeward, for whatever that was worth.

Emirates Team New Zealand's second AC72, named Aotearoa after the Maori word for her home country. (© 2013 ACEA/Photo: Gilles Martin-Raget)

OTUSA's Grant Simmer admitted they were shocked by ETNZ's speed upwind in the early races.

With upwind speed now an all-out priority, adjustments were made that would have been obvious on any cat. Raking the mast aft moved the center of effort, loading up the after parts of the hulls, letting the boat track better, and generally improves pointing ability. OTUSA's hull shapes seemed to respond better to sailing a little less bow down. Removing the bowsprit, in addition to reducing windage, appeared to aid the fore-aft balance, too. The combination of daggerboard foils and rudder wings was also sensitive to the balance of the boat, and OTUSA was seeking a configuration that would help the boat foil efficiently on the downwind legs as well.

Starts

The starts were a visible issue. Leading at Mark 1 and defending was much better than having to pass. In the Louis Vuitton Cup, Dean Barker had been having his way with his opponents by Mark 1. OTUSA at first looked no better than Luna Rossa had against the Kiwis, regardless of windward or leeward position in the usual drag race on the reaching leg. With coaching from Phillipe Presti, and careful attention to crew work, including studying their opponent, OTUSA developed similar techniques to maximize acceleration, and to get the boat up on foils as soon as possible, leveling the playing field at the start. Ultimately, even though the starts received a lot of attention, leading at Mark 1 wasn't decisive by itself. ETNZ led at Mark 1 in 5 of their 8 wins, and OTUSA led at Mark 1 in 7 of their 11 wins, averaging about 63% success for both teams, significant in a close match, but not as vital as constant discussion of starting results in the press might have suggested. Port versus starboard entry statistics were nearly dead even, too, another hint that speed around the racecourse was deciding the outcome of races in the long run.

But the techniques for quickly foiling at the starting gun were also applicable to an AC72 coming out of a tack, or getting back up on foils after other maneuvers, and as OTUSA perfected their techniques, they closed out another one of ETNZ's advantages.

Tacking

Tacking was one of the most critical aspects of the matchup. In the early races, ETNZ was faster through their tacks, losing less velocity going through the eye of the wind and getting back up to speed quicker than OTUSA. And once they realized they were better at it, the Kiwis tried to make the Defender tack at every opportunity, gaining several seconds each time. ETNZ had some built-in advantages, including a self-tacking jib, but a lot of tacking is coordination among the crew, and how they respond with the wing and the foils as the helm goes over. After some careful analysis of the telemetry data, and hours spent on the water, OTUSA managed to solve the issue.

In later races, OTUSA appeared to sail slightly higher angles just before tacking, then moved more quickly through their turns and came out with greater speed. The more sharply the boat could be turned without scrubbing speed, the shorter the maneuver and the less distance lost.

As long as they were able to execute crisply, tacking was no longer a weakness and OTUSA could engage ETNZ upwind.

As OTUSA sorted out their crew work, they were able to take it a few steps further, too. The AC72s had been able to foil upwind only intermittently and make it pay off. Usually the apparent wind angles that made foiling possible were too far off the wind to have any advantage over sailing

ORACLE TEAM USA's second AC72, 34th Defender of the America's Cup.(© 2013 ACEA/ Photo: Gilles Martin-Raget)

conventionally to windward with the hull in the water. In August, OTUSA had been developing a foiling technique that could work, but in the turmoil surrounding the cheating scandal, had fallen back to the proven methods of sailing the boat. As they got other aspects of the matchup with ETNZ sorted out ORACLE TEAM USA was able to return to upwind foiling and make it work, finding the slightly lower angles that were actually faster to the mark. ETNZ wasn't able to do it consistently, and OTUSA gained an effective tool for closing out New Zealand in the later races.

Foiling upwind was a weapon that the Challenger just couldn't match.

"Their boat was better suited for doing that for extended periods," Dean Barker said. "They certainly were doing a better job finding that extra gear that we simply couldn't."

And even when not foiling, as the OTUSA crew learned their boat, they also became more adept at the small changes, such as finding a "point mode" to sail closer to the wind than normal for short periods of time, which can be essential in close tactical situations.

Gaining Time

But what made it all work was the time to get better. Starting the race at a two-point disadvantage to ETNZ—due to the penalty—was nearly the end. The turning point in most accounts was the call that Spithill received the most heat for at the time, his decision to post-pone Race 6, the second race of the day on September 10, when ETNZ had just gone ahead to 4-1 after catching OTUSA, forcing them to the left boundary, passing them, and sailing off to a big lead. Even admitting miscues in tactics, ETNZ had looked clearly faster. A second race would have almost certainly been a loss, and as events turned out, ETNZ might have clinched the regatta before the Defender had a chance to make their dramatic improvements pay off in victories.

The postponement gave OTUSA time for technical improvements. The most significant change that OTUSA has revealed involved a modification to the rudders. A limiting factor on the AC72s was emerging: cavitation around the lifting surfaces of the daggerboard and the rudder, a phenomenon caused by the extremely low pressure a foil generates when moving at high speed through the water. Bubbles form, essentially the water boiling at low pressure, and then collapse, potentially causing a loss of lift, making the boat unstable, not to mention creating shock waves that could damage the surface of the foil over time.

OTUSA adapted a small torpedo shape placed at the intersection of the rudder's vertical blade and the horizontal wing. Protruding slightly ahead of the rudder, and continuing back along the joint between the two surfaces, the retrofitted piece altered the high-speed flow over the rudder enough to delay the onset of cavitation. More stability via the rudder may have also then allowed more efficient angles of attack for the daggerboard foils.

The wind limits, too, were a significant influence. By the time ORACLE TEAM USA's winning streak began on September 19, down 8-1 with no room for error, four missed races had already been lost to high winds. One of the races got as far as the upwind leg, with New Zealand leading by 7 seconds before being called off. More races earlier in the schedule, before the relative performance profiles of the boats crossed over, might have made the difference in the match.

Human Factors

On the heels of making the call for the postponement, another tough decision was taken by OTUSA, pulling tactician John Kostecki off the boat, replacing him with Ben Ainslie, and bringing Tom Slingsby into the mix on tactics. Whether it was his helming experience, changes in grinding responsibilities, or just a fresh start, Ainslie and Slingsby developed a good interpersonal dynamic on tactics, working issues out, and communicating with Spithill but letting him concentrate on helming the boat. Kostecki worked hard onshore to prepare the two sailors to take over his duties. It was of course easy to look smart once the boatspeed issues were fixed, but throughout the match Ainslie and Slingsby were at least the equal of Ray Davies on ETNZ.

Secret Weapon

Despite theories to the contrary, no credible secret technology emerged to explain ORACLE TEAM USA's remarkable turnaround. The boats had actually been very closely matched even from the first race, but making it a contest was a case of accumulating enough small advantages that could add up to wins. By the end of the match, the Defender had tapped the potential of their boat to be effective at foiling upwind, gaining an advantage that Challenger ETNZ couldn't match.

ORACLE TEAM USA had proven again just how much racing in the America's Cup still a development game. Even with one of the most advanced boats on the planet, the team was still learning until the end how to sail better, and how to make their boat faster, with no margin for error in the last eight races.

"The guys on board changed a lot," said Russell Coutts. "For sure there was a use of the technology change where we manipulated the force or manipulated the balance of those forces, but the guys on board the boat changed their technique, so there's this fantastic human element to this which really won the day in the end, which is great."

EPILOGUE
The Next America's Cup

Larry Ellison confirmed at the post-race press conference following ORA-CLE TEAM USA's victory that a Notice of Challenge for the 35th Defense of the America's Cup had been accepted, deferring announcement to a later date. Hamilton Island Yacht Club (HIYC) of Australia was revealed on September 30th as the next Challenger of Record. The Notice of Challenge had been received on the water as the winning yacht crossed the finish line in the last race of the 2013 America's Cup. Representatives of GGYC and HIYC will negotiate the terms of challenge and establish the initial rules to accept additional challengers for the 35th defense.

Specifics involving the types of boats and other aspects like format, timing, and location will be explored with the potential challenger community to help increase participation and build on the successes of America's Cup 34. Expectations are not for any firm announcements until the early months of 2014.

Timing for the next cup is likely 2016 or 2017 depending on some of the decisions about the boat and the venue. There may also be an effort to avoid conflicting with the 2016 summer Olympics, which will create difficulties for some of the top sailors.

While praising San Francisco, and saying he would love to come back, Ellison did not commit to where the next defense would be held, saying that the topic would need to be explored with the city.

Piers 27 to 29, the location of the 2013 America's Cup Park, will become the cruise ship terminal they were originally designed to be. And Piers 30 to 32 south of the Oakland Bay Bridge are earmarked now for an NBA stadium. Ellison joked, or so it seemed, about holding the next defense off the Hawaiian island of Lanai, which would be spectacular sailing but a bit light on accommodations and infrastructure. Of course Jimmy Spithill joked that Ellison had promised to give him the island of Lanai if Spithill won the America's Cup.

The boats selected stand a good chance to be multihulls, thanks to the excitement generated by the closeness of the 2013 match. Even the possibility of a return to the AC72 Class has been met with positive responses in the sailing world, something unthinkable at the start of the summer of 2013. The wingsail is less likely to be retained as a feature than the foils, which with proper provisions for in-race adjustment might become less intimidating to sailors.

TEAMS FOR THE 35TH AMERICA'S CUP

Defender: ORACLE TEAM USA

Golden Gate YC , San Francisco, USA

James Spithill is likely to continue as skipper. Russell Coutts is expected to remain team CEO. Ben Ainslie may depart to form his own British team; see below.

Background: Golden Gate YC will be the Defender of the America's Cup in the 35th Match, having won the trophy in 2010 from Société Nautique de Genève, and successfully defended it in 2013 against Royal New Zealand Yacht Squadron. The club was represented in 2003, 2007, 2010, and 2013 by ORACLE TEAM USA (variously known as Oracle BMW Racing [2003] and BMW Oracle Racing [2007 and 2010]).

Challenger of Record

The Challenger of Record (COR) is the first Challenger accepted by the Defender of the America's Cup. The COR has lead position in negotiating the mutual consent terms of the next Defense with the Defender/Trustee, such as time, location, type of yachts, match format, and details rules, though in the past additional prospective Challengers have sometimes also participated in the shaping of the conditions for the next match. Traditionally, the Defender and COR set the initial terms and then Notices of Challenge from additional yacht clubs and their representatives will be submitted. For the 35th Cup, the COR's Notice of Challenge was accepted as the winner crossed the finish line in the most recent America's Cup match.

AUSTRALIAN CHALLENGE | HAMILTON ISLAND YC, AUS An official announcement of Hamilton Island YC as Challenger of Record was issued September 30, 2013. Bob Oatley is an active yacht racer, winning the Sydney-to-Hobart race multiple times with his 100-footer *Wild Oats XI*, the latest in a string of yachts to carry the name. Oatley is the head of Wild Oats Wines, his family business, and a real estate developer of Hamilton Island. Oatley's son Sandy is also reported as a principal in the challenge. The Oatleys have said that a central goal of the next America's Cup cycle from their point of view is retaining much of the excitement of the 2013 America's Cup, but with the budgets at more accessible funding levels in order to encourage more teams. "We can put some boxes around the boats and the sails so it doesn't become a race of money," Oatley told Reuters on October 2. As for their own funding, the Challenger will seek support from corporate sponsors and the Australian government.

An all-Australian crew is a possibility, which would fit with other reports of trying to restore a greater sense of national representation to America's Cup competition, though Sandy Oatley told *Perth Now* that the composition of a crew will ultimately depend on the talent available as the challenge takes shape.

Iain Murray, who in 2013 served as Regatta Director and head of America's Cup Regatta Management, sails with Oatley and has a professional history with Hamilton Island. Murray was designer, skipper, and leader of Taskforce America's Cup Defence '87, the Australian Defender of the America's Cup in 1987. There is no word on whether Murray might be associated with the new Australian Challenger, or if he will remain with America's Cup Regatta Management for the next Cup. This is the first Australian Challenger for the America's Cup since Young Australia in 2000.

Challengers from 2013

ARTEMIS RACING / *ROYAL SWEDISH YC* (KUNGLIGA SVENSKA SEGEL SÄLLSKAPET) SWE. Iain Percy has been re-signed, promoted to team manager. Nathan Outteridge is being kept on as skipper. Officially these signings are only for team patron Torbjörn Törnqvist's other sailing programs for now, but continuity in personnel is an early sign of hope for a second Artemis America's Cup effort. "We're going to have a core of people from the existing team and see what happens with the next Cup before we go on," Törnqvist told *Bloomberg News* in mid-September 2013.

EMIRATES TEAM NEW ZEALAND / *ROYAL NEW ZEALAND YS* NZL. Continuing the team in the short term relies on having funding available quickly in order to retain key personnel. For 2003, the government of NZ provided this financial package to help bridge from one Cup cycle to the next. NZ Economic Development minister Steven Joyce told the press shortly after the regatta ended that the country will consider fully funding the team again once they have more details of the next America's Cup. The government voted TNZ $5 million NZD in bridge funding to help prevent top talent from being poached by other teams for the next Cup until more is known. Anticipation was for an approximately $35 million NZD package if the challenge proceeds. The amount contributed for the 2013 challenge was similar, adding up to about one third of total team budget.

Though Dalton looked crushed, "gutted," speaking before the media after the final race of 2013, both he and Barker expressed heartfelt appreciation for the welcome they received upon their return to Auckland. Though they had lost in a somewhat unprecedented fashion, and expected a potentially unhappy New Zealand public attitude after their defeat, their fans turned out in huge numbers for a welcome home celebration. The New Zealanders were disappointed to lose of course, but understood how remarkable their team had been, how extreme the effort had been, and that TNZ had done everything possible. The reception breathed new life into Dalton's outlook on the team, and he began working on additional fund-raising.

ETNZ's America's Cup record: Challenger (won 5-0), 1995; Defender (won 5-0), 2000; Defender (lost 0-5), 2003; Challenger (lost 2-5), 2007; Challenger (lost 8-9), 2013.

LUNA ROSSA CHALLENGE (PRADA) / *CIRCOLO DELLA VELA SICILIA* **ITA.** Had ETNZ won the America's Cup in San Francisco, Luna Rossa and ETNZ were simpatico enough that the Italian team was widely believed to have been lined up by ETNZ as the next Challenger of Record. Team patron Patrizio Bertelli was critical of the AC72 yachts and other aspects of the regatta as staged for 2013, as was ETNZ's Grant Dalton, though not resistant to another Cup held in a multihull class.

Luna Rossa has been a major team in the Cup since 2000, and the Italian sporting passion has always been on prominent display, including a strongly national crew. Following previous America's Cups, Bertelli has not been quick to commit to the next campaign. Their 2013 entry was made past the standard entry deadline, but welcomed by GGYC and OTUSA. Likely more needs to be understood about America's Cup 35 before Luna Rossa's future is known.

Luna Rossa's America's Cup record: Challenger, 2000 (lost 0-5); Challenger of Record, 2003; Louis Vuitton Cup Finalist, 2007 (lost 0-5 to ETNZ). 2013 Louis Vuitton Cup Finalist (lost to ETNZ).

2013 ACWS Only Teams (Racing AC45s)

ENERGY TEAM CHALLENGE / *YACHT CLUB DE FRANCE* **FRA.** That this team of French multihull experts did not field an AC72 entry to the 2013 America's Cup was one of the greater disappointments of the regatta. Leaders Bruno and Loïck Peyron may have future plans. After Energy stood down, Loïck was drafted by Artemis Racing to help skipper the Swedish AC72, and provide guidance to Nathan Outteridge, who sailed the boat in their Louis Vuitton Cup races. His time with Artemis was certainly a learning experience for Peyron as well. Loïck also has embarked on a foiling Moth campaign, suggesting he is working up the skills necessary to take the wheel of a foiling catamaran somewhere down the road.

Potential New Challengers

BEN AINSLIE RACING (BAR) / *ROYAL CORNWALL* **YC GBR.** When *Team Origin*, billed as the British America's Cup team, pulled the plug in October 2010, two reasons were cited either directly or in press reports: money and the commitments that key sailing team members including Ben Ainslie had to 2012 Olympic campaigns. Ainslie, now a four-time Olympic gold medalist, had been Team Origin's skipper and helmsman.

Ainslie joined ORACLE TEAM USA, but competed on his own AC45, and in the process hoped to possibly help secure backing for a full-on challenger campaign in the next America's Cup. Funding for the AC45 effort came from Larry Ellison at first, and some from name sponsor JP Morgan, according to Ainslie.

Following the end of the 2013 America's Cup, Ainslie has been exploring funding for a British challenge, and wants to sign top design talent as soon as possible. A decision on whether to challenge is expected to be made by the end of 2013.

In the America's Cup World Series, BAR represented the *Royal Cornwall YC*, which Ainslie has been associated with since he was a junior sailor. It is not known whether that is the same club BAR would represent if an entry is made for the 35th America's Cup.

CANADIAN CHALLENGER / *ROYAL VANCOUVER YC* CAN. A Canadian yacht club was reported to be interested in being the Challenger of Record for the 35th America's Cup, but that the GGYC deferred their offer, accepting Hamilton Island YC since the Australian club had expressed interest first. Presumably a team willing to be Challenger of Record also has intentions of being a Challenger otherwise, but no public statement has been made at the end of 2013.

CATS ARE LOOSE—WHERE DO WE GO FROM HERE?

The 34th America's Cup was everything organizers dared to hope it would be—close, exciting racing, lead changes, and enough drama to put this Cup into the history books. But now comes decision time: do the Defender and the new Challenger of Record decide to give the AC72 another try, go with a smaller, more manageable version, or change direction altogether and return to a keelboat? Time will tell, but after such an exciting America's Cup, it prompts the question—can you put the "cat" back in the bag?

If anyone had been asked back in August 2013, the decision would have been an easy one: the AC72 had been deemed too big, too expensive, requiring too many shore crew, and, more than anything, did not yield exciting racing. But an America's Cup like no other, one that featured close racing at nearly 50 mph, thrills, near spills, and perhaps the greatest comeback in sports history, has changed more than a few minds about the monster catamaran.

So the America's Cup sits at a crossroads: stay with the known, albeit expensive, AC72; move to a version smaller than 72 feet but larger than the AC45 used in the America's Cup World Series; or return to a monohull keelboat, which would require a substantially smaller shore team.

Naturally, if you ask Emirates Team New Zealand designer Pete Melvin, the direction is pretty clear.

"It would be a little hard to go back," said Melvin, one of the preeminent multihull designers in the world. "These boats are so exciting. I think that as time goes on, as the sailors get more used to them, the sailing will only get better.

"People still haven't made up their minds about them. I think that having some closer racing was key to making it more exciting, but the jury is still out. Perhaps if the boats were a little more one-design next time, maybe smaller, that could reduce cost somewhat, but if we retain the same class of boat, the teams would be much closer together next time. This is just the first iteration, so we were bound to see some pretty large differences. I wasn't in the America's Cup game back in 1992, when they first introduced the America's Cup Class keelboat, but apparently some of the races were complete blowouts at that stage as well."

One of the biggest complaints about the AC72—and perhaps the largest factor keeping Challengers away—was the sheer cost involved. The AC72 requires nearly 40 shore crew to step the 130' mast and launch the boat, meaning each team had a huge outlay in personnel alone. But for each pundit demanding a cost reduction comes another aghast at the very idea of one-design parts. The America's Cup is, after all, a design game—and with innovation comes cost. Designer Melvin believes there are ways to rein in cost without losing the essence of the game—especially since the AC72 has not come anywhere near its full potential yet. Added to that mix will be the knowledge that each of the four current teams will have an advantage over new teams, should the AC72 remain.

"I think that since we first launched our boat, we're going 20 or 25 percent faster and you just don't know where that development curve is going to end. It feels as though we're still on the steep part; it doesn't feel as though we've hit the plateau yet. I think it's a tough call between keeping the basic AC72 design and changing the rules inside that box to reduce cost. It could come from any number of areas—from making components one design to limiting how many boats teams can build, where they can sail them, etc.

"The other solution would be to go to a smaller boat, starting from scratch. That way the teams from this last Cup would have a technological advantage but it would level the playing field a bit. But it would probably be easier to start again with the AC72; everyone knows those boats a bit better now and the development wouldn't be nearly as intense this cycle, in terms of knowing what works and what doesn't. You wouldn't have such a broad canvas to start with. The boats would be a little bit closer—and that would be inviting to new teams."

Nathan Outteridge became one of the breakout stars of the 34th America's Cup—as much for his actions off the water as on. Becoming the Artemis Racing helmsman in the fall of 2012, it was Outteridge who, with skipper Iain Percy, helped keep the Swedish team going after Andrew Simpson's tragic death. As the team regrouped and finished construction on their second AC72, Outteridge spent a great deal of time watching and learning about the other teams—including stints in New Zealand "spying" on the Kiwi foiling technique.

That knowledge base was put to good use during the Louis Vuitton Cup Finals and the America's Cup match itself, as Outteridge joined the television coverage to offer his perspective. He's become a face of the new America's Cup, a young Olympic Gold medalist who parlayed a career in the 49er dinghy into a chance at the helm of the sport's most recognizable boat in yachting's most famous regatta. But the answer Outteridge gives to the question of the choice of boat for AC35 is as thoughtful as you'd expect from the young man who grew into a team leader under the worst of circumstances—and earning kudos for his insight and honesty.

"I've thought about it a lot," said Outteridge, "and I've been asked about it a lot. You can go in two ways: you can take this as a version of a new class for the America's Cup or you can return to keelboats. With the AC72, I do think they overshot the mark—they made them too big, too expensive, and too hard to manage with too much power.

"These boats have also taken out any kind of crew work that's visible for the public to watch. It's extremely technical sailing and you have to be on your game, but it's mostly grinding, with a few people doing controls. So I would say the first thing to do is to make the boats smaller."

Outteridge would prefer a new boat that brings the sailor back into the equation, where winning relies more on crew work than design. A boat that requires a headsail and a spinnaker, Outteridge believes, is a good place to start.

"I don't think the price will ever go down, whether you've got a keelboat or these boats. The cost is always going to be there because people have budgets and they just spend money developing stuff that doesn't even help in the long run. But I don't think money is the only issue. You go a little bit smaller and then you try to make the power a little bit less so that you do need a sail to go downwind, at least under 15 knots, so you have to choose what to do. At the moment, the crossover is eight to ten knots and it's never under ten in San Francisco—that's why we cut the spinnaker pole off; you're never going to use that sail. You make the wing smaller and then you do need that front sail. Then you have teams hoisting sails, dropping sails, the potential for the foils to come undone, you can see more things go wrong that aren't catastrophic. You can drag a sail in the water—you used to see spinnakers go in the water and that was cool to watch. Whereas now, we've got these boats that just zip around really fast. The technology is awesome, but you're missing that small element.

"The other alternative would be going back to keelboats, ones that go under ten knots upwind and twelve knots downwind. You will get extremely close, tactical, hard-fought racing, just like the Version Five boats in 2007. You'll get interesting stuff in the pre-start and the whole way around the course and sure, there will be technological advancements. The added bonus is there are a lot more designers in the world who can design keelboats. There aren't a lot of designers who can design foiling multihulls; that's a pretty small market.

"But if you put them in high-performance keelboats that go fast, you're going to have the exact same problem we saw earlier in the summer—boats going in different areas, boats going different speeds and racing that's not going to be close. It depends on what people think the America's Cup should be—and I always thought the America's Cup should be cutting-edge design with a race at the end and hopefully it's a good race. But I think all the America's Cups have been the fastest boat wins and the slower boat can get in front and slow them down for only so long."

The question of the next America's Cup boat was posed to the ultimate combatants of the 34th America's Cup at the final press conference following ORACLE TEAM USA's stunning comeback victory. New Zealand's Grant Dalton was understandably reluctant to offer more than a perfunctory opinion on the subject while USA's Larry Ellison addressed criticism of the decision to go with the 72-foot catamaran and offered thoughts on its future.

"It's too expensive," said Dalton. "I've always said you need something that's more realistic, price-wise. Oracle has done an amazing job with their technology and that would be quite scary to other teams."

"The worst part for me was the loss of Andrew Simpson," said Ellison. "It was such a freak accident—sailing is a very small community and all of us took that pretty hard. These boats were meant to be extreme but they certainly weren't meant to be life-threatening. There was a lot of criticism about these boats and I thought that rather than me responding, I would let the guys show what these boats are like out on the water—let the regatta get started and let the people judge for themselves what we've done.

"We'll talk about the boats we want to use going forward. This was the most magnificent spectacle I have ever seen out on the water. San Francisco was a great backdrop for a sailboat race. These 40-plus-knot catamarans are absolutely amazing—I think a lot of people who were never interested in sailing suddenly got interested in sailing. I think a lot of young kids will get interested in sailing and maybe they'll jump into a Hobie Cat instead of a Laser. I think this regatta has changed sailing forever. There are more people who watched the first race of this America's Cup than all the America's Cups in history.

"We tried going to catamarans to make sailing a bit more extreme, a bit friendlier for the viewing audience, moving it into a confined area so more people could watch it firsthand. We tried to make it popular for a television audience. The television announcers' explanation and the graphics on the screen really made sailing accessible to a large number of fans for the first time. We loved that part of the regatta. It's no secret that these boats are expensive, and we'd like to have more countries competing next time, so we'll have to figure out how to accomplish both—get more countries competing but keep it as spectacular as this last regatta."

One of the fascinations of the America's Cup is that you never know what it will be next. And you never know if it will be the same again. Anybody who missed seeing the 2013 America's Cup really missed something special. The boats were incredible. The achievement necessary to build them, sail them, and race them no less so. We may never see this sort of thing again.

Some may say "Good!" and mean it. The days of two opponents competing to see who can haul 45,000 pounds of lead around a course at 12 nautical miles per hour for two hours may return.

For all the glorious warm light of nostalgia that the 12-meter era is now bathed in, when the Twelves were on the verge of being adopted for the Cup in the 1950s Harold "Mike" Vanderbilt was wistful for the J-Class to the point of offering to build a second boat from his beloved *Ranger*'s plans if the NYYC would turn back the clock.

Every era is due their own glories, and for a few weeks, we had something really special, historic actually, in front of us in San Francisco. Enjoy it, truly enjoy it, on its own magnificent terms for what it was. The America's Cup will go on.

NOTES

Chapter One

Page 4 **"Like Jupiter among gods, America is first and there is no second!"** Daniel Webster, Speech at the Massachusetts House of Representatives, 1851.

Page 9 **The first is fun; the second is work."** "A Cup Defender Needed," *The New York Times* (March 28, 1890): 5, col. 5.

Page 10 **Challengers had to source their components from their own country once again.** In 1980, the NYYC overturned the 1962 resolutions to allow Challengers to once again use foreign components and foreign research and design facilities.

Page 11 **The whole thing has become deadly, deadly serious."** Tony Fairchild, *The America's Cup Challenge: There Is No Second* (London: Nautical Books, 1983), 115.

Page 13 **To beat them we must be even faster."** Fairchild, *America's Cup Challenge*, 199.

Page 14 **the price more often than they reap the rewards."** Dennis Conner and Michael Levitt, *Sail Like a Champion*, 37.

Page 14 **two or three matches of the 1970s, however.** Doug Riggs, *Keelhauled*. 202.

Page 14 **and a long counter like *Courageous*.** Riggs, *Keelhauled*. 209.

Page 15 **Thirteen years' experience beat thirteen months experience."** Nancy Trimble, "America's Cup News," *Yachting*, 161, no. 3 (March 1987): 22-24.

Page 16 **the International America's Cup Class (IACC).** Subsequently known as the "America's Cup Class" (ACC).

Page 18 **with both the Australians and the Americans in 1983.** Dutchmen Peter van Oossanen and Joop Slooff assisted Australian Ben Lexcen. Johan Valentijn, although he was made a U.S. national to design the boats for U.S. America's Cup teams, was born and raised in The Netherlands.

Page 18 **was in many ways the pinnacle of nationalism in the America's Cup.** There were exceptions in 1987, such as Frenchman Laurent Esquier, who served as a manager with New Zealand's challenge, but they were few and far between.

Page 19 **123 teams that competed for the Cup from 1870 to 1980.** The first 123 campaigns, from 1870 to 1980, spent a total of $481 million in 2013 U.S. dollars.

Page 19 **spent $315,000 ($5.5 million).** Figures of J-Class campaign costs based on data from *The New York Times* (September 12, 1936), 13-1, and from author's estimates.

Page 19 **runs around $13 million.** America's Cup Event Authority pro forma budget estimate.

Page 19 **1983 defense spent around $12 million** Edward du Moulin, spreadsheet of cost of Freedom-Liberty syndicate, 1983.

Page 21 **three more months of sailing everyday, all day."** Robert N. Bavier, *A View from the Cockpit* (New York: Dodd, Mead, & Co., 1965-6), 2.

Page 21 ***Defender*, in 1895, amounted to $75,000 ($2,040,000).** Cost of maintenance of *Defender*, 1895, C. Oliver Iselin Papers, Mystic Seaport Museum Manuscripts Collection.

Page 21 **approximately the same, at $125,000 ($588,000).** Richard du Moulin, "Organizing to Win," The Society of Naval Architects and Marine Engineers, paper presented at the Second Chesapeake Sailing Yacht Symposium, Annapolis, Maryland, January 18, 1975, 2, 3.

Page 21 **the total design cost was a mere $73,000 ($178,500).** Edward du Moulin, spreadsheet of cost of Freedom syndicate, 1980.

Page 24 **noted, "If she is right, then all of us are wrong."** John Rousmaniere, *The Low Black Schooner: Yacht America 1851-1945* (Mystic, CT: Mystic Seaport Museum, 1986), 24.

Page 24 **"[The designers] either got it horribly wrong or it's terrifically right!"** Russell Coutts with Paul Larsen, *Course to Victory* (Auckland: Hodder, Moa, and Beckett, 1996), 171.

Page 27 **Alinghi would select the umpires on the water and the jury who would judge the races.** Julian Guthrie, *The Billionaire and the Mechanic* (New York: Grove Press, 2013), 195.

Page 28 **and the shape doesn't distort. It is a much more efficient shape."** Steven Tsuchiya, *33rd America's Cup. Deed of Gift Match*, privately printed. 2010.

Chapter Two

Page 35 **to help raise $270 million from corporate sponsors**. This plan was eventually scaled down to a plan to raise $32 million privately in order to offset the City of San Francisco's direct expenses.

Chapter Three

Page 37 **The IACC had been a compromise between two factions.** Proposals for other variations were at least presented, including one from the multihull contingent, but dismissed after early consideration.

Page 40 **and the concept briefs given to the rule writers reflect that feedback."** GGYC Press Release, July 2, 2010.

Page 41 **while being able to sail in a wide range of conditions."** GGYC Press Release, July 2, 2010.

Page 46 **could last for many years in the future."** GGYC Press Release, Sept. 13, 2010.

Page 46 **we need the best sailors racing the fastest boat in the world,"** Russell Coutts said. GGYC Press Release, Sept. 13, 2010.

Page 47 **Valencia announcement was not due to be published for another three weeks,** The Class Rule publication deadline would in fact be extended by two weeks until October 15.

Chapter Seven

Page 104 **technically be scored Did-Not-Start (DNS).** Procedures were changed to allow a non-starting boat to be disqualified (DSQ) after a period of time and the race terminated upon the request of her opponent.

Chapter Nine

Page 124 **because the AC45 Class rules** AC45 Class rule C.1.5 states that components, including the kingpost and forward kingpost, "shall not be modified or replaced unless specifically permitted by the Measurement Committee."

Page 124 **and angry at what had happened,"** Jury Case AC33. Jury Notice JN117. Section 87. Sept. 3, 2013.

Page 124 **that the boat was being raced out of measurement."** Jury Case AC30. Jury Notice JN096. August 8, 2013.

Page 124 **retired retroactively from the ACWS series,** There were four regattas in the ACWS that they retired from: in Newport, July 2012; San Francisco, August and September 2012; and Naples, April 2013.

Page 124 **without the permission of the Measurement Committee."** OTUSA Press Release. "OTUSA Withdraws from Past AC45 Regattas." August 8, 2013.

Page 125 **"the modifications had no impact on the performance of the boats."** OTUSA Press Release. "OTUSA Withdraws from Past AC45 Regattas." August 8, 2013.

Page 125 **and a similarly small detriment to downwind speed."** "Weighing in on WeightGate," Sailing Scuttlebutt Exclusive, August 15, 2013.

Page 126 **Sailor X (OTUSA sailor)** Allegations of gross misconduct against "Sailor X" were dropped, so his name was redacted from the jury reports.

Page 127 **five incidents of breaching the AC45 Class rule.** Jury Case AC33, Jury Notice JN117, Sections 56-60, September 3, 2013.

Page 127 **inside the forward kingpost** The "forward kingpost" is a vertical compression member mounted on the underside of the spine below the forestay attachment point.

Page 127 **was found inside the main kingpost** The "main kingpost" is a vertical compression member mounted on the underside of the spine, immediately below the wing rotation point.

Page 127 **The jury concluded the following** Jury Case AC33, Jury Notice JN117, Sections 63-65, September 3, 2013.

Page 128 **and appropriate for the conduct involved."** Email correspondence between R. Steven Tsuchiya and David Tillett, October 1, 2013.

Page 129 **"outrageous, ridiculous" and "grossly unfair."** Julia Prodis Sulek, "America's Cup: Cheating scandal docks ORACLE TEAM USA two races before main event starts Saturday," *Mercury News* (September 3, 2013).

Page 129 **He's a big loss for those guys."** Duncan Johnstone, "Cheating scandal will hurt Oracle boss Ellison," Stuff.co.nz (September 5, 2013).

Chapter Twelve

Page 196 **The certainly were doing a better job finding that extra gear that we simply couldn't** Alden Bentley, "Oracle sailors learned flying for America's Cup comeback." September 29, 2013, Reuters.

Page 197 **so there's this fantastic human element to this which really won the day in the end, which is great** Christopher Clarey, "Oracle Completes Voyage to History, Winning America's Cup," *The New York Times*, September 25, 2013.

APPENDIX

DEED OF GIFT OF THE AMERICA'S CUP

This DEED OF GIFT made the twenty-fourth day of October, one thousand eight hundred and eighty-seven, Between GEORGE L. SCHUYLER as sole surviving owner of the Cup won by the yacht America at Cowes, England, on the twenty-second day of August, one thousand eight hundred and fifty-one, of the first part, and THE NEW YORK YACHT CLUB, of the second part, as amended by orders of the Supreme Court of the State of New York dated December 17, 1956,[1] and April 5, 1985,[2] WITNESSETH:

THAT the said party of the first part, for and in consideration of the premises and of the performance of the conditions and agreements hereinafter set forth by the party of the second part, has granted, bargained, sold, assigned, transferred and set over, and by these presents does grant, bargain, sell, assign, transfer and set over unto the said party of the second part, its successors and assigns, the Cup won by the schooner yacht America at Cowes, England, upon the twenty-second day of August, 1851. To Have and To Hold the same to the said party of the second part, its successors and assigns, IN TRUST NEVERTHELESS, for the following uses and purposes: -

This Cup is donated upon the condition that it shall be preserved as a perpetual challenge Cup for friendly competition between foreign countries.

Any organized yacht Club of a foreign country, incorporated, patented, or licensed by the legislature, admiralty or other executive department, having for its annual regatta an ocean water course on the sea, or on an arm of the sea, or one which combines both, shall always be entitled to the right of sailing a match for this Cup with a yacht or vessel propelled by sails only and constructed in the country to which the challenging Club belongs, against any one yacht or vessel constructed in the country of the Club holding the Cup.

The competing yachts or vessels, if of one mast, shall be not less than forty-four feet nor more than ninety feet on the load water line; if of more than one mast, they shall be not less than eighty feet nor more than one hundred and fifteen feet on the load water line.

The challenging Club shall give ten months' notice in writing naming the days for the proposed races; but no race shall be sailed in the days intervening between November first and May first if the races are to be conducted in the Northern Hemisphere; and no race shall be sailed in the days intervening between May first and November first if the races are to be conducted in the Southern Hemisphere.

Accompanying the ten months' notice of challenge, there must be sent the name of the owner and a certificate of the name, rig and the following dimensions of the challenging vessel, namely, length on load water line; beam at load water line, and extreme beam; and draught of water; which dimensions shall not be exceeded; and a custom-house registry of the vessel must also be sent as soon as possible. Centreboard or sliding keel vessels shall always be allowed to compete in any race for this Cup, and no restriction nor limitation whatever shall be placed upon the use of such centreboard or sliding keel, nor shall the centre-board or sliding keel be considered a part of the vessel for any purposes of measurement.

The Club challenging for the Cup and the Club holding the same may by mutual consent make any arrangement satisfactory to both as to the dates, courses, number of trials, rules and sailing regulations, and any and all other conditions of the match, in which case also the ten months' notice may be waived.

In case the parties cannot mutually agree upon the terms of a match, then three races shall be sailed, and the winner of two of such races shall be entitled to the Cup. All such races shall be on ocean courses, free from headlands, as follows: the first race, twenty nautical miles to windward and return; the second race, an equilateral triangular race of thirty-nine nautical miles, the first side of which shall be a beat to windward; the third race, (if necessary), twenty nautical miles to windward and return; and one week day shall intervene between the conclusion of one race and the starting of the next race. These ocean courses shall be practicable in all parts for vessels of twenty-two feet draught of water and shall be selected by the Club holding the Cup;

and these races shall be sailed subject to its rules and sailing regulations so far as the same do not conflict with the provisions of this deed of gift, but without any time allowances whatever. The challenged Club shall not be required to name its representative vessel until at the time agreed upon for the start, but the vessel when named must compete in all the races; and each of such races must be completed within seven hours.

Should the Club holding the Cup be for any cause dissolved, the Cup shall be transferred to some Club of the same nationality, eligible to challenge under this deed of gift, in trust and subject to its provisions. In the event of the failure of such transfer within three months after such dissolution, said Cup shall revert to the preceding Club holding the same, and under the terms of this deed of gift. It is distinctly understood that the Cup is to be the property of the Club, subject to the provisions of this deed, and not the property of the owner or owners of any vessel winning a match.

No vessel which has been defeated in a match for this Cup can be again selected by any club as its representative until after a contest for it by some other vessel has intervened, or until after the expiration of two years from the time of such defeat. And when a challenge from a Club fulfilling all the conditions required by this instrument has been received, no other challenge can be considered until the pending event has been decided.

AND the said party of the second part hereby accepts the said Cup subject to the said trust, terms and conditions, and hereby covenants and agrees to and with said party of the first part that it will faithfully and fully see that the foregoing conditions are fully observed and complied with by any contestant for the said Cup during the holding thereof by it; and that it will assign transfer and deliver the said Cup to the for-eign yacht Club whose representative yacht shall have won the same in accordance with the foregoing terms and conditions, provided the said foreign Club shall by instrument in writing lawfully executed enter with said party of the second part into the like covenants as are herein entered into by it, such instrument to contain a like provision for the successive assignees to enter into the same covenants with their respective assignors, and to be executed in duplicate, one to be retained by each Club, and a copy thereof to be forwarded to the said party of the second part.

IN WITNESS WHEREOF, the said party of the first part has hereunto set his hand and seal, and the said party of the second part has caused its corporate seal to be affixed to these presents and the same to be signed by its Commodore and attested by its Secretary, the day and year first above written.

In the presence of H. D. Hamilton.

George L. Schuyler {L.S.}
The New York Yacht Club

by Elbridge T. Gerry, *Commodore*.
{Seal of the NYYC}

John H. Bird, *Secretary*

---

1 The deed of gift was amended to allow the 12-meter class to be eligible for the America's Cup: the minimum waterline restriction was reduced to 44 feet and the condition that required the challenger to sail to the site of the match on its own bottom was eliminated.

2 With Australia winning the Cup in 1983, the deed of gift was amended to allow the America's Cup match to be held during the summer in the Southern hemisphere.

AMERICA'S CUP WINNERS

AMERICA'S CUP

Winner in Bold

YEAR	MATCH	CHALLENGER (Sail #)	CHALLENGING CLUB (Nation)	DEFENDER (Sail #)	DEFENDING CLUB (Nation)	RATING BASIS*	VENUE	SCORE
1870	1st	*Cambria* (tenth place)**	Royal Thames Yacht Club (GBR)	***Magic*** (first place)**	New York Yacht Club (USA)	Waterline-Area	New York City	1-0
1871	2nd	*Livonia*	Royal Harwich Yacht Club (GBR)	***Columbia*** (2-1), ***Sappho*** (2-0)***	New York Yacht Club (USA)	Cube-Root-of-Displacement	New York City	4-1
1876	3rd	*Countess of Dufferin*	Royal Canadian Yacht Club (CAN)	***Madeleine***	New York Yacht Club (USA)	Cubical-Contents	New York City	2-0
1881	4th	*Atalanta*	Bay of Quinte Yacht Club (CAN)	***Mischief***	New York Yacht Club (USA)	Cubical-Contents	New York City	2-0
1885	5th	*Genesta*	Royal Yacht Squadron (GBR)	***Puritan***	New York Yacht Club (USA)	Length-and-Sail-Area	New York City	2-0
1886	6th	*Galatea*	Royal Northern Yacht Club (GBR)	***Mayflower***	New York Yacht Club (USA)	Length-and-Sail-Area	New York City	2-0
1887	7th	*Thistle*	Royal Clyde Yacht Club (GBR)	***Volunteer***	New York Yacht Club (USA)	Length-and-Sail-Area	New York City	2-0
1893	8th	*Valkyrie II*	Royal Yacht Squadron (GBR)	***Vigilant***	New York Yacht Club (USA)	Length-and-Sail-Area	New York City	3-0
1895	9th	*Valkyrie III*	Royal Yacht Squadron (GBR)	***Defender***	New York Yacht Club (USA)	Length-and-Sail-Area	New York City	3-0
1899	10th	*Shamrock*	Royal Ulster Yacht Club (IRE)	***Columbia***	New York Yacht Club (USA)	Seawanhaka	New York City	3-0
1901	11th	*Shamrock II*	Royal Ulster Yacht Club (IRE)	***Columbia***	New York Yacht Club (USA)	Seawanhaka	New York City	3-0
1903	12th	*Shamrock III*	Royal Ulster Yacht Club (IRE)	***Reliance***	New York Yacht Club (USA)	Seawanhaka	New York City	3-0
1920	13th	*Shamrock IV*	Royal Ulster Yacht Club (IRE)	***Resolute***	New York Yacht Club (USA)	Universal	New York City	3-2
1930	14th	*Shamrock V* (J/K3)	Royal Ulster Yacht Club (N. IRE)	***Enterprise*** (J4)	New York Yacht Club (USA)	Universal J-Class	Newport	4-0
1934	15th	*Endeavour* (J/K4)	Royal Yacht Squadron (GBR)	***Rainbow*** (J4) (J5)	New York Yacht Club (USA)	Universal J-Class	Newport	4-2
1937	16th	*Endeavour II* (J/K6)	Royal Yacht Squadron (GBR)	***Ranger*** (J5)	New York Yacht Club (USA)	Universal J-Class	Newport	4-0
1958	17th	*Sceptre* (K-17)	Royal Yacht Squadron (GBR)	***Columbia*** (US-16)	New York Yacht Club (USA)	International 12-Meter Class	Newport	4-0
1962	18th	*Gretel* (KA-1)	Royal Sydney Yacht Squadron (AUS)	***Weatherly*** (US-17)	New York Yacht Club (USA)	International 12-Meter Class	Newport	4-1
1964	19th	*Sovereign* (K-12)	Royal Thames Yacht Club (GBR)	***Constellation*** (US-20)	New York Yacht Club (USA)	International 12-Meter Class	Newport	4-0
1967	20th	*Dame Pattie* (KA-2)	Royal Sydney Yacht Squadron (AUS)	***Intrepid*** (US-22)	New York Yacht Club (USA)	International 12-Meter Class	Newport	4-0
1970	21st	*Gretel II* (KA-3)	Royal Sydney Yacht Squadron (AUS)	***Intrepid*** (US-22)	New York Yacht Club (USA)	International 12-Meter Class	Newport	4-1
1974	22nd	*Southern Cross* (KA-4)	Royal Perth Yacht Club (AUS)	***Courageous*** (US-26)	New York Yacht Club (USA)	International 12-Meter Class	Newport	4-0
1977	23rd	*Australia* (KA-5)	Sun City Yacht Club (AUS)	***Courageous*** (US-26)	New York Yacht Club (USA)	International 12-Meter Class	Newport	4-0
1980	24th	*Australia* (KA-5)	Royal Perth Yacht Club (AUS)	***Freedom*** (US-30)	New York Yacht Club (USA)	International 12-Meter Class	Newport	4-1
1983	25th	***Australia II*** (KA-6)	Royal Perth Yacht Club (AUS)	*Liberty* (US-40)	New York Yacht Club (USA)	International 12-Meter Class	Newport	4-3
1987	26th	***Stars & Stripes '87*** (US-55)	San Diego Yacht Club (USA)	*Kookaburra III* (KA-15)	Royal Perth Yacht Club (AUS)	International 12-Meter Class	Fremantle	4-0
1988	27th	*New Zealand* (KZ-1)	Mercury Bay Boating Club (NZL)	***Stars & Stripes '88*** (US-1)	San Diego Yacht Club (USA)	No rating; Deed of Gift	San Diego	2-0
1992	28th	*Il Moro di Venezia V* (ITA-25)	Compagnia Della Vela di Venezia (ITA)	***America³*** (USA-23)	San Diego Yacht Club (USA)	America's Cup Class	San Diego	4-1
1995	29th	***"Black Magic"*** (NZL-32)	Royal New Zealand Yacht Squadron (NZL)	*Young America* (USA-36)	San Diego Yacht Club (USA)	America's Cup Class	San Diego	5-0
2000	30th	*Luna Rossa* (ITA-45)	Yacht Club Punta Ala (ITA)	***Team New Zealand*** (NZL-60)	Royal New Zealand Yacht Squadron (NZL)	America's Cup Class	Auckland	5-0
2003	31st	***Alinghi*** (SUI-64)	Société Nautique de Genève (SUI)	*Team New Zealand* (NZL-82)	Royal New Zealand Yacht Squadron (NZL)	America's Cup Class	Auckland	5-0
2007	32nd	*Emirates Team New Zealand* (NZL-92)	Royal New Zealand Yacht Squadron (NZL)	***Alinghi*** (SUI-100)	Société Nautique de Genève (SUI)	America's Cup Class	Valencia	5-2
2010	33rd	***USA*** (USA-17)	Golden Gate Yacht Club (USA)	*Alinghi 5* (SUI)	Société Nautique de Genève (SUI)	No rating; Deed of Gift	Valencia	2-0
2013	34th	*Aotearoa*	Royal New Zealand Yacht Squadron (NZL)	***ORACLE TEAM USA*** (17)	Golden Gate Yacht Club (USA)	AC72 Class	San Francisco	9-8****

* During each of the first thirteen defenses, the boats had different ratings; formulas determined the rating value and the time allowance. Beginning with the J-Class in 1930, the boats had the same rating due to class rules (and, thus, the races were no longer held on corrected time). In 1988 and 2010, there was no rating rule in effect because the competitors could not agree to the terms of the match. See Deed of Gift.

** The 1st Defense was a fleet race: the challenger, Cambria, raced against a fleet of seventeen New York Yacht Club defenders.

*** The 2nd Defense was a fleet race. However, in 1871, the New York Yacht Club alternated two defenders against the lone challenger.

**** ORACLE TEAM USA started the "first-to-win-nine" match with a deficit of two races due to a penalty incurred for violating the AC45 Class Rule and the Protocol during the 2012-13 ACWS.

AC72 CLASS CATAMARAN TYPICAL FEATURES

(Illustration: ©CupInfo.com)

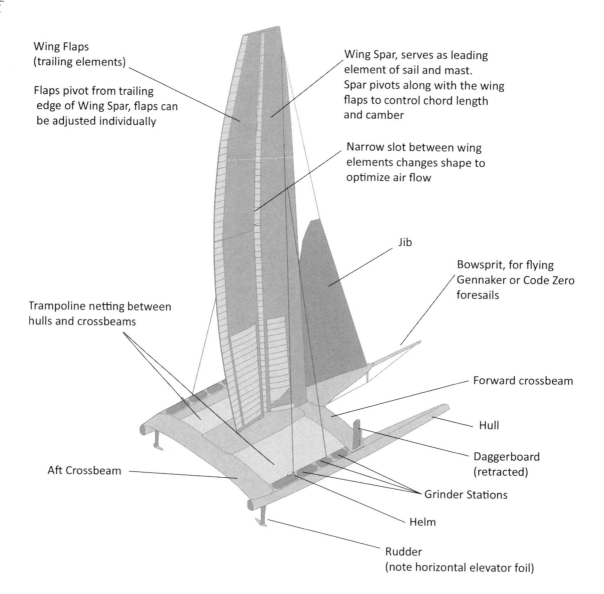

Wing Flaps
(trailing elements)

Flaps pivot from trailing
edge of Wing Spar, flaps can
be adjusted individually

Wing Spar, serves as leading
element of sail and mast.
Spar pivots along with the wing
flaps to control chord length
and camber

Narrow slot between wing
elements changes shape to
optimize air flow

Jib

Bowsprit, for flying
Gennaker or Code Zero
foresails

Trampoline netting between
hulls and crossbeams

Forward crossbeam

Hull

Daggerboard
(retracted)

Aft Crossbeam

Grinder Stations

Helm

Rudder
(note horizontal elevator foil)

TACKING RACES 3&4

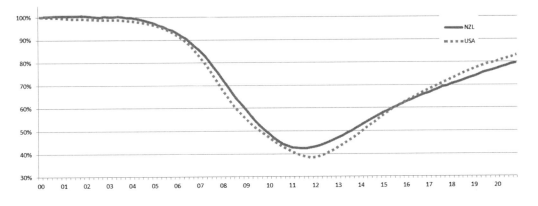

Average Speed during a Tacking Phase (Base 100: 10s before Tack) - Races 3 & 4

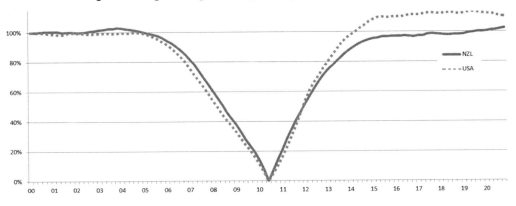

Average Wind Angle during a Tacking Phase (Base 100: 10s before Tack) - Races 3 & 4

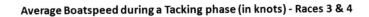

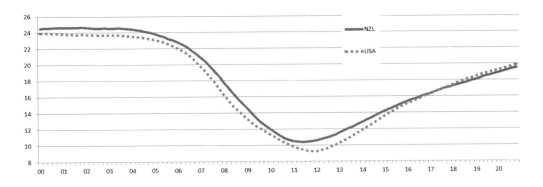

Average Boatspeed during a Tacking phase (in knots) - Races 3 & 4

TACKING RACE 10

(©CupInfo.com/cupstats)

Average Speed during a Tacking Phase (Base 100: 10s before Tack) - Race 10

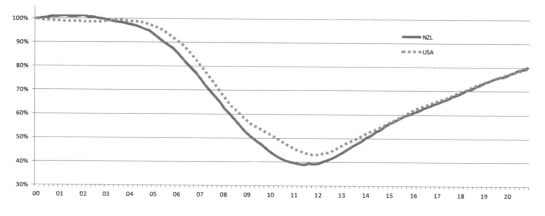

Average Wind Angle during a Tacking Phase (Base 100: 10s before Tack) - Race 10

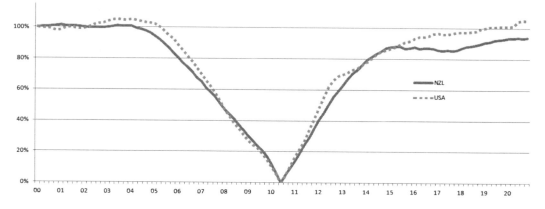

Average Boatspeed during a Tacking phase (in knots) - Race 10

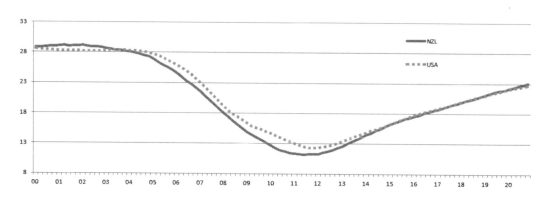

MATCH POINT SUMMARY

34th Defense of the America's Cup, September 2013
First to score nine points wins the America's Cup match.
ORACLE TEAM USA lost the points from their first two wins due to penalty.

Date	Race	Winner	Margin (min:secs)	Wins USA	Wins NZL	Points USA	Points NZL
Sep 7	Race 1	NZL	0:36	0	1	-2	1
Sep 7	Race 2	NZL	0:52	0	2	-2	2
Sep 8	Race 3	NZL	0:28	0	3	-2	3
Sep 8	Race 4	USA	0:08	1	3	-1	3
Sep 9	Lay day						
Sep 10	Race 5	NZL	1:05	1	4	-1	4
Sep 10	*USA postpones Race 6.*						
Sep 11	Lay day						
Sep 12	Race 6	NZL	0:47	1	5	-1	5
Sep 12	Race 7	NZL	1:06	1	6	-1	6
Sep 13	Lay day						
Sep 14	Race 8	USA	0:52	2	6	0	6
Sep 14	*Race 9 abandoned; wind limit exceeded with NZL leading on Leg 3.*						
Sep 15	Race 9	USA	0:47	3	6	1	6
Sep 15	Race 10	NZL	0:16	3	7	1	7
Sep 16	Lay day						
Sep 17	*Race 11 and Race 12 postponed; wind limit exceeded.*						
Sep 18	Race 11	NZL	0:15	3	8	1	8
Sep 18	*Race 12 postponed; wind limit exceeded during pre-start.*						
Sep 19	Race 12	USA	0:31	4	8	2	8
Sep 19	*Race 13 postponed; wind limit exceeded.*						
Sep 20	*Race 13 abandoned; time limit expired with NZL leading near Mark 4.*						
Sep 20	Race 13	USA	1:24	5	8	3	8
Sep 21	*Races 14 and 15 postponed; winds too southerly to set race course.*						
Sep 22	Race 14	USA	0:23	6	8	4	8
Sep 22	Race 15	USA	0:37	7	8	5	8
Sep 23	Race 16	USA	0:33	8	8	6	8
Sep 23	*Race 17 postponed; too late in the day to start.*						
Sep 24	Race 17	USA	0:27	9	8	7	8
Sep 24	Race 18	USA	0:54	10	8	8	8
Sep 25	Race 19	USA	0:44	11	8	9	8

Golden Gate Yacht Club, represented by Oracle Team USA, wins the America's Cup

INDEX

(Numbers in **bold** indicate photos or illustrations.)